Ringtone

Ringtone

Exploring the Rise and Fall of Nokia in Mobile Phones

Yves L. Doz and Keeley Wilson

OXFORD
UNIVERSITY PRESS

OXFORD
UNIVERSITY PRESS

Great Clarendon Street, Oxford, OX2 6DP,
United Kingdom

Oxford University Press is a department of the University of Oxford.
It furthers the University's objective of excellence in research, scholarship,
and education by publishing worldwide. Oxford is a registered trade mark of
Oxford University Press in the UK and in certain other countries

Published in the United States of America by Oxford University Press
198 Madison Avenue, New York, NY 10016, United States of America

British Library Cataloguing in Publication Data
Data available

Library of Congress Control Number: 2017939839

ISBN 978–0–19–877719–9

Printed in Great Britain by
Clays Ltd, St Ives plc

Preface

From banking services via a mobile phone in Africa, to the pressures to respond to work emails 24/7, to being able to find the nearest Thai restaurant in a strange city, to a president with a penchant for Tweeting his thoughts and ideas direct to the world—whether for good or bad, there is no denying that in less than three decades mobile communications have changed the world and the way we live. Whereas once economic development was paced by the ability to build vital fixed-line telecommunications infrastructure, mobile telephony has offered new opportunities to billions of people in emerging markets. And whereas those of us over a certain age vividly recall the public phone box (with its attendant problems of finding one available and in service, having the right change, not being deafened by passing traffic, and turning a blind eye—or nose—to the questionable hygiene) as the only means to make a call outside the home or office, a younger generation could not imagine the deprivation of being without their smartphone.

At the forefront of this transformation in mobile telecommunications was Nokia. While they successfully provided the infrastructure for mobile communications (and continue to do so today), this book is about the more visible part of Nokia—the innovative business which gave us iconic mobile phones, and at its height dominated the industry with a global market share of over 40 percent. The mobile phone was one of the most successful product innovations ever, its rate of adoption faster than any other physical device. And so, the story of Nokia's rapid rise in mobile phones and its equally rapid decline is one which needs to be told.

Nokia's dramatic journey in mobile phones is intrinsically fascinating as there are few comparable high-profile companies who have led the growth of a world-changing industry, built one of the most valuable global brands, and then failed so spectacularly and quickly. What this book offers is not only a history of Nokia's rise and fall in mobile phones, but an analysis that opens the proverbial "black box" of why and how decisions are made by senior managers at the top of organizations. Beyond understanding what happened to Nokia, this offers valuable and important lessons for all managers.

We have been fortunate to write this book from a unique perspective: that of outsiders who have been given privileged access to the managers who led

Nokia from the early 1990s but have not had to have our final manuscript "approved" by anyone at Nokia, past or present. As well as interviews specifically for researching this book, Yves Doz was involved with various projects for Nokia managers over a long period from 1996 (greater detail about our research and a list of the people we interviewed can be found in Appendix 6). This access has been invaluable. It has given us insight into the dynamics of the management teams, and the processes and behavior that drove Nokia's strategy. In turn, this allows us to describe how and why real people made the decisions they did.

In writing this book, during the process of gathering and making sense of our research and taking the first tentative step of putting pen to paper, we made a somewhat unusual decision (for a book with two authors) to write from the first-person perspective of one author only. The interviews and long research journey had been Yves's alone, with Keeley becoming involved at the point of analyzing the mass of data ahead of planning the structure of the book. In telling the story of Nokia in mobile phones and recounting instances from experience Yves had of Nokia as well as quotes from the many managers he had interviewed, it seemed more natural to do this in a first person narrative. We hope this gives the reader a clearer sense of events as they unfolded, the people who played prominent roles in Nokia's story, their motivations, and the decisions they made.

Acknowledgments

Our research benefited from the support and contribution of many people. First and foremost the former Nokia leaders collectively known as the "dream team," Jorma Ollila, Matti Alahuhta, Sari Baldauf, Olli-Pekka Kallasvuo, and Pekka Ala-Pietilä. Also Anssi Vanjoki, Marko Ahtisaari, Juha Äkräs, Jyrki Ali-Yrkkö, Jean-Francois Baril, Timo Ihamuotila, Pertti Korhonen, Paula Laine, Teemu Malmi, Tero Ojanperä, Erkki Ormala, Juha Putkiranta, Risto Siilasmaa, Mikko Terho, and Alberto Torres. All contributed their time, volunteered valuable perspectives, and provided open and frank accounts of the evolution of Nokia in mobile phones and of their own roles over time. They also gave valuable feedback on intermediate findings in the course of the research. Risto Siilasmaa, Nokia's current chairman, also provided a clear account of his experience over recent years, and gave us his support in this work. We are grateful to all.

Finnish researchers, in particular Katja Kolehmainen, Eero Vaara, Martti Häikiö, and Saku Mantere were very helpful, and some provided valuable feedback at a seminar in Helsinki in June 2016. So was Tom Murtha and participants in research seminars at the Ivey Business School in London, Ontario, at the Carlson School at the University of Minnesota, and at the Institute for Manufacturing at the University of Cambridge.

Many others helped us directly and made completing this book possible. Petra Turkama selected and translated Finnish-language documents, Jaana Ekström scheduled interviews and meetings in Finland, Kim Wilkinson and Melanie Camenzind provided administrative assistance, and Caro Fry worked through endless interview notes and first-draft chapters. Sabine Lozachmeur made invaluable contributions to the manuscript completion and finalization. Muriel Larvaron, who had contributed to earlier research on strategic agility, including on Nokia, was a source of support and a friendly sounding board, as was Patrick Butler, who provided valuable feedback through many iterations and remained patient and supportive throughout.

We are grateful to INSEAD, in particular to Dean Mihov, Research Dean Tim van Zandt, and Professor Ziv Carmon, chair of the R&D Committee, and to the Solvay Chair Fund for providing resources and support for this unconventional work. David Musson, then editor for business books at Oxford

University Press, was supportive since the minute he heard of the idea, well before the actual research started. Adam Swallow and Clare Kennedy have been very supportive since David retired.

Our INSEAD colleague, Professor Jose Santos, deserves a special mention—he was a very insightful intellectual sparring partner throughout the research work and a frequent stimulant for going deeper and developing sharper findings.

And finally, more than anyone else, Mikko Kosonen, a co-author on a previous book and former senior executive at Nokia, decisively contributed to our work. He not only helped set up interviews with ex-colleagues and others in Finland and hosted a feedback seminar in Helsinki, but he was endlessly willing and patient as a source for fact checking and provided constant feedback on tentative interpretations and emerging findings. Without his unfailing support and advice this book might not have been written.

Of course, despite all the help and support we received from so many quarters, all errors and oversights remain our own.

Table of Contents

List of Figures

List of Tables

1

A Shooting Star

In 1993, when Nokia's ringtone was installed on its phones for the first time, few people would have expected the short melodic phrase from Francisco Tárrega's 1902 "Gran Vals" would become one of the most recognizable, not to mention most played, tunes in history. No large industrial company has ever grown as fast as Nokia did in the 1990s and few have fallen quite as rapidly: Nokia's mobile phone business went from posting record results in 2007 to almost dragging the whole company into bankruptcy in 2012. Like a shooting star, Nokia appeared in our sky traveling at great speed, shining brightly, and then disappearing just as fast.

In following that trajectory at such speed, Nokia is unique; an "outlier" when compared to the rise and decline of average firms which take place over much longer periods. While Internet or platform-based businesses can scale up to dizzying levels in short time frames, as a product-based industrial company, the rate of Nokia's extraordinary growth was unprecedented. In less than a decade, the firm which few outside its home market in Finland had heard of became the dominant player in the mobile phone industry, with one of the world's most powerful brands.

Nokia's remarkable growth was punctuated by just three small blips. The first occurred in 1995 when growing pains in the supply chain led to problems with product availability and a consequent slowdown in sales. The second saw sales growth plateau in 2001 when the whole industry slowed following the dotcom crash. And finally in 2004, Nokia was hit by major telecom operators briefly boycotting its products in retaliation to Nokia moving into value-added services and to punish the firm for not introducing a folding phone to rival the runaway success of Motorola's RAZR.

In 2013, with sales and margins having been falling since 2010, the threat of bankruptcy looming and management in disarray, Nokia deftly sold its mobile phone business to Microsoft. This gave Nokia the resources to reposition itself and invest in its network equipment business. After two decades of being synonymous with mobile phones, the Nokia brand all but disappeared, as Microsoft failed to leverage its acquisition to become a smartphone player.

The repercussions of Nokia's rise and fall were spread far and wide: investors who stuck with Nokia for too long and then sold before its refocused network business began to pull the company back to recovery, were badly hit. Tens of thousands of Nokia employees saw their jobs disappear and their stock options evaporate. Many suppliers were left struggling to find new customers. And in Finland, where Nokia's success had for many years been synonymous with the growth of the national economy, the firm's failure contributed significantly to the country's economic woes in the mid-2010s.

The Nokia story is obviously a fascinating one, and in the tradition of the best "whodunit" leaves the observer intrigued to explore why and how the story unfolded as it did, and who and what was responsible for its meteoric rise and its equally dramatic decline.

From a management standpoint there are three different and obvious lines of reasoning we can draw upon to attempt to answer these questions:

1. Could Nokia's decline have been *unavoidable*—just an extreme case of Schumpeterian creative destruction?

2. Was it an instance of *organizational evolution and adaptation gone astray* down a dead end in the face of disruption and business model change?

3. Was this a *failure of management volition*—the wrong strategic decisions, poor choices of organization, inadequate management processes, weak leadership, and bad timing?

Nokia's success in the 1990s was primarily the result of visionary, courageous, and thoughtful management choices, made in a fortuitous context that had developed in Finland at a particular point in time, as digitalization and deregulation unleashed the value-creating potential inherent in mobile phones. A combination of Nokia's entrepreneurial leadership—a team with very complementary skills—its early innovative lead in key technologies such as radio frequency, a series of smart opportunistic strategic moves since the 1960s, strong "can-do" energy, collective commitment, and effective management processes positioned Nokia to lead the charge toward the dream of mobile phones as a mass-market consumer product.

The downturn in Nokia's fortunes in the 2000s is more intriguing and requires more complex analysis. Observing from a distance, a Schumpeterian explanation would be tempting. New competitors, primarily Apple and Google, arrived with different skills and business models that were better suited to a new software-driven, Internet-based communication industry. And then Samsung and other Asian manufacturers stole the show in hardware. Although this simple explanation is seductive, it overlooks a most critical point: Nokia was already in decline before the arrival of these new competitors.

So, if Nokia's downfall was not just a product of Schumpeterian disruption, to what extent did adaptation running astray down a dead end play a role?

There is some face validity to this line of reasoning. Around 1990 Nokia deftly moved from analog to digital phones, captured a key role in emerging GSM (Global System for Mobile Communications) alliances, was active in Japan and the US, developed outstanding products, and quickly built and scaled up a formidable, and unmatched, global supply system. It also successfully expanded into emerging markets. It pioneered smartphones (with the "Communicator" introduced in 1996) and was among the first to offer camera phones, radiophones, and other feature-rich products.

Yet, by the mid-2000s, Nokia was reaching strategic stasis—it was hyperstable and rigidly set on a disastrous trajectory well before Apple and Google changed Nokia's world. This strategic stasis did not develop in a vacuum, but largely resulted from a co-evolutionary lock-in with major European telecom service operators around 3G (third-generation) telephony and the widespread introduction of data communications. In a book written with Mikko Kosonen (Doz and Kosonen, 2008) we explained how this type of stasis could easily develop as a toxic side effect of great success (and there have been similar conclusions about other firms, for instance see Collins, 2009; Sull, 2003).

The third line of reasoning—managerial errors and leadership weakness—is also a useful lens through which to observe the unfolding events. Here though, one has to be careful about undertaking "what if" reasoning with the benefit of hindsight, as to consider the road not taken calls for a form of intellectual speculation. Speeches and presentations given in 1999–2000 by key leaders within Nokia denote a keen understanding of trends and discontinuities and a well-informed foresight of their industry, implying any leadership and managerial failure was not one of cognition. However, there are a few key turning points where a different road could have been taken, or at least the dangers of the twists and turns in the road ahead better assessed.

Just as success often results from many small positive steps, the roots of failure can usually be found in multiple small mistakes, which seem manageable when viewed in isolation. However, overlooked interdependencies can result in these small errors converging to create serious problems (Perrow, 1984; Weick, 1990; Taleb, 2007). Nokia's management failure therefore cannot be ascribed to a single "wrong" decision, but to multiple and successive decisions each of which was made for what appeared to be the right reasons but within too narrow a framing of each managers' limited context. Systemic interdependencies that led to unfolding second- and third-order consequences of decisions were not taken into account.

The explanation of Nokia's success and decline cannot be reduced to a single, simple answer, be it inevitable creative destruction, organizational evolution, or poor managerial choices. Elements of each of the three logics outlined above are relevant, showing complementary facets of the unfolding events and contributing to our understanding. Even though they may appear *a priori* to be mutually exclusive and incompatible (having different theoretical premises), we will endeavor throughout this book to combine the explanatory power of each to describe and analyze Nokia's success and failure in mobile phones. More broadly, by highlighting these three alternative explanations we hope to shed further empirical light on what is perhaps the most central theoretical debate in the field of strategic management: How much does management matter?

Population ecologists, in a pure Schumpeterian creative destruction logic, would argue it does not. From their perspective it is the quality of "fit" between demands from the environment and the organization that determines success—if the environment changes and that "fit" deteriorates the organization will ultimately perish (Hannan and Freeman, 1984). Management is seen as powerless, acting in a reality they do not control and perhaps do not even fathom—rearranging the proverbial deckchairs on the *Titanic* as the ship sails full steam ahead into an iceberg. In fact, population ecologists go so far as to argue that the actions management take to adapt organizations in the face of decline actually accelerate rather than stave off demise, as they trigger negative consequences resulting from breaking interdependencies that were never understood when the "fit" was good (Hannan and Freeman, 1984).

Students of organizational adaptation develop a more nuanced argument. The evolutionary paradigm suggests that even though managers are limited in their ability to shape how their organization evolves, they are not powerless. Organizational rules and routines largely drive how the organization adapts (Nelson and Winter, 1982). In adhering to behavioral decision-making models (Cyert and March, 1963), managers in an organization seek solutions that involve only "proximate" and incremental changes to existing routines and activities, often in a trial and error mode, with limited *ex ante* strategic deliberation. According to that logic, organizational adaptation is constrained by current activities and resources and is highly path-dependent.

In trying to explain the differences in firms' performances, strategic management scholars, on the other hand, obviously give primacy to management volition. They see the organization as a tool for the CEO and key corporate executives, who craft and implement well thought-through strategic decisions working in an environment they understand. The founding "environment–strategy–structure" paradigm of the strategic management field reflects the primacy of this view (Chandler, 1962; Andrews, 1971).

It would be surprising if managers reading this book didn't naturally lean toward the managerial volition logic, although it is interesting that in retrospect many of Nokia's ex-leadership team now argue that Schumpeterian disruption was key to Nokia's demise, bolstering their argument with conceptual developments about how difficult it is for an incumbent to resist disruption (Christensen, 1997). In adopting this perspective they are exonerating themselves from responsibilities in what they characterize as an unavoidable failure.

Our own perspective in approaching the research for this book is definitely managerial. Through dissecting and analyzing Nokia's story, our objective is to make observations of potential general value to inform management action. But we also recognize that there are insurmountable limits to what managers can do, and so we place managerial volition and action in a context where changes to the environment may ultimately render management ineffective.

With this brief introduction to the three approaches through which to view the success and failure of Nokia in mobile phones concluded, we hope to whet the reader's appetite with a potted history of Nokia intended to highlight key points in Nokia's journey in mobile phones.

A Capsule History

Although it could trace its origins to back to 1865, it wasn't until the 1990s, when that ubiquitous ringtone began to fill streets and cafes from Paris to Shanghai to New York (and most places in between), that Nokia became known outside its home market of Finland. And even then there was some confusion, as many people assumed the firm with an unusual name that created these new and exciting mobile phones was Japanese. Japan being the home of innovative, well-designed consumer electronics, this made more sense than the reality of Nokia emerging from Finland, a small Nordic country which was best known for forestry products, reindeers, and Lapland—the home of Santa Claus!

Nokia's rise in mobile phones was truly astonishing. Throughout the early 2000s, Nokia seemed unstoppable. In 2001, when its competitors stumbled as the dotcom and telecom overinvestment crises caused the industry's first dip in growth, Nokia kept growing and capturing further market share, up to nearly 40 percent of the world market for handsets. It gained dominant market positions in two of the largest and fastest emerging markets: China and India.

Such was Nokia's success that Jorma Ollila, the group's chairman and CEO, became an iconic corporate leader in Europe. He was sought after at Davos, the European Roundtable, the Aspen Institute, and other high-level arenas not only as a pundit, famous for presiding over the largest European success in the ICT (information and communication technology) industry, but also for his penetrating analyses of the geopolitical and economic environments.

Innovation was at the core of Nokia's dominance. It made its phones small and portable, invested in creating a unique brand design, and added new features so users could personalize their phones. It introduced the first smartphone (the "Communicator") in 1996. And although Sharp launched the first camera phone in 2001, it was Nokia's camera phone released the following year which really changed the landscape, providing not only superior picture resolution but also picture-sharing applications that paved the way for multimedia communication.

This product innovation came from fifteen labs around the world and a number of technical cooperation projects and partnerships. In the US, for instance, its R&D (research and development) was strategically located in San Diego (the epicenter of innovation in mobile communication in the US, with the leading research university for telecom technologies and home to Qualcomm, a major innovator in the architecture of telecom chips) and Palo Alto (the heart of Silicon Valley). Year after year, Nokia overwhelmed the competition by introducing a broader array of products faster and faster, with one new product per week on average by the mid-2000s.

Beyond product innovation, Nokia's success was supported by an innovative and highly efficient supply chain system that had been built in the 1990s. Through this, Nokia was able to achieve much lower prices from suppliers than its competitors and ramp up new production lines to full capacity in a matter of days. In the 1990s it had also mastered lean production and Japanese quality processes, and organized its integrated manufacturing around a few key regional hubs in Europe (Finland, Germany, Hungary), Asia (China), and North America (Mexico).

By 2001, Nokia's brand had grown into one of the best known and most valuable in the world. To many inside Nokia it almost felt like the company could walk on water. It knew its industry and was at the top of its game. When Apple introduced its first iPhone (in 2007), many Nokians dismissed it as a "pocket computer with poor phone features." Not only did they feel the product was extremely expensive and technologically represented a backward step—relying on intermediate 2.5G standards, known as GPRS, while the mobile incumbents were already rolling out 3G worldwide, and beginning to work on the next-generation 4G—they felt that Apple's "vertical" business model (from hardware components to operating system (OS) and content and application provision) was obsolete and bound to fail. When prior to announcing Android, Google informally sounded out Nokia about the idea of a possible alliance, Nokia's management declined to engage in a serious conversation.

However, by 2010 Nokia's sales in the highly profitable smartphone market were struggling, while Apple, with an improved product and increased distribution, had seen sales of its iPhone soar. Google's Android was emerging as the main platform competitor to Apple, with Samsung leading the onslaught of Android-based phone makers, followed by new entrants from China. Confusion prevailed at Nokia: product quality had deteriorated and products were being introduced late. While the limitations of Nokia's Symbian OS were becoming more painfully obvious, a new

OS under development was making slow progress and, as a result, application developers began deserting Nokia.

In a bid to try and halt the decline, Nokia's board fired their CEO and replaced him with Canadian national Steven Elop—a Microsoft executive who had rather unsuccessfully led Microsoft's efforts to grow into the mobile software market. Based on what he saw at Nokia, in 2011 Elop issued an internal memo to all staff comparing the firm to a burning oil platform. Designed to spur the firm into action, this backfired as the memo was leaked to the press—the world now knew how bad things had become at Nokia. Sales of Nokia's Symbian phones declined rapidly.

Shortly after, Nokia entered an alliance with Microsoft to use the Windows Mobile OS on its phones. However, this was beset with problems and delays and resulted in the collapse of Nokia's competitive position. In 2013, with the firm suffering from a massive cash drain in mobile phones, and threatened with bankruptcy, a great chapter in Nokia's history ended as it sold its mobile phone activities to Microsoft.

Although this heralded the end of Nokia's spectacular journey in mobile phones, it marked a new beginning for its network infrastructure business, as Nokia bought out Siemens to take full control of the joint venture Nokia Siemens Networks. Shortly after, it began talks to acquire Alcatel and, once the acquisition was complete, this positioned Nokia as the world's second-largest telecoms network infrastructure firm, just behind its old rival Ericsson.

Research Focus

Obviously, faced with such a huge research subject and vast quantities of data, if this book were ever going to see the light of day it was essential to focus our research on certain critical periods, achievements, events, and challenges where managerial action or inaction played a crucial role in shaping subsequent events.

The foundations for Nokia being able to move into mobile telecommunications had been laid by two strategies of an early CEO: one to buy consumer electronics businesses, and the second to internationalize Nokia so it was not so reliant on its neighbor and old foe, the Soviet Union. Although the later decision to focus all of Nokia's efforts on telecommunications equipment, with a strong emphasis on mobile communications, can be formally dated to 1991, this was in fact the culmination of multiple technology development efforts, strategic commitments, organizational alignments, and key managerial appointments, some made as early as the 1960s.

The 1990s were important on a number of fronts. A young and energetic leadership team took the helm. Talented and driven, but with little managerial experience and few industry orthodoxies to slow them down, they essentially ran Nokia like an entrepreneurial start-up. They played a pivotal role in the rapid international expansion of both sales and manufacturing, and imbued the firm with a strong organizational energy and "can-do" culture. The processes put in place during this period, in particular in response to the near breakdown of the supply chain, positioned Nokia to be able to scale up production and sales much faster than all of its competitors.

There were a number of decisions made between 2001 and 2005 that had significant consequences. The continued focus on an ever-greater user lifestyle-based approach to market segmentation resulted in product proliferation and difficulties achieving high enough levels of differentiation between products. The decision to continue investing in and using the Symbian OS not only slowed down new product development but further contributed to a lack of differentiation.

The 2004–8 period was one of strategic stasis that had its genesis in a poorly implemented reorganization into a matrix structure. The departure of key senior executives after the reorganization left a vacuum in both strategic thinking and informal yet powerful integration mechanisms. Poor implementation of the matrix combined with the introduction of short-term metrics resulted in internal competition for shared resources and further product fragmentation with a lack of differentiation.

While Nokia posted some of its strongest financial results in 2007, internally it was struggling. The period up to 2010 was characterized by management's attempts to stem the decline. The board stepped in and for the first time in Nokia's history brought in an outsider to head the firm. But this change in leadership did nothing to alleviate the deep problems and resulted in the sale of the mobile phones business.

The research journey to understand these important periods and critical decisions was a long and detailed one—although when Yves began his exploration of Nokia back in 1996, it was certainly not with this book in mind. For readers who wish to understand more about the research process, a description can be found in Appendix 6.

Organization of the Book

To enable the reader to explore the history of Nokia, and hopefully get a sense of the context in which events unfolded and decisions were made before our own analysis comes into play, each chapter comprises two parts. The first is a broadly chronological narrative history of the period in question. In the space given, the narratives do not pretend to provide an exhaustive history of Nokia. But neither are they just a recalling of specific events or actions. Each narrative dives into the underlying causal mechanisms behind the organization and its workings, and the relationships between senior executives, which made effective decisions and commitments either easier or more difficult.

To avoid the risk of focusing the narratives on data which supported any preconceived ideas we might have had about Nokia's rise and decline, we carefully separated the development of the narratives for each chapter from their interpretation, developing each of the narrative chapters before attempting any conceptualization based on the data.

The second part of each chapter is an analytical commentary based on the analysis and interpretation of data gathered for the narratives. These commentaries do not necessarily contribute "new to the world" conceptualizations, but they do draw together multiple aspects from Nokia's experience and frame these in such a way as to allow for more generalizable lessons to be learned. Selected references to other publications are made in the commentaries—these do not aim to provide a review or synthesis of the academic literature or existing research relating to these points. The intention is that they further deepen and enlighten our own analysis and point the reader to the most relevant research findings and conceptualizations. In each chapter, apart from Chapters 8 and 9, the commentary either explicitly or implicitly analyzes events along what we call the "CORE" dimensions: *Cognition, Organization, Relationships,* and *Emotions.*

Although it is easier to discern patterns in strategic outcomes than to identify and analyze the various mechanisms that interact to create these outcomes, a narrative that ignores the details of these mechanisms would be seriously wanting. Potentially generalizable implications for action would not be reliable. So in developing the narratives we did not limit ourselves to strategic actions or discourses, but decided to dive into the underlying mechanisms, along four dimensions: the perspectives and mental models managers developed and adopted; the organization and its workings; the relationships between senior executives that impacted the ability to make effective decisions and commitments easier or more difficult; and the emotional engagement that provides the energy and will to act.

A Cognitive Dimension

In the strategist's mind (the CEO, or part of the executive team), strategy is a theory of how to succeed. As such, it is a cognitive construct, an intellectual reasoning about the causes and effects of actions and understanding of a firm's environment. This includes clear or fuzzy, accurate or mistaken foresight about the future of that environment. In exploring Nokia's evolution, we need to be sensitive to what its leaders saw, how they interpreted what they perceived, what conclusions they drew, and what decisions they made.

An Organizational Dimension

Strategy is not just thought and planning but is about action—what actually gets done. And in large, complex organizations like Nokia, strategy in action involves many people in the organization. In our exploration, we therefore develop an understanding of not only how the organization worked in implementing strategic decisions, but also the equally important but less visible area of how it generated operational actions and drove behavior, the consequences of which were strategic. An organization filters strategic choices and, in many cases, may drive actions that only get rationalized *ex post* as an "intellectual" strategy. It is therefore important to understand what managers did in the context of their roles, responsibilities, and relationships in an organization, not just what they thought.

A Relational Dimension

Relationships among people are thus also important. In mature, long-standing bureaucratic organizations, relationships are often codified, formalized, well established, and likely to have become routine. Managers are the proverbial "cog in the machine" of a bureaucracy with set rules and norms. But in younger, fast-growing organizations like Nokia in mobile phones, which are still being built and striving to succeed in wholly new domains, relationships need to be explored more carefully. The interpersonal dimension matters more than the institutional one—how leaders complement each other, how well they work together, and the ambitions they harbor are all important elements in exploring and explaining success or failure.

An Emotional Dimension

It is not only relationships that are instrumental in rapidly emerging businesses, emotions matter too. They are critical to the quality of strategic sense-making, as the majority of our cognition is intuitive and therefore affected by our emotions. Emotions are also vital to collective commitments where interpersonal likes and dislikes play a role. And as emotions are contagious, they influence everybody's commitment and attitudes in the organization. Joy or fear spread easily, sometimes in the absence of good analytical justification. So, we cannot ignore the emotional dimension in our exploration.

The interplay of these CORE elements determines the ability of a company's leadership to be strategically adaptive or to fall prey to growing rigidity and strategic stasis in the face of conflicting pressures and priorities.

Chapter Outlines

Each chapter covers a distinct period in Nokia's rise and fall in mobile phones.

Chapter 2: The Planetary Alignment Was Right

This chapter provides historical background on the growth of Nokia and the co-evolution of an emergent ICT cluster in Finland. It carefully distinguishes what is unique and idiosyncratic and what is generalizable from that co-evolution.

It explores how smart opportunism, rather than a grand strategy, drove Nokia's adaptation from traditional industries to mobile telecoms and how the group took advantage of unique features of the geopolitical, institutional, and industrial contexts of Finland, post-World War II. It highlights the dominant logics and heuristics from formative experiences in the early evolution of the company.

Chapter 3: We Were the Only Ones to See It

Alone among key early competitors (in particular Ericsson and Motorola), Nokia's executives perceived the full potential of mobile phones as a consumer product. Nokia progressively foresaw the development of a mass market. This chapter describes and analyzes how this more perceptive framing emerged over time, and why other firms (the leading incumbents at that time) did not develop a comparable framing.

Conceptually, the key points highlighted in this chapter are that innovative winning strategies result from clear, lucid, and determined strategic opportunism and are built from increasing insights as an innovation process or as new competitive situations develop, not from grand plans or a sudden awakening to a new reality. They evolve and develop incrementally and often iteratively. We also conceptualize how negotiation skills in a new consortium—GSM—opened a new strategic window. The chapter shows that the most important innovations are not necessarily technological: perhaps most critical to Nokia's success in that period was understanding the needs of new recently licensed mobile service operators—how different they were from those of traditional incumbent telecoms and how they fostered business model innovations that helped Nokia grow globally very rapidly.

Chapter 4: A Rising Star

Nokia was able to scale up remarkably quickly in the 1990s, faster than any producer of a complicated product ever had (a mobile phone has about 200 to

300 components and subsystems). By 1995, however, Nokia lost control of its supply chain, going through what it refers to as a "logistics crisis." This chapter reviews and analyzes the factors that allowed extremely fast growth, and also discusses how Nokia was able to recover from the logistics crisis by bringing greater discipline to how Nokia Mobile Phones was run and greater sophistication, in particular, to supply chain management. Nokia also decided to create a New Venture organization, initially with a mission to search for a "third leg," beyond Mobile Phones and Networks. This chapter analyzes how these developments enabled the continuation of extraordinarily rapid growth through the late 1990s but also sowed the seeds of later difficulties.

Chapter 5: Attracting the Planets

In the late 1990s, after Nokia had developed the first smartphone (then dubbed "Communicator"), executives became increasingly sensitive to the importance of operating systems. At the same time, as data communications and multimedia were gaining importance, they were well aware of the dangers of mobile phones following a similar evolutionary path to that of personal computers, in which Microsoft captured nearly all the value leaving hardware producers with very little. It was also becoming clear that more complex business models would be needed to tap into new opportunities and applications beyond voice transmission.

This chapter describes and analyzes how Nokia managed this transformation. It describes the development of the Communicator smartphone, the establishment of the Symbian OS, and the creation of an innovative camera phone. As the nature of the industry was changing and becoming more complex, it also looks at how Nokia responded by engaging with a wider ecosystem to develop the visual radio concept. These examples highlight the challenges the new world of software platforms and application ecosystems raised for Nokia.

Chapter 6: A Supernova

This chapter reviews the period 2004–6, opening with a description of problems Nokia was facing due to a boycott of its products by operators. It goes on to analyze the implications of a reorganization into a matrix structure in 2004, which led to wide-ranging top-management changes over the following two years and a subsequent deterioration of strategic thinking and strategic leadership. We also see a growing bureaucratization and loss of agility during this period, along with increasing internal competition and difficulties as Nokia grappled with the challenges of shifting from a "hardware-first" to "software-first" approach.

Chapter 7: A Fading Star

Covering the period 2006–11, in this chapter we see how the seeds of destruction that were unknowingly sown in the early 2000s came to fruition. Nokia was collapsing from within well before Apple or Google became competitors, leaving Nokia's new management team in a difficult position in which developing a successful managerial response to the changed external environment had become all but impossible.

Successive reorganizations, a lack of technology leadership, and the collapse of the strategy process all contributed to Nokia rapidly losing its leadership position. We look at the options Nokia's management team considered with regard to its smartphone strategy before ultimately choosing an alliance with Microsoft.

Chapter 8: Toward a New Alignment?

This chapter covers the demise of Nokia's phone business under the group's first non-Finnish CEO, and the ultimate failure in strategy which led to significant losses and the sale of the phone business to Microsoft. It also describes how under new chairmanship, the board began to play a much stronger strategic role which resulted in the rebirth of Nokia as a telecoms infrastructure player.

Chapter 9: The Astronomer's Perspective

The bulk of this chapter is conceptual more than descriptive and analytical. It focuses on the research questions raised in Chapter 1 and how analyzing and conceptualizing the story of Nokia in mobile phones helps address these and shed valuable light on their managerial implications. Of course, this also provides a way to summarize the main findings and conceptual implications from the research, and brings a logical closure to the book.

References

Kenneth R. Andrews, *The Concept of Corporate Strategy* (Richard D. Irwin, Homewood, 1971).

Alfred Chandler, *Strategy and Structure: Chapters in the History of the Industrial Enterprise* (MIT Press, Cambridge, MA, 1962).

Clayton M. Christensen, *The Innovator's Dilemma* (HarperCollins, New York, 1997).

Jim Collins, *How the Mighty Fall and Why Some Companies Never Give In* (Random House Business Books, London, 2009).

Richard Cyert and James March, *A Behavioral Theory of the Firm* (Martino Fine Books, Eastford, CT, 1963).

Yves Doz and Mikko Kosonen, *Fast Strategy: How Strategic Agility Will Help You Stay Ahead of the Game* (Wharton School Publishing, Harlow, 2008).

Michael T. Hannan and John Freeman, "Structural Inertia and Organizational Change" (*American Sociological Review*, Vol. 49 Issue 2, April 1984) pp. 149–64.

Richard Nelson and Sidney Winter, *An Evolutionary Theory of Economic Change* (Harvard University Press, Cambridge, MA, 1982).

Charles Perrow, *Normal Accidents: Living with High-Risk Technologies* (Princeton University Press, Princeton, 1984).

Donald Sull, *Revival of the Fittest: Why Good Companies Go Bad and How Great Managers Remake Them* (Harvard Business School Press, Boston, 2003).

Nassim Nicholas Taleb, *The Black Swan: The Impact of the Highly Improbable* (Random House, New York, 2007).

Karl Weick, "The Vulnerable System: An Analysis of the Tenerife Air Disaster" (*Journal of Management*, Vol. 16 Issue 3, September 1990) pp. 571–94.

2

The Planetary Alignment Was Right

Mention the name Nokia to its legions of loyal customers around the world during the height of the firm's success, and most would likely have assumed that the company responsible for putting an innovative phone in their pocket and transforming the way they communicate was a young, entrepreneurial firm which, unlike the incumbent telecoms equipment firms, was hungry for success, with a bold vision of the future and unafraid to take risks to play a leading role in realizing that future. On many counts Nokia's customers would have been right, but for the fact that Nokia existed long before it made its brand ubiquitous with mobile phones. In fact, far from being a start-up or even a relative newcomer, the company's origins stretch back to 1865.

Informative though the history of Nokia is in understanding what drove both the rise and fall of Nokia in mobile phones, it isn't the purpose of this book exhaustively to pore through the annals of Nokia's past. Yet neither can its history be entirely ignored, because understanding Nokia's incredible success from the 1990s to mid-2000s, and even its later decline, requires knowledge of critical aspects of the company's history that played an important role in shaping subsequent events. What follows in this chapter, therefore, is a selective journey through Nokia's history, introducing the key events and leaders that had a direct impact on the firm's evolving strategic commitments, competency development, culture, and people.

The Origins of Nokia

Nokia Corporation as we know it, was born in 1967 from the merger of forestry, paper, and pulp group Nokia Ab (established 1865 and named after the town in which it was founded), Finnish Rubber Works (established 1889), and Finnish Cable Works (FCW, established 1912). By far the biggest constituent in the newly merged entity, FCW can also be viewed as the real forerunner of the modern Nokia due to a series of opportunistic strategic moves taking advantage of the unique Finnish context to shift from producing telegraph cables to radio communications and electronics.

FCW's initial foray away from purely cables and into the wider telecoms sector came in 1930 when it began designing telephones and automatic switches for Finland's burgeoning fixed-line telephone networks, which by the end of the decade had over 800 local operators—this in a country with a population of just under 3,700,000! Unusually, at the time, without a national champion, the Finnish government had promoted an open competitive market for telecoms equipment, which meant Nokia was just one of many suppliers, the largest of which was Sweden's Ericsson.

A policy of eschewing a state monopoly (prevalent in other countries) in favor of this unusual and rather fragmented approach to telecoms had been pursued with good reason. Finland had long been under Swedish rule when in 1808 it was attacked by Russia, and after a successful Russian campaign the following year it became a Grand Duchy of Russia (essentially a protectorate). Even though Finland was granted its own senate, all major decisions had to be approved by the Russian Tsar. After centuries of foreign control, the Finns understandably felt vulnerable and recognized that a telephone network could be a vital tool for national security (to put this into context, Finland was and continues to be a sparsely populated country that, in terms of land mass, is only slightly smaller than modern-day Germany). To circumvent the requirement for Russian approval of a major telecoms project and keep the new network under Finnish control, the Finnish Senate promoted a local, decentralized approach run by municipal authorities.

The Bolshevik revolution in 1917 led to Finland gaining independence. But just over two decades later, the Soviet Union would once again assert its influence over Finland through what became known as the Winter War, and in doing so contributed to shaping modern Finland's national identity. Stemming from the Nazi-Soviet non-aggression pact, Stalin wanted to take over Finnish territory in the Baltic for military bases. The Finns refused, and in November 1939 a huge, well-equipped Soviet Army invaded Finland. The Finnish Army was tiny and lacked arms, munitions, and even uniforms, yet working in small teams, in the densely forested border territories during one of the coldest winters in memory, they initially inflicted huge casualties on the Soviets. By mid-March, however, the Finnish Army could no longer hold back the Soviet Army and a peace treaty was sought in which the Finns were forced to concede even more territory along their eastern border than Stalin had originally demanded.

Ironically, it was the Soviet Union that would later provide the bedrock for the expansion of FCW's telecoms business. Finland had fought alongside Germany during most of World War II. At the end of the war, although Finland escaped becoming a Soviet "satellite" state, significant reparations were nonetheless imposed by the Soviet Union, including the supply of telecoms equipment, which was largely met by FCW. By the end of the 1940s, even after the reparation payments had ended, around half of FCW's output headed to its eastern neighbor.

In 1948, when the Marshall Plan was being introduced to help rebuild Western Europe's post-war economies, Finland declined to receive aid on the grounds that it needed to remain neutral in the eyes of its biggest trading partner, and very powerful neighbor, the Soviet Union (with which it shared a 1,340 kilometers (833 mile) land border). This could have put Finnish companies at a technological disadvantage against their European competitors, who were the recipients of technology transfers as part of the Marshall Plan. But Finland, long used to self-reliance, determination, and willpower to overcome obstacles (characteristics that Finns sum up in the term *sisu*), believed the right combination of public policies and private enterprise would enable the country to develop its own technologies. The spirit of *sisu* was further called upon to develop the technologies and competencies for military equipment, as not being a member of NATO (North Atlantic Treaty Organization) when it was established in 1949, Finland was excluded from importing military equipment from NATO countries.

In this climate of national self-reliance and determination, FCW's cable business went from strength to strength, growing production capacity and efficiency, but it wasn't until 1956 and the appointment of Björn Westerlund as CEO that FCW began to lay the foundations critical for the emergence of Nokia as a global player in mobile telecoms. A graduate of Helsinki University of Technology and son of a prominent industrialist, Westerlund had joined FCW as an engineer in 1936. He was of a generation born shortly before Finnish independence that had grown up surrounded by the ghosts of the country's turbulent past. The desire to help create a strong and stable Finland was just as important to Westerlund as transforming FCW (and later Nokia) into a resilient international player. He saw that while the Soviet Union was an important market, and that the cable business was profitable, for FCW to survive in the long term it would need to diversify into adjacent product areas and expand into other export markets.

In 1960, Westerlund took the important step of establishing an electronics department at FCW. The new unit imported computers, ran data processing services for the Finnish public sector and private firms, conducted R&D covering a wide range of electronics-related areas, and designed and manufactured minicomputers. Accounting for a tiny fraction of the firm's sales and making a loss for its first fifteen years, many CEOs would have abandoned this fledlging business. But for Westerlund, the electronics unit was creating new competencies for Nokia in an industry that was growing rapidly.

Throughout this period, close collaboration between the Finnish government and industry saw a coordinated push to upgrade national technical capabilities (the fact that Westerlund briefly took on the role of minister of trade and industry in 1961, gives an indication of the strength of the relationship between state and industry). In addition to the Helsinki University of Technology (established 1849) and the University of Tampere (established in 1925 in Finland's main industrial center), in 1958 a third technical university was founded at Oulu, near the northern tip of the Baltic. And in 1967, the government established Sitra, a national fund for innovation mandated among other things to promote and financially support future-oriented R&D in private firms.

Nokia: Post-Merger Collaborations

The newly merged Nokia Group was a direct beneficiary of the government's push to transform the Finnish economy from one reliant upon forestry-related industries to one based on high value-added technologies. After the merger, Westerlund had become CEO of Nokia, and although the group retained its diversified portfolio of businesses, he was firmly focused on pursuing opportunities in the telecoms and electronics arenas. Nokia's telecoms and electronics research units received government subsidies to support innovative research programs, and the group attracted Finland's best and brightest engineers and technologists graduating in ever-greater numbers from the country's expanding technical universities.

A series of challenging tenders from the Finnish military and government put the firm on the path toward mobile communications. In 1963, FCW had developed a forerunner of the mobile phone with a radio-telephone it created for the army. Then, in 1968, the government announced its intention to build a national mobile network. With almost 75 percent of the country being dense forest, over 180,000 lakes, and a similar number of small islands, Finland has a particularly challenging topography which, combined with low population density, made it untenable to connect all of the telephone services in small dispersed communities into a national fixed-line system. So a national mobile network seemed a much quicker, more cost-effective, and easier-to-maintain alternative. This gave the newly merged Nokia additional stimulus to explore mobile technologies, and the following year it unveiled the world's first pulse code modulation (PCM) digital data transmission equipment that conformed to international standards (PCM transforms analog signals into digital ones and would prove to be critical for later digital switching platforms).

When Westerlund retired as CEO in 1977 he left a very different firm to the one he had joined forty-one years earlier. He had set the firm on a new path toward a more technology-intensive future, and had recognized that the best prospects of both Nokia and Finland lay not in a tightly coupled relationship with the Soviet Union but with the wider world.

This was a belief that was shared and expanded upon by Kari Kairamo, Nokia's director of international affairs, who succeeded Westerlund as CEO. Kairamo was flamboyant, charismatic, and unusually for a Finn, particularly at that time, had spent time living and working abroad selling Finnish paper-manufacturing machinery in Poland, Brazil, and New York. Kairamo's personality, energy, sales experience, and international exposure would have an enormous impact on shaping Nokia well beyond his tenure at the helm. As Pekka Ala-Pietilä (later head of Nokia Mobile Phones and of whom we shall hear much more in later chapters) explained when we met early in 2015, "Kairamo was a very visionary and inspiring leader and thanks to his leadership I chose to come to Nokia like many other young people at that time. Kairamo had the vision that Nokia could conquer Europe—it was completely unprecedented in Finland that someone could state such an ambition aloud."

Like Westerlund before him, Kairamo relied less on a detailed strategic roadmap than a broad vision of where Nokia was headed, which was realized through successive opportunistic moves. Toward the end of 1977, for example, Nokia formed an R&D joint venture with Televa (Finland's loss-making state telecoms company) to develop digital switching technologies. This was an area of growing importance, as computer networks which sent digitally coded data packets relied on telephone systems for connectivity, and to cope with this, telephone exchanges would need digital switches. Nokia's larger competitors, Ericsson, Alcatel, and Siemens, were all working on digital switching and so it seemed logical for Nokia to combine its computing experience from the electronics division Westerlund had established with Televa's electromechanical and electronic switching exchange knowledge to enter the fray.

The following year, Nokia formed another joint venture that would prove critical to later success, with Salora, one of Finland's larger radio-telephone suppliers. Until this point, radio telephony had been the preserve of the military and emergency services. With this move Nokia and Salora formed a new company, Mobira, which would combine the latter's radio-telephone handset knowledge with Nokia's expertise in base stations and switching technologies to commercialize mobile technologies for wider applications.

Mobira didn't have to wait long for a large market for its products to emerge. In 1981, Sweden, Norway, Finland, and Denmark collaborated to launch the NMT (Nordic Mobile Telephone). This cross-border mobile network, which relied on analog technology, was the most advanced system in the world at the time and offered roaming between the countries in the network. This required cooperation around standards and technical specifications, and as a result opened the supplier market to intense competition. In addition to a number of small players, Nokia found itself competing directly against the much larger Ericsson for both infrastructure contracts and handset sales.

At this point, it is probably worth a detour to revisit early mobile phones, as it is easy to forget quite how far mobile communications have come in the three and half decades since NMT attracted its first customers. The phones in use on the early NMT network were car phones—Mobira's first dedicated car phone, the Mobira Senator 450, came to the market in 1982. It was connected to a huge battery pack and weighed around 10 kilograms (22 pounds). It wasn't long before handheld portable phones were available on the NMT network, but even these were bulky, heavy, and had a short battery life (the Mobira Cityman 900 for example—made famous by the image of Mikhail Gorbachev using one to call Moscow from Helsinki in 1987—weighed 760 grams).

NMT had provided not only an impetus for Mobira to speed up the development of handsets, but put pressure on the Nokia Televa joint venture to deliver a digital switch. Yet, unlike their large competitors, this small joint venture faced a disadvantage in that they had neither the financial resources nor the time to design their own proprietary semiconductor chips for the switch. Instead, they designed their switch around a standard Intel processor chip, and in 1982 introduced the DX200 digital switching platform. Although this came to the market slightly later than its competitors' offerings, the DX200 was an immediate and long-lasting success. It was highly reliable, it was significantly cheaper than its rivals (costing about two-thirds less) thanks to the use of the Intel chip, and its modular architecture made it easily scalable to cope with increased capacity. In fact, Nokia sold DX200 platforms globally until the technology began to be phased out in 2013.

A year after the successful launch of NMT, in 1982 the Confederation of European Posts and Telecommunications (CEPT)—a body formed by Europe's monopoly state telecoms firms in 1959 to coordinate regulations, standards, and operational issues across the region—established the Groupe Spécial Mobile, later renamed Global System for Mobile Communications (GSM). There were nine different and incompatible analog systems in use by Europe's twenty-six phone companies, and the GSM advisory group had a mandate to design a single pan-European digital set of standards. Being from a small country with a very limited market, Nokia could only grow by expanding its horizons geographically, and so GSM, with the promise of twenty-six European markets adopting the standard, was a collaboration that Nokia wanted to be at the heart of.

Being involved in NMT, Nokia already had pioneering research programs underway looking at FDMA (Frequency Division Multiple Access) and TDMA (Time Division Multiple Access) digital systems. As an active member of a number of international GSM collaborative working groups, Nokia had positioned itself at the center of GSM development, and in 1986 delivered the first GSM digital test system, which was formally adopted by CEPT the following year.

International Expansion Under Kairamo

The 1980s were not only a period of growth through technical advancements and local collaborations—under Kairamo's leadership the decade saw Nokia grasp every opportunity to internationalize, as he felt that growth opportunities in Finland would be limited for Nokia and that European integration would expose the group to strong international competition. True to his entrepreneurial drive, Kairamo decided to take the initiative and internationalize Nokia around three growth areas he foresaw would converge in the future: consumer electronics, computers, and telecom equipment.

In 1983, Mobira formed an alliance with Tandy, at the time the largest consumer electronics retailer in the US, in which they would supply handsets for Tandy to sell in its 7,000 Radio Shack stores under the Tandy and Radio Shack brands. Until this point, Mobira's focus had been on technology innovation, but its encounter with Tandy exposed it to the importance of cost efficiency in manufacturing when Tandy rejected Mobira's proposal to manufacture phones in Europe in favor of setting up a low-cost production facility in South Korea.

In the US, sales of mobile handsets were dominated by the big operators as part of customer contracts, as only the operators could get products certified by the US regulator, the Federal Communications Commission (FCC). Having gained a foothold in the market through the Mobira-Tandy alliance, Nokia approached US operators as a new channel to distribute its handsets—initially under the Mobira brand and later when Nokia acquired UK handset firm Technophone under that brand too. As he had spent much of his career in sales, one of Kairamo's early moves on becoming CEO had been to instill the importance of listening to customer requirements across the Nokia Group. Even though in later years Nokia would struggle with sales in the US, during this earlier period a focus on customers as well as technological innovation paid dividends, as Nokia was eager and willing to adapt its products to meet individual operator requirements, and as a result rapidly grew its market share as well as its know-how.

Not all of Nokia's international growth plans during this period were so successful though. Unlike mobile telecoms, in which Nokia had technical expertise and an early-mover advantage it could exploit in order to grow, when Kairamo decided to push into consumer electronics, Nokia was a relative newcomer to the sector. It entered the market at a time when Japanese manufacturers were gaining strength and the market in Europe was already saturated and consolidating around Philips and Thomson. Nokia had neither the expertise nor the time to grow organically, and so sought expansion via international acquisitions.

Driven by a lethal combination of Kairamo's infectious enthusiasm to see Nokia become an international player and a lack of experience in both the sector and merger and acquisition activity, Nokia rushed headlong into buy-ing the "leftovers" of Europe's consolidation without conducting thorough due diligence. Consequently, it ended up with a hotchpotch of weak brands, poor distribution channels, and multiple manufacturing processes across the brands that proved impossible for the Finns to integrate. Even though these acquisitions would prove to be a major cash drain on the company for several years and were ultimately a failure, they did provide Nokia with some critical lessons. First, strong global branding was key for consumer goods. Second, in consumer electronics, margins were low and so success was dependent upon high-volume sales. Finally, the lessons from Tandy about the importance of low-cost, efficient manufacturing processes were reinforced.

Finland and Nokia: Growing Together

Like Westerlund before him, Kairamo played a very active public role in helping to shape Finnish industrial policy toward a more technology-intensive future. Partially motivated by the need to create a high-tech cluster to provide the suppliers and partners needed for Nokia's growth, Kairamo also had a genuine desire to see an independent Finland flourish after centuries of being held back by foreign rule. Although Nokia did not yet dominate the Finnish economy, by the 1980s it was already a big enough and serious enough player for the Finnish administration to take Kairamo's suggestions very seriously. Throughout the 1980s, in addition to his "day job," Kairamo was also chairman of the Confederation of Finnish Industry, and in this capacity lobbied very hard for the policies and public sector support needed to assist the emergence of a strong high-tech sector in Finland.

His discussions with the Ministry for Employment and the Economy played a role in the establishment in 1983 of Tekes (the Finnish Funding Agency for Technology and Innovation), which was set up to support R&D financially in areas identified as being strategically important and broker research partner-ships across private and public bodies.

Over the following decade in particular, Tekes would prove vital to Nokia's innovation capability in more ways than one. Throughout the 1980s, Tekes-funded research projects within Nokia represented on average around 8 percent of the firm's R&D budget. Depending upon the size and number of projects this could vary vastly from year to year. What was constant though, was that Tekes-funded research was at the more innovative end of the R&D spectrum and so gave the firm a little more latitude to undertake higher risk, higher reward research.

Tekes also introduced Nokia to research partners that would make a critical contribution to building the firm's capabilities. For example, an early joint project with the VTT Public Technical Research Center developed the foundation for Nokia's later GSM technologies; and by partnering with universities, public research institutes, and other private firms, Tekes projects gave Nokia access to a valuable recruitment pool of some of the country's most talented scientists and engineers.

During this period, growth at Nokia also came from the consolidation of its two joint ventures in mobile communications. First, in 1984, Nokia bought out Salora to take full control of the handset joint venture, Mobira—four years later this was renamed Nokia Mobile Phones. Then, in 1987, it acquired the Finnish state's share in the R&D joint venture with Televa that a few years earlier had so successfully developed the DX200 digital switching platform. Combined with Nokia's existing competencies, taking control of these two joint ventures gave the firm the full set of in-house capabilities in mobile infrastructure and handsets. This was to prove a great advantage for Nokia's expansion related to GSM technologies when a standard was agreed in 1987.

Management, Governance, and Reorganization

During the 1980s, the Nokia conglomerate was ostensibly made up of two very different sides. On the one hand, the rubber and forestry parts of the firm displayed all of the attributes of mature, established businesses. But on the other side, everything related to the old FCW portfolio of telecoms businesses—electronics, mobile handsets, and telecoms infrastructure—behaved very much like a series of entrepreneurial start-ups, and this wasn't an accident. Kairamo strongly believed that formal management processes and systems, managerial hierarchies, and strong central oversight would hinder the growth of the new technology-intensive parts of Nokia, preventing them from investing in experimentation and seizing new opportunities. Instead, decentralization, entrepreneurialism, and a flat organization were the bywords for how these parts of Nokia were managed. It is interesting to note that very few of the people joining the telecoms-related businesses in Nokia at this time had experience of management in multinational corporations, or any large company for that matter, and those that did had only held junior positions.

Unfortunately, there was a stumbling block to Kairamo's vision of operational freedom and flexibility in the form of board members from Nokia's largest shareholders, the Union Bank of Finland and KOP Bank. With financial deregulation yet to take hold, it was very common at the time for local banks to dominate shareholdings in large Finnish firms. Kairamo hatched a plan to reduce shareholder control over Nokia, and in 1986 formally proposed a new governance structure in which a new internal board with Nokia's CEO acting as chairman would be established in between the existing supervisory board and the management board. This new board, made up of senior Nokia executives, would take on much of the work of the supervisory board, leaving it to focus on "big issues." At the same time, the management board would be headed by Nokia's president/chief operating officer (COO) and include the business division heads.

As Kairamo was a very vocal and public figure, widely revered for putting both Nokia and Finland on the international stage, the supervisory board felt it would be unwise to risk a public furor by refusing his proposal. And so they agreed to the new governance structure that in essence reduced their involvement in and control of Nokia.

Freed from the constraints imposed by a conservative board, most of whose members had neither experience in international business nor the new mobile telecoms sector, Kairamo and his deputies could move much more certainly and swiftly in positioning Nokia to take advantage of emerging opportunities. Deregulation in the telecoms market, for example, which began with the US and UK in 1984, would open up the nascent mobile telecoms sector to competition and also provide an opportunity for new equipment firms to offer cost-efficient end-to-end solutions. Nokia's experience of working with Finland's many small and demanding operators positioned it well to move into this segment. Having developed its own very successful digital switching platform, digitization was another emerging opportunity that Nokia's entrepreneurial managers felt the firm was well positioned to exploit.

A working group of young managers from the handset, base stations, and switches sides of the businesses produced a report outlining the opportunities they saw arising from market liberalization and digitization. For instance, they anticipated that rather than being merely network terminals—which was the unquestioned, prevailing view at the time—mobile phones, or handsets, could become a business in its own right. One of the group, Sari Baldauf (who at the time was working as a Nokia Group-level strategist and would go on to become a key figure in Nokia's success on the network infrastructure side), also concluded that Nokia was not optimally structured to meet the new strategic opportunities. She recognized there was a risk that the "old" analog business lines would resist the development of "new" digital ones, and so made a recommendation that a new, separate business unit for mobile handsets be established.

Convinced that the working group was right in predicting the telecoms sector would be revolutionized in the coming years, in 1987 Nokia restructured its mobile telecoms activities into two distinct groups. All base station and digital switching activities were grouped into a mobile infrastructure division called Nokia Cellular Systems (NCS), which sat within Nokia Telecommunications (NTC). Following Baldauf's recommendation, handsets became a standalone business unit—Nokia Mobile Phones (NMP). These two divisions would, over the following decade, become the core of Nokia Corp.

External Events and Internal Crisis

With a new structure in place to support its vision for growth, the future should have looked bright for Nokia. But a rapid succession of internal problems, exacerbated by external geopolitical and economic events, would expose the group's fragility and put its very survival in peril.

Kairamo's decentralized approach to running Nokia made it difficult for corporate management to get a true picture of how various parts of the firm were performing except in terms of aggregate financial control. Added to this, the acquisition-fueled international growth over the preceding decade, which had been financed by Finnish banks, had resulted in a lot of persistent red ink in Nokia's balance sheet, and pre-tax profits were down around 40 percent from the previous year. It certainly looked like Nokia had overextended itself.

Things were made worse when in 1988, KOP Bank, one of Nokia's biggest investors and itself in trouble, proposed not only withdrawing funding but divesting its stake in Nokia. A reprieve was granted by Nokia's other large shareholder, Union Bank of Finland, persuading KOP to maintain the status quo for the time being.

The pressure of this looming crisis on Nokia's management was tremendous. Although Kairamo was known for his optimism, enthusiasm, charisma, and energy, he had for many years suffered from bipolar depression. In December 1988 he committed suicide. Tragically, Timo Koski, the person being groomed as Kairamo's successor, had died from a brain hemorrhage earlier that year and this led to a vicious political battle between four young sector heads all now vying for pole position. By all accounts, Kairamo had been very shaken by the death of Koski and unimpressed by the sector heads competing for his attention and approval, and he had failed to put an alternative succession plan in place.

The continuing battle for leadership based on pure self-interest was a cultural shock for Nokians who had been used to a collegiate culture in which everyone pulled together for the benefit of their firm and their country. Rather than allow the destructive succession battle to further weaken the firm, Nokia's supervisory board overlooked the four young executives competing for the role in favor of appointing Nokia's COO, Simo Vuorilehto, as CEO. Having a strong operational background, Vuorilehto was seen as a safe pair of hands to integrate Nokia's acquisitions and steer the firm out of the danger zone.

Vuorilehto began to rationalize Nokia, cutting the workforce in half (to 22,000) over the next two years. But progress was stalled by unfolding external events. The Soviet Bloc had begun to unwind in 1989 with the fall of the Berlin Wall. Within two years, the Soviet Union collapsed and Europe had entered a deep recession. The impact of these events on the Finnish economy was devastating. Gross domestic product fell by 10 percent, unemployment reached 18 percent, exports dried up, and Finnish banks were near to collapse. For Nokia, which was already in trouble, its options seemed very limited. The Union Bank of Finland saw a potential lifeline in selling Nokia to Ericsson, but negotiations broke down as the Swedish group felt Nokia's data and consumer electronics divisions were too great a liability.

All of this was taking place against a background of senior management infighting. Two years into Vuorilehto's tenure, Nokia's supervisory board had begun to exercise greater influence on strategic choices. Without Vuorilehto's knowledge, they had appointed the chairman's son-in-law, Kalle Isokallio, as president of Nokia, dividing the loyalties of senior managers between the two men, eroding trust within the senior ranks, and resulting in stalemates over urgent and critical decisions.

In a last-ditch attempt to find a way out of the crisis, Nokia's board hired Boston Consulting Group (BCG) to assess Nokia's strategic options. Instead of providing a hoped-for panacea, the resulting report painted a bleak future. BCG suggested the only sector in which Nokia was involved that could offer sustainable growth was mobile communications, but felt that Nokia was far too small to survive and compete in that sector against the likes of Ericsson, Motorola, and the Japanese players.

Commentary

When Jorma Ollila, pouring coffee early in the morning while being interviewed for an earlier research project over a decade ago, at a time when Nokia was still a stellar success, opened the conversation with, "Yves, before we start, do not forget that back in the 1990s the planetary alignment was right," little did I realize how apt his metaphor was. As planets are constantly on the move, a planetary alignment is a rare and brief occurrence, something unlikely to repeat itself for a very long time. And as such, seizing the opportunity presented by a "planetary alignment" when it arises is essential as timing conditions success.

And indeed the timing was right for Nokia. In the 1990s, one often heard bewilderment from distant observers at Nokia's success out of the "barren tundra" of Finland (actually quite an inaccurate comment in topographical terms, as Finland is mostly forest and lakes). Nokia's surprising success sprung from a highly fortuitous and very supportive context, creating a planetary alignment in the firm's favor. In more conceptual terms, Nokia's success in mobile phones was made possible by circumstances specific to Finland, where a remarkable innovation cluster emerged around mobile telecommunications, mobile devices, and infrastructure. There was no great plan, no overriding strategic logic or guiding architecture, just smart opportunistic collective adaptation.

But as human beings, we are programmed not only to find recurrent causes but also to look for repeatability and rules for action, so to accept an outstanding success as stemming from an alignment we cannot do much about is hard. At a conference I spoke at in Ljubljana in the early 2000s with Mikko Kosonen, our session was titled (not by us), "Can Europe Create Another Nokia?" The question came from the observation that except for SAP, started in the 1970s by former IBM engineers, Nokia was the only big ICT success story in Europe, and it was the only truly indigenous one. But Europe did not create Nokia, Nokia's leaders created Nokia! Much of the audience felt disappointed that we could not offer a repeatable recipe for European companies.

The very fortuitous alignment did not just come about by itself, but was the result of a long sequence of problem-solving actions and visionary initiatives, in which explicit consideration of an innovation ecosystem came into play only very late in the game. In his classic essay on the competitiveness of nations, Porter (1990) identifies a set of conditions that drive international competitiveness in specific industries. In summary form, Porter describes these as demand conditions (characteristics of the home-country market and regulatory context), factor conditions (such as skilled labor, public R&D, and national infrastructure), the nature of related and supporting industries (e.g. competitive suppliers and complementers), and the firms' strategies, industry structure, and competitive rivalry in the home market. The stimulating interplay between productive factors, leading and demanding customers, high-quality suppliers, and intense competitive interactions drives the development of an internationally competitive industry. These apply to Finland for mobile communications (Sölvell and Porter, 2011).

The fragmented and localized structure of the Finnish telephone service network resulted from concerns with the risk of full Russian control back in the nineteenth century. This led to the devolution of phone services to municipalities so they would fall under the purview of the local Senate, to which the Russians had delegated territorial administration, thus escaping control by the central Tsarist administration. Small local operators, adjudicated by municipalities, often set up as subscribers' cooperatives, provided more resilience against Russian control than a centralized ownership and network architecture would have. (Actually, a century later, Arpanet, the precursor to the Internet, was developed from very similar resilience considerations, with US military research guidance and funding.) Municipal control could have resulted in fragmented, sleepy, and stodgy bureaucratic services, but the fact that stronger, more efficient operators were allowed to acquire their weaker siblings, and municipalities could invite new operators, created a dynamic market not only for customers but for corporate control. This forced all these small companies to invest in the most up-to-date technologies and leading-edge equipment, lest they were threatened with take-over.

Unlike Sweden with Ericsson, or Germany with Siemens, Finland, at the time, did not have an obvious "national champion" to take on the telecom challenge and supply the necessary equipment. The fragmentation of the operators also made the vertical integration from services to equipment impossible, contrary to what happened in the US (with AT&T and its equipment manufacturing affiliate, Western Electric) or in Canada (Bell Canada). This meant that both the Finnish municipal market side and the international equipment supply side remained quite fragmented and intensely competitive.

Early partial deregulation (in 1987) in Finland, responding to a possible shift to mobile communication, was very timely. It allowed the creation of Radiolinja, as a new nationwide mobile communication cellular network operator, emanating from the association of local telecom operators (Finnet). In 1989, Radiolinja became the first customer of Nokia for a digital network.

While a dynamic and demanding competitive open market played a role in Finland, it alone was not enough for a domestic industry to flourish—in fact, quite the contrary. Finland could have gone down the same route as Belgium—a highly competitive open market for testing innovations, but not one in which domestic companies could easily flourish against multinationals (with the exception of Solvay, Belgium has produced few strong enduring national champions).

Two more planets were aligned to stimulate the development of a domestic industry in Finland. First, post-1917, Soviet threats and various difficult battles of the 1939–44 period, where Finnish forces displayed high mobility and held their own against superior forces, had convinced the Finnish military of the importance of quality communication, including mobile radio communications on the battlefield. The military initiated research into radio communications—later to become the cornerstone of mobile phone networks. This led to an early interest in mobile communication technologies, and to R&D work both in public military labs and in private corporations. Finland's neutral status, not being a beneficiary of the Marshall Plan, nor part of NATO or the European Community, made reliance on local research necessary.

Second, another aligned planet, this one driven by cooperation rather than conflict with the Soviet Union, was essential. In the peace treaty that followed World War II, which allowed Finland to escape Soviet occupation, Finland committed to pay "reparations" in kind to the Soviet Union. A large part of these were in the form of power and telecom cables, encouraging FCW to increase capacity and productivity, given the need to reduce costs to meet Soviet requirements.

Beyond cables, with the advent of digital switching in the 1970s, a new window of opportunity opened in small fixed-line digital switches. At a time when industry leaders such as Ericsson, ITT (the international arm of Western Electric later merged with French Compagnie Générale d'Électricité to form Alcatel), and Siemens were focusing on large urban digital switches, this left an opening for small local switches of the type needed in large numbers in Finland and also in the Soviet Union, which had similarities to Finland geographically and demographically and had been starved of Western tech-nologies (in particular after it invaded Afghanistan). This created the impulse for Finnish companies to invest in digital switching, and gain familiarity and competence in the new technology.

In another fortuitous development, it turned out that Nokia's smaller digital switches could rely on standard microprocessors. Where competitors had developed expensive, complex proprietary circuits, made in small volumes for large switches, Nokia adopted the Intel x86 processors and their architec-ture to power its DX200 digital switch. This decision—made from resource scarcity and competence deficiency (necessity being the mother of invention), not superior foresight—turned out to be critical. First, Nokia could move fast, and second, it could piggyback on the formidable success of Intel and personal computers (following Gordon Moore's famous "Moore's Law" on rapid expo-nential performance improvement and cost reduction with accumulated experience). Where competitors did not benefit much from economies of scale, scope, and experience, Nokia did. The mastery of digital switches, with the expertise in PCM it bred, would prove vital later on in the development of cellular networks. Indeed, Finland turned a constraint into an advantage.

More generally, in the 1980s, Finland could be regarded as a crucible for mobile phone development. There was no grand plan, no mastermind or impresario overseeing the process up to the mid-1980s following the creation of Tekes and the strategic perspective its leadership developed. Different entities, public and private, and the individuals leading them were just trying their best to address the problems at hand: infrastructure resilience, national defense, trade with the Soviet Union, technological independence, upgrading of Finland's technical skills, a national mobile network capability, and regional development. These problem-solving actions came together in space and time to allow, but not drive, the development of mobile phone networks and handsets in Finland. Major trends and discontinuities could well have remained unconnected, with no one putting them together via an integrated awareness.

But they were informally integrated, often in an emergent rather than planned mode. This informal adaptive approach was facilitated by Finland being a small country where everyone knows everyone else who matters, hence critical trends and discontinuities do not remain unseen, nor are they only recognized and framed narrowly in a fragmented fashion. Collective awareness was possible (Korhonen, 1996). Finland was one of the world's most homogeneous societies, with a strong identity, a nearly unique language (related only to Estonian, Hungarian, Basque, and the Inuit language), and a history of having to protect itself against powerful and aggressive neighbors. All of these factors led to corporate leaders such as Björn Westerlund and Kari Kairamo having a strong sense of national interest and a powerful voice in Finnish politics.

Finland was quick to develop critical technical universities (regional development policies also led to new research domains being pursued to stimulate highly skilled employment in secondary cities such as Oulu, in the north of Finland at the tip of the Baltic Sea), and to establish R&D-funding vehicles, such as Sitra and Tekes, to support Nokia's ambitions by providing skills and resources. These specialized agencies spearheaded industrial and innovation policy thinking. This reflected a characteristic of Finland (and even more so of Nokia) to seize on the importance of innovation and new technologies. For example, the original Nokia paper pulp plant adopted an innovation from Germany and used wood as its raw material at a time when rags were generally used in paper production. Similarly, just a few years later and soon after its invention by Graham Bell, Finns were prompt in seeing the importance of the telephone and introducing telephony to Finland. Another early precursor to Nokia was a rubber product company that very quickly saw the new value that vulcanization (a process invented by Michelin to harden rubber) brought to rubber products, from boots to tires.

Finland would also prove supportive of Nokia by having a high-enough competence in industries complementary to ICT, but essential to mobile phones, such as plastic molding, electronic circuit assembly, and the like. Nokia was also able to access key international suppliers such as Texas Instruments, Philips, and ST Microelectronics early in its development.

Another very propitious aspect of Finland's context was its participation in the NMT standardization process and collaboration project in the 1970s and 1980s. This provided specific "firsts" in mobile telecoms, such as roaming services across the Nordic area. But, even more importantly, it offered collaboration experience and a precedent for GSM collaboration. This could almost become a process "blueprint" for GSM, conferring an advantage to Nordic companies in this new standardization alliance. Nordic PTTs (postal, telegraph, and telephone) and equipment makers had also devoted more attention to mobile communication and bandwidth use than their Western European counterparts in GSM, conferring them an advantage in negotiations. They were better prepared and more thoughtful. GSM came to be influenced by a Nordic way of thinking (inclusive, open, egalitarian) that drove its success and opened the way to mobile phones becoming a consumer good.

However, contrary to market learning and technical competence-building, Finland did not provide a fortuitous context or a strong precedent in terms of management learning. Linguistic barriers, national pride, *sisu*, a belief one could learn from books (for instance on Jorma Ollila's part), and a sense of self-sufficiency all contributed to relative isolation. A distinctive form of management combining hierarchical organizations and bureaucratic processes with a sense of autonomy and independent entrepreneurial action became a hallmark of several Finnish companies. Further contributing to this isolation, contrary to countries that developed earlier, Finland did not grow multi-national companies until Kone (a crane and elevator maker) and the paper companies internationalized in the 1960s and 1970s. Managers with international experience, or the experience of large firms, were in short supply. Furthermore, these could not be developed as fast as electronics researchers could be trained. There were few opportunities for international careers, and Finns were often attached to their home country and reluctant to become expatriates.

Financial resources were also a challenge, with conservative banks playing a dominant role, both in holding shares in companies and in providing credit. Their executives neither benefited from experience in communication technologies nor international experience, both essential ingredients for Nokia's development. Limits to foreign investments and privileged voting rights for existing shareholders over new ones made foreign participation difficult. This was one of the key challenges Nokia had to address in order to grow rapidly.

In sum, all of these factors contributed to forging Nokia's mobile communications success. Nokia is not the product of a strategically thought-out and systematically implemented industrial policy. So the question raised in Ljubljana was not the right question. In an adaptive, incremental fashion, various institutions in Finland took steps to solve specific problems and address focused needs, and these steps cumulatively allowed Nokia's development. Nokia's leaders took smart actions to make Nokia the focal firm and capture the advantage the local context offered to them. Put differently, we observed the adaptive emergence of an innovation cluster in Finland, over a long period of time, through loosely connected actions and networking. This suggests that the emergence of innovation clusters is neither random nor planned (Enright, 1998). It relies on a form of clever strategic opportunism: seizing the opportunities the situation offers as it unfolds, and perhaps informally nudging aspects of the situation (for instance, government policies) toward favorable outcomes.

Nokia's development was largely the result of two successive visionary leaders. Björn Westerlund, the first CEO of Nokia—after its three constituent companies merged in 1967—had seen the potential of electronics very early. As CEO of FCW, he had started a "beyond the scene" effort to master electronics technologies. A military contract for the development of radiophones in 1963 allowed these technologies to see the light of day.

Second, Kari Kairamo, who succeeded Westerlund as CEO, coming from the pulp and paper business, saw that a purely Finnish "home-country" base would be very vulnerable to foreign competition and foresaw a convergence between industries which Nokia could benefit from by being active in consumer electronics as well as telecoms and computers. He decided to take the offensive by turning Nokia into a European technology group, with companies like Electrolux or Philips as models. Of course, except for telecoms, he was too late, but forays into consumer electronics and computers provided valuable experience: consumer electronics brought lessons of how difficult but important mass manufacturing was and a concern with unit costs and manufacturing scale. It also brought a keen sense of the need for branding in consumer products (Nokia had bought, through various acquisitions, a hotchpotch of weak brands in TV sets and brown goods, and found their integration impossible given the structure of electronics retail distribution). Computers brought a sense for digital technologies and the importance of software. Pekka Ala-Pietilä, who was later to play a key role, began his career in Nokia's computer business, and so did the handful of research engineers who took Nokia into smartphones. But the unfortunate acquisition spree in consumer electronics also bred an awareness of how difficult acquisition integration was, resulting in an enduring reluctance toward acquisitions.

In terms of our four CORE enablers—*Cognition, Organization, Relationships,* and *Emotions*—the situation at the end of the 1980s offers a mixed picture of Nokia's strategic capabilities. Its former CEOs, Westerlund and Kairamo, had been visionaries, foreseeing the role of electronics and the importance of internationalization. Both had acted on this strategic foresight. The firm's late entry into both consumer electronics and computers proved unsuccessful, however, and consumed significant resources. The BCG report of 1990 suggested that only mobile communications would offer a high future growth potential and a situation where the competitive game had not been played yet. But it also intimated that Nokia had too weak a hand in that game to succeed.

But Nokia had been amassing stronger cards, in a favorable and demanding Finnish context, than was obviously visible: radio technology, digital coding and switching, the experience acquired with the NMT network, the development of a cellular network, and the experience of dealing with myriad small, demanding customers with limited technical experience. Through alliances and acquisitions in Finland, and the alliance with Tandy internationally, Nokia had positioned itself as a competitive company for smaller switches and mobile phones.

Creating a separate business unit for mobile phones in a decentralized flat organization left the strategic freedom and the space to build a new business—only a conservative board, and ownership by major banks in the 1991 economic crisis, compromised development.

Relationships among senior executives were at a crisis point following Kairamo's sudden death and that of his most likely successor. Rivalry among business unit heads flared up, and conflicts erupted over resource allocation and CEO succession. The company was in disarray, with its management demoralized and the collapse of the Soviet market now putting it at risk of bankruptcy. Figure 2.1 summarizes this analysis graphically.

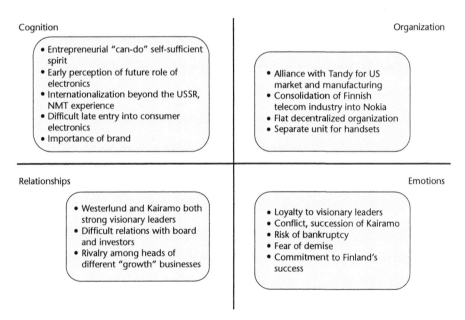

Figure 2.1. 1967–91 CORE profile

References

Michael J. Enright, "Regional Clusters and Firm Strategy," in *The Dynamic Firm: The Role of Technology, Strategy, Organization, and Region*, edited by Alfred Chandler, Örjan Sölvell, and Peter Hagström (Oxford University Press, Oxford, 1998), pp. 315–42.

K. J. Korhonen, "Finland's History of Networking," in *Networks of Enterprises and Local Development*, edited by Organisation for Economic Co-operation and Development (OECD, Paris, 1996), pp. 149–70.

Michael Porter, *The Competitive Advantage of Nations* (Free Press, New York, 1990).

Örjan Sölvell and Michael Porter, "Finland and Nokia: Creating the World's Most Competitive Economy" (Harvard Business School case study 9–702–427, revised March 7, 2011).

3

We Were the Only Ones to See It

Vuorilehto had not been involved in commissioning the BCG report and certainly did not agree with the consulting group's implicit recommendation that the best prospect for the various Nokia businesses lay in dismantling the Finnish conglomerate. General performance problems prompted him to sell off some businesses in 1991, including the information systems unit to ICL, but he was not prepared to preside over the complete breakup of Finland's national champion. Nor did he agree with BCG's assessment that Nokia's telecoms businesses were too small to have a viable future, as the young management team in NMP, headed by Jorma Ollila, had made a convincing argument that the mobile phone-related operations could play a major role in Nokia's future growth.

So rather than cry defeat, in early 1991, in a bid to bolster the mobile phone operations, Nokia acquired the UK-based mobile phone manufacturer Technophone for £34 million. As well as being innovative—it was the first producer in the world to launch a phone small enough to fit in a shirt pocket—Technophone was the second-largest producer in Europe by sales volume behind Nokia, and the acquisition propelled Nokia to being the second-largest mobile phone supplier globally after Motorola (though unlike Motorola, Nokia's mobile phones were sold under multiple brand names, including Mobira, Nokia, Radio Shack, and now Technophone).

Later that same year, NMP received another boost when it hired a smart, savvy, ambitious young manager, Anssi Vanjoki, from 3M to head its sales and marketing activities. Vanjoki immediately began to consolidate NMP's products into one global brand that would have a consistent design style and marketing message. It was hoped the new "Nokia" brand would be a powerful tool in helping Nokia close the gap between itself and Motorola.

A Change in Management

By the end of 1991, despite some progress being made in the mobile-related divisions, overall, Nokia was still in trouble. Group-wide results were worsening and Vuorilehto had yet to outline a strategy to steer the group back to growth. Having lost patience with his indecision, at the beginning of 1992 the board announced that Vuorilehto would retire in June and be replaced by the forty-one-year-old head of NMP, Jorma Ollila.

Like Kairamo before him, Ollila had a more international background than most Finns at the time. From 1967 he attended Atlantic College in Wales, before returning to Finland to study political sciences at Helsinki University. After a Master's degree in engineering at Helsinki University of Technology, he moved back to the UK to complete a Masters in economics at the London School of Economics, and then joined Citibank in London for two years before being transferred to their Helsinki office. In 1985, Ollila joined Nokia as head of international operations, the following year became the group's CFO (chief financial officer), and in 1990 was appointed head of NMP.

In addition to a sharp intellect, drive, and boundless energy, Ollila brought a wider economic and geopolitical perspective to Nokia. His easy mastery of numbers, as well as of the interpersonal and political intricacies of situations, enabled him to challenge and drive his colleagues and staff. He was as demanding of others as himself, and when people failed to perform to his high expectations they could expect to feel the full force of what he later described in his autobiography as his "volcanic" personality. Unpleasant though his temper was, and however disturbing his outbursts, Ollila's colleagues and staff had great respect for him as his explosive anger tended to die down very quickly to be replaced by a type of objective reflection that led to valuable insights and action.

Although there were many talented managers who would play significant roles in the success of Nokia over the coming years, the four senior managers Ollila assembled, which collectively became known inside Nokia as the "dream team," were of particular importance. They had diverse personalities and cognitive styles, and yet socially they formed a homogeneous unit. Together Ollila, Kallasvuo, Ala-Pietilä, Alahuhta, and Baldauf made a formidable team.

CFO Olli-Pekka Kallasvuo had been Ollila's number two when he was CFO and remained extremely loyal to Ollila throughout his career. Although Kallasvuo, a former lawyer, was a rigorous and disciplined finance and operations man who shared Ollila's belief that "numbers tell a story," he was not consumed by the detail and was always able to see the bigger picture. An introvert by nature, Kallasvuo found it difficult to inspire people inside and outside Nokia.

In contrast, the three members of Ollila's inner circle who were heading the businesses were all highly charismatic characters as well as inspirational leaders. They formed a tightly knit, cohesive, and complementary unit and were as loyal to each other as they were to Nokia.

At the age of thirty-five, Pekka Ala-Pietilä replaced Ollila as head of NMP. Like Ollila, he was trained as an economist and had clearly made an impression as head of strategy and then marketing in NMP when Ollila was in charge of the unit. The most strategic mind in the "dream team," Ala-Pietilä had a rare skill in being able to cope well with uncertainty and ambiguity. Known for being quietly thoughtful, patient, and reflective, his approach to dealing with complex situations was always analytical and balanced.

Matti Alahuhta, who was appointed head of NTC, was one of Ala-Pietilä's favored intellectual sparring partners. The two men had very complementary skills and approaches. Alahuhta, an action-oriented manager from an engineering background, was very performance-focused and took a systematic approach to measuring and improving performance at every level. While he was thus naturally drawn to solving operational problems, he had a broad architectural and systemic sense of how actions interacted and how they were interrelated.

The final member of Ollila's new senior management team was the head of NCS, Sari Baldauf. Having joined Nokia in 1983, she had worked in a number of strategy roles in Helsinki and the US before gaining prominence in the late 1980s as one of the chief architects behind the reorganization of the group's telecoms activities into two divisions: infrastructure and handsets. A talented strategist with a keen intellect, Baldauf was also an extremely shrewd negotiator who was known for her tireless energy and dogged determination.

GSM: The Fulcrum of the New Growth Strategy

On becoming CEO, Ollila inherited a firm that was in crisis strategically and financially. Due to the senior management problems since Kairamo's death, Nokia had been left with low morale and high levels of uncertainty. One of Ollila's first actions was to form a task force of thirty managers from across the group to outline the strategic direction the firm should take. Time being of the essence, the group worked closely and intensively to outline the "Nokia Vision 2000," and invested much time communicating the outcomes to all Nokia employees.

Despite the telecoms businesses representing less than a third of Nokia's sales, and having global market share of only 12 percent, the task force concluded that mobile communications should spearhead Nokia's growth. With the benefit of hindsight, this seems a simple logical conclusion for the task force to have reached, yet as Ala-Pietilä recalled, the decision was seen as risky at the time, "we were criticized for overfocusing but we believed telecoms would be a huge industry with several legs. Back then it took real guts to say that telecoms would offer enough of a growth path." Nokia's large investors were particularly cautious about heading in this direction, having been badly stung by Nokia's earlier forays into electronics and televisions and having no appetite to go head-to-head with large, innovative Japanese consumer electronics firms again.

The new digital GSM standard lay at the heart of Nokia's decision. In 1991, Radiolinja, a Finnish consortium of local operators and their corporate customers, had been granted the license to develop the world's first GSM network in Finland and turned to Nokia to provide the network equipment. The following year Nokia delivered both the infrastructure and the world's first GSM handset (though not to Radiolinja but a Turkish customer who had placed an urgent order), giving the firm valuable early experience in the new technology and the conviction that GSM would transform the industry.

The analog systems in use prior to GSM imposed serious limitations on the potential growth of mobile communications. Restricted capacity inherent to analog signal connections resulted in high equipment and service costs that in turn limited the market—back in 1991 mobile communications were the preserve of emergency services, large businesses, and the very wealthy. Managers at Nokia, in particular Ala-Pietilä and Baldauf, argued that digitization would lead to a virtuous circle in which the removal of capacity limitations which digital coding enabled would increase volumes, thereby significantly lowering costs and prices in both networks and handsets. And this was where they saw a huge opportunity to create a mass consumer market for mobile telephony.

At a conference in London in 1992, Ala-Pietilä dared to share his vision with industry delegates from around the world. When we talked about this period some years later, he chuckled as he recalled, "I'd said that mobile penetration could reach around 25 percent of the population in the most advanced economies by 2000. I was almost laughed out of the room. This thinking was so out of the box that most people there thought I was a lunatic!"

Yet it wasn't just the prospect of huge markets in advanced economies that had inspired Nokia's belief in mass consumer mobile markets. Through their sales of network equipment, Baldauf and Alahuhta had developed a good relationship with Chinese authorities and a clear understanding of the issues they were facing in trying to build a national radio communications network. The two Nokia managers believed that digital mobile telephony could be the alternative to fixed-line networks the Chinese were looking for. The potential mass market was vast in China and other emerging economies.

Another aspect of GSM that convinced Nokia's managers that this was where the firm's future lay was the fact that the new standard provided a balance between competition and collaboration. Rather than fully standardize GSM, a model had been adopted whereby only technical interfaces between functional modules were standardized, leaving infrastructure suppliers to develop their own proprietary technologies for the various modules. So while the GSM system as a whole was a collaborative effort, by developing superior and lower cost technologies to underpin its proprietary modules Nokia could gain a larger market share across multiple markets.

As a small firm from a small country, competing in foreign telecoms markets against large incumbent players had always been difficult. But with GSM being a pan-European standard in which Nokia had been involved from the very beginning, and with the opportunity to build on its earlier experience of collaboration on the NMT network, the prospect of playing a bigger role emerged. Unlike many of its competitors at the time, Nokia was able to provide end-to-end solutions with both network infrastructure and handsets. As governments across Europe began to sell GSM licenses, more often than not the new entrepreneurial operators that bought them did not have the expertise to specify the technical aspects of the networks they were building. Nokia recognized it had an advantage in positioning itself as the only firm ready and able to provide end-to-end "turnkey" GSM network solutions.

Not Everyone Saw the Opportunity

Reflecting on his early days as CEO and the decision to focus the conglomerate on telecoms, Ollila explained, "1991 to 1993 were the defining years for who understood what that business was really about." And Nokia saw the industry very differently to its large, incumbent competitors. Although Nokia could trace its history back to 1865, the mobile telecoms units were young businesses, unencumbered by strong industry orthodoxies or legacy investments. Ollila and his senior managers saw GSM as an enabler for a new consumer industry, while their main competitors, Motorola and Ericsson, were focused elsewhere.

In the early 1990s Motorola was the world's largest supplier of mobile phones. It had a large patent portfolio, strong brand recognition, brilliant engineers with a "can-do" attitude in its R&D centers, and the benefit of being located in the largest single market for mobile telephony—the United States. Motorola saw itself very much as a technology company. It was vertically integrated, producing most of the components for its mobile phones in-house. This gave the firm a real advantage as it was able to design smaller components than were available through suppliers and so produce smaller and lighter phones than any of its competitors.

But Motorola did not see the potential for a mass consumer mobile telecoms market, and so all of the firm's considerable technical strengths were directed toward high-end mobile communications. The fated Iridium project is a good example—Motorola invested over US$5 billion creating a mobile satellite network with sixty-six dedicated low-orbiting satellites, only for the project to declare bankruptcy two years after the launch of the first satellites. It had failed to attract enough customers due to prohibitive call costs coupled with bulky, heavy equipment—it hadn't recognized that the type of customer interested in using satellite communications was likely to be in a remote or inhospitable location and unlikely to want to carry a heavy phone pack around.

On a more down-to-earth front, in 1989 Motorola had launched the world's smallest and lightest mobile phone, the high-end Microtac. Despite costing up to US$3,500, the Microtac was a great success and much lauded for its performance and design, which incorporated a revolutionary flip-down mouthpiece. An interesting aside, on looking at a Microtac, Nokia's engineers were astonished by the small size of the components and knew that their own suppliers would not be able to come close to creating anything so small.

Impressive though it was, just like all of Motorola's other products the Microtac was an analog phone. And this was the firm's Achilles heel. Motorola was so focused on perfecting technology and on the top end of the US market that it had dismissed GSM due to its inferior digital chips and high power consumption. As Ollila put it, "Consumer business knowledge was never in Motorola's DNA. They had an aversion to thinking from a mass consumer and brand perspective." Where Motorola had been strong in consumer goods, such as television sets, it had been battered by the Japanese, and so it did not see that digital had the potential to lower costs and reach a mass market. They believed the future for the next few years lay in improving analog offerings, even if that meant redesigning phones to meet the different technical specifications of each analog market.

Compounding the strategic short-sightedness of focusing on analog technologies, Motorola was also experiencing severe problems with the speed of its development and production activities. In 1986, Motorola engineer Bill Smith had developed and introduced "six sigma" as a set of tools to radically improve quality within the firm. But by the early 1990s, Motorola's obsession with quality left the firm almost paralyzed by six sigma—they lost sight of the importance of speed and struggled to launch new products.

Unlike Motorola, Ericsson understood the benefits of GSM and had been involved in its conceptual predecessor, NMT. A Swedish firm, Ericsson was a leading global player in fixed and mobile network technologies and in particular digital switches, with which it had made significant inroads into the US market. Its focus on supplying infrastructure to large, incumbent national telecoms providers meant that, like Motorola, Ericsson saw itself as a technology company, and accordingly it invested significant sums in R&D but little effort went into building marketing capabilities.

This technology and infrastructure bias was so strong within Ericsson that it viewed GSM as providing an opportunity to develop and sell more network equipment. Not only did the firm lack the skills or vision to see the world through the lens of a potential consumer industry, but it actually saw handsets as peripheral to infrastructure—a mere "terminal" provided to users by operators.

In fact, in 1989, Ericsson's view that handsets were not of great strategic importance led to it moving its handset development activities to a joint venture with General Electric in the US (it wasn't until 1994 that the joint venture was broken up and Ericsson transferred its handset development back to Europe). A serious consequence of this was that Ericsson was so busy playing catch-up with Motorola's analog phones in the US that it failed to develop digital phones compatible with the GSM infrastructure it saw as being so crucial to the future of the industry.

The Threat from Japan

The benefit of hindsight has shown that the Japanese never obtained global success with mobile telecommunications, but at the time they were considered a real threat to Nokia, and as Ala-Pietilä explained, "The Japanese were a powerful competitor group and we were constantly asked how we would fight against the Japanese consumer electronic giants." In fact, genuine concern over Japanese competition was one of the reasons Ollila and his team had not received the full support of their Finnish investors when they proposed to focus Nokia on mobile telecoms. Not many years previously, these same investors had seen Japanese consumer goods firms like Sony and Matsushita come to dominate the sector in Europe while Nokia's own consumer electronics businesses had gone from bad to worse. The lesson learned had been that a combination of Japanese innovation and quality was unbeatable.

Nor were the Japanese seen merely as a threat to Nokia's vision of the mobile phone as a consumer good. Nippon Telegraph and Telephone (NTT) had introduced Japan's first mobile service in 1979 and went on through significant capital investment combined with deep R&D capabilities to release a series of innovations in technologies and services to create an advanced domestic market.

Transforming Nokia to Shape an Emerging Industry

Although Nokia was ahead of most of its competitors in terms of strategic vision, toward the end of the 1980s Nokia's telecoms businesses, which were organized around functions and regions, still lacked process discipline. At one level, in the mobile phones business, differing technical standards for analog networks in different countries had led to a proliferation of engineering and development processes. Not only was this inefficient, but it created product/market silos and prevented functions upstream of R&D from being able to form a comprehensive picture of the product pipeline. The situation wasn't much better at the management level. Both NMP and NCS were internationalizing so quickly and without any blueprint to work from that recalling the early piecemeal approach to creating management processes, Baldauf explained, "It was during long-haul flights that we built a set of management processes, writing standard operating procedures and reports. We were so busy and growing so fast, this was the only time we had to focus on the underlying processes needed to support the business."

Part of the reason Nokia seemed so lacking in process and discipline capabilities in 1991 was due to a legacy of international expansion that had resulted in the firm being regionally organized to match diverse analog standards, often with different management approaches between regions. However, the decision to focus on GSM had centralized all key activities in Finland, and so for the first time Nokia was organized as a home-centric global firm in need of the structures and systems to support this arrangement.

It wasn't until 1991, under the guidance of Ala-Pietilä while he was still head of strategy for both NMP and Nokia Telecommunications (and just before he became head of NMP), that a more consolidated and thorough approach to building strong core processes began. Looking at Nokia as a consumer-focused, global product company, Ala-Pietilä defined three core processes. The first, global logistics, included everything related to sourcing, manufacturing, and distribution. The second, customer satisfaction, brought together product planning, marketing, and sales activities. Both of these fed into the final one, concurrent engineering. Borrowed from the Japanese, concurrent engineering essentially brought upstream functions and external partners into the R&D process, resulting in faster cycle times, greater efficiencies, and a more focused product development effort. So for the first time at Nokia, from the conception of a new product onwards, engineers were working closely with the sourcing, manufacturing, and marketing functions.

From this integrated process approach, detailed individual product plans were drawn up. When combined into a full product road map, these would give Ala-Pietilä a vital management tool when he became head of NMP. During our discussions, some years later a still very animated Ala-Pietilä, keen to stress the importance of the product road maps, urged me to, "Write this in bold letters: NOKIA IS A PRODUCT COMPANY. OUR SUCCESS IS DOWN TO THE COMPETITIVENESS OF THE PRODUCT AND NOTHING ELSE. So when I was running NMP, the product road map gave me peace of mind. It was my strategic map. From it, I knew what we were going to produce in the future and the steps we needed to take to get there." Everything from discussions with potential new technology partners and information from component suppliers to details throughout the internal value chain was included in the product road map, and this gave Nokia a pretty clear rolling picture of the coming thirty-six months—something that was seen as critical for catching up with Motorola, which was at least one generation ahead of Nokia at the time.

At this critical stage, while the mobile market was in its infancy and Nokia was still a young challenger company in the sector, the firm's internal process capabilities took yet another, unexpected leap forward thanks to a larger-than-life Scot, Frank McGovern. McGovern had joined Nokia with the Technophone acquisition, and was later described by Ala-Pietilä as the most valuable part of the acquisition. The outspoken McGovern brought with him years of experience in manufacturing (including being head of Hitachi's manufacturing operations in Europe), a mastery of the Japanese continuous quality improvement processes, and a passion for leadership development.

Experience from Nokia's joint venture with Tandy and its troubled foray into the consumer electronics sector had made managers keenly aware that if their vision of a mass consumer mobile industry were to be realized, efficient, world-class manufacturing would have to lie at its heart. Yet knowledge about how to achieve this was lacking within the firm, as few of the largely Finnish workforce and management had ever worked for the type of large multinational firm that excelled in manufacturing. McGovern brought that knowledge, along with energy and enthusiasm, to transform Nokia's manufacturing skills through Japanese-style continual learning and improvement assessment and reassessment. He not only introduced processes to ensure consistency, efficiency, quality, and reliability in manufacturing, but identified and mentored talented production managers to ensure manufacturing became as important and valued a competence in Nokia as any other function.

With progress being made on upgrading core processes and manufacturing, Ollila and his team began tackling the softer elements of transformation. The bitter management infighting since Kairamo's death had left its mark on Nokia. Coupled with weakening performance and a lack of strategic direction during Vuorilehto's tenure at the helm, morale had been further dented. In a bid to reverse the negative impact of the previous few years on Nokia's culture and redefine the firm as entrepreneurial, decentralized, and flexible, the beginning of 1993 saw the launch of "Nokia Values," the first of what would become the group's Annual Transformation themes.

"You need company values," Ala-Pietilä explained, "Without these energy and risk-taking won't be there and there won't be innovation. To deal with uncertainty and ambiguity you need a culture of sharing and trust with the right support incentives." Encompassing aspects of Finnish culture, Nokia's experience, and its ambition, a group of Nokia managers defined four key values: customer satisfaction, respect for the individual, achievement, and continuous learning. These four values, which were intended to inform the group's strategy as well as individual behavior, created the foundation of the "Nokia Way." Over the course of the year the working group went on to define key processes, working practices, and a mission statement as further aspects of the "Nokia Way."

One of the tangible outcomes of Nokia's process, manufacturing, and culture improvements was that between 1990 and 1994 the firm's mobile phone output grew from 500,000 units per annum to five million.

Although Ollila and his team had decided to focus the group's future growth around telecoms back in 1991, it wasn't until 1994 that Nokia's board finally gave the go-ahead for all non-mobile telecom-related businesses to be divested.

The impact this would have on the composition of the firm was profound. In less than two years, Nokia experienced a 60 percent turnover in staff. A large cohort of young engineers from Finland's technical universities joined Nokia's ranks and were rapidly inculcated into the "Nokia Way." By international and industry standards, remuneration packages at Nokia were low. But for many ambitious graduates this was more than compensated for by the prospect of early responsibility in development projects, regular job rotations (something Ollila believed not only built knowledge and competence, but also reduced the likelihood of silos emerging and political rivalries destabilizing the business), and the personal development this would lead to.

A New Era of International Expansion

The adoption of a new strategic direction and a focus on improving operational aspects of the firm, together with the reintroduction of a strong values-based management approach, had enabled Nokia's new management team to steer the firm away from near bankruptcy in 1991 toward strong growth. From a group-wide operating loss of FIM 96 million in 1991, Nokia posted an operating profit of FIM 1,465[1] million in 1993—87 percent of which came from Nokia Telecommunications and NMP.

Plans for future growth, however, were constrained by a lack of access to capital. Although Nokia had been listed on the Helsinki Stock Exchange since 1915, foreign investment in Finland was heavily restricted and so the firm's main shareholders remained Finnish financial institutions—none of which were in a position to meet Nokia's funding requirements, as they were grappling with their own problems resulting from a deep recession in Finland. It wasn't until November 1993 and the signing of the Maastricht Treaty that curbs on foreign investment in Finnish firms were removed.

This timing couldn't have been more fortuitous for Ollila—at the very moment Nokia needed the kind of large capital injection to fund ambitious international growth plans, which wasn't forthcoming domestically, he was finally able to turn to foreign markets. On July 1, 1994, Nokia was listed on the New York Stock Exchange (NYSE).

The growth plans for Nokia's internationalization, however, flew in the face of conventional wisdom. Ollila and his team knew that any time they spent building a multinational firm through a network of overseas subsidiaries would erode their early lead in offering end-to-end digital mobile solutions. The recent PhD theses of two senior managers, Matti Alahuhta and Mikko Kosonen, who had been encouraged to engage in doctoral studies and make them relevant to Nokia, offered an alternative approach.

Alahuhta's PhD looked at global growth strategies for high-tech firms. He argued that it was possible for companies with strong R&D capabilities to be "born global" if they entered new markets early when technologies were in their infancy and consumer adoption was only beginning to emerge. Kosonen's PhD had focused on internationalizing and adapting business systems to differentiated local demands while maintaining global integration. These research theses, together with Ollila's willingness to experiment and be bold, provided Nokia with a potential alternative and rapid route to internationalization. And it wasn't long before their findings were put to the test.

Despite being advised that, as a firm without a strong local presence (and with only three staff on the ground), they stood little chance of success, Nokia submitted a tender to supply an end-to-end system in Thailand. Against all the odds, and to the surprise of Ericsson which had a local staff approaching 3,000, Nokia won the contract and went on successfully to deliver a system tailored to the customer's needs.

Over the coming years, time and time again, new fast-growing mobile operators around the world chose the customer-centric Nokia to supply new systems over its large rivals with established local subsidiaries and ties to incumbents. One of the reasons Nokia was so successful at building an international business in the early 1990s, according to Baldauf, was also a consequence of the "Nokia Way" combined with their agile approach to global expansion, "Our approach was not, 'we know everything and this is how you do things.' Instead, we'd go to a country, explain our values, basic beliefs, and products. We'd try and find people who were interested in this way of cooperating and build respectful, trusting relationships with them." A good example of this was in 1994 when Nokia won a tender with Cellnet despite being £25 million more expensive than rival Motorola. The message from the UK operator was that they had chosen Nokia because they trusted them more.

In tandem with expanding their customer base across the globe, Nokia was busy internationalizing in other areas. It pursued key suppliers across Europe and the US, and built manufacturing plants in China and Mexico. It also established R&D centers in other markets, though the lion's share of development remained in Finland.

Throughout this fervor of rapid internationalization (the New York listing, new customers and suppliers across the globe, and new international production and R&D facilities) it is worth noting that one aspect of Nokia—the board—remained resolutely Finnish. It wasn't until 1998 that the first two non-Finns joined the board of Nokia.

Turning Mobile Phones into a Consumer Product

The early 1990s were a particularly pivotal time for NMP in terms of the design and branding of its products. Under Vanjoki, multiple handset brands had been consolidated into the Nokia brand and a new marketing slogan, "Connecting People," had been introduced. A keen Mac computer fan, NMP's new head, Ala-Pietilä, understood that to turn mobile phones into a desirable consumer product, Nokia would need to achieve the same consistent usability and quality design for its phones that Apple had achieved with its computers. The aim, entirely new to the mobile phone industry at the time, was to ensure that all Nokia phones shared the same look and feel.

To achieve a distinctive look to its phones, in 1993 Nokia hired a new head of design, Frank Nuovo, from the Pasadena School of Design. Nokia's first mass-produced GSM phone, the Nokia 1011, launched in 1992, had had a clunky design with a small screen, a short antenna on the top, weighed just under 500 grams, and came in black. Working closely with engineers in Finland, Nuovo and his team radically redesigned and re-engineered Nokia's phones, culminating in the launch of the Nokia 2100 in 1994—a phone which even today would be easily recognizable as a modern Nokia design. The 2100 was packed with innovations: it had a rounded, slimline, "soap bar" design, an internal antenna, a large screen with a scrolling text menu, battery and signal indicators, multiple ringtones, and changeable covers in a large variety of colors. It weighed under 200 grams and measured around 10 cm by 4.5 cm by 2 cm—tiny in comparison to its predecessors. On the technical front the new phone had better radio frequency technology and a longer battery life than any of the digital phones on offer from Nokia's competitors. Here was a phone that people wanted to own, and as it was compatible with every digital standard around the world at the time, the potential market for the 2100 was global.

A large, and enduring, part of Nokia's drive to transform its mobile phones business into a consumer industry was based around market segmentation. Vanjoki and Ala-Pietilä both felt that, based on lifestyle requirements, different groups of consumers would value different features on their phones. To identify these nascent needs, they began carrying out customer clustering exercises to segment the market.

Not only was this approach innovative from a product marketing stand-point, but the design and manufacturing process to deliver a range of phones with different features was a first in the industry too. Nokia adopted a modular, platform approach to design and production so that while the basic bones of its phones were standardized, allowing for economies of scale in design, sourcing, and production, the features in each range were different. Modularity also enabled Nokia to vary its phones to meet local standards, frequencies, languages, and customer preferences in different markets around the world, both quickly and at relatively low cost—although the success of this hinged upon a complex global supply chain.

At the beginning of 1995, Nokia was on a very fast and successful growth trajectory. Under a young, bright, and enthusiastic new management team, it had taken on its much larger competitors with a bold strategic global vision and had introduced clear processes to support this. As an indicator of how well this new direction was going, the group's operating profit in 1994 increased 145 percent from the previous year to FIM 3,596 million, with strong sales growth up 23 percent in Europe, 76 percent in North America and Mexico, 38 percent in Asia, and 74 percent in the rest of the world.

Looking to Nokia's future, analysts had positive messages for investors. In March 1995, Credit Suisse First Boston stated, "We are highly confident that Nokia will not disappoint investors in 1995 on either top line growth or operating profit growth" (Brau, 1995). While at the end of the previous year, a Bear Sterns report had advised," Nokia currently sells its products in over 110 countries [and] is one of a few telecom equipment companies that have been successful without the luxury of a large, protected home market. We believe Nokia's success solidly positions it for the remainder of the decade [and it] should continue to benefit from the growth of wireless communications and macroeconomic trends of privatization and deregulation of telecommunications" (Theodosopoulos, 1994).

Commentary

When I met him back in 2005 to discuss Nokia's success in mobile phones, Jorma Ollila completed his opening sentence, "The planetary alignment was right" with, "but we were the only ones to see it." Although this was a great summary *ex post*, it was in fact a bit of an overstatement of how Nokia perceived the opportunity at the time. Confidence in the possibility of a very large consumer market did not come about from the start. A key supplier to Nokia remembered his first visit to Helsinki in 1991, when Jorma Ollila asked him to design a specific phone circuit for Nokia. Toward the end of the conversation, the would-be supplier asked what volume Nokia could guarantee, and after a long silence recalls being told, "We are really not sure, but 300,000 a year is a safe bet." Just a few years later, Nokia would produce and sell that many phones every day.

It's clear from this exchange that the full awareness of the opportunity only developed over time. But what set Nokia apart as an innovative outlier in the telecom equipment industry was the fact that its management recognized earlier than any of its competitors that mobile phones could be a mass-market consumer product opportunity selling many more than 300,000 phones a year. Nokia was unique not only in the emergence of that framing, but also in gaining sufficient confidence to drive a commitment to growth. A fresh and different understanding of both market and technological opportunities that developed over the crucial early 1990s shaped that framing.

From a market standpoint, this came to be driven by the progressive recognition of a consumer product opportunity in mobile phones. The strategic frame other potential contenders used—chiefly Ericsson and Motorola—had been shaped by analog and heavy mobile phones for professional use. Their attention and focus were largely on the military, civil emergency services, and car phones for which bulk, weight, and limited battery capacity were not insuperable obstacles.

In other words, Nokia enjoyed the huge advantage of an innovative consumer-oriented framing of the opportunity at a time when the whole industry had a professional/security services framing that restricted their perception of the opportunity. These framings were largely driven by past experience. Of course, Motorola did have consumer experience, but its trouncing by Japanese competitors in TV and consumer electronics had driven its leaders toward a "never again" perspective. A strong and enduring commitment to analog phones also contributed to preventing Motorola's key managers from perceiving the full potential of digital phones in the early days—in particular how digitalization would support many more subscribers and thus lower both handset and call costs. The Japanese mobile phone suppliers, all divisions of consumer electronic companies such as Matsushita, Sharp, and Sony, perhaps did bring mass-market consumer experience, but the development of unique national standards in Japan, combined with the leading role of network operators, led them astray, blunting their attack on international markets.

Nokia therefore stood alone as a strategic innovator—drawing its framing largely from analogy with personal consumer electronics inspired by Sony's Walkman and Apple's Macintosh computer (Mac). Nokia saw that if portable phones could be made lightweight, small, and with sufficient battery autonomy, they could become a pocket-sized mass-market device. Technophone's innovations, and its subsequent acquisition by Nokia, provided a "halfway house" on that path, as Technophone had developed the first (almost) pocket-sized and lightweight analog phone.

Of course, what Nokia attempted with its new consumer-focused devices was not unprecedented. Apple had been a precursor a few years earlier, with the first Mac setting new standards of design and user-friendliness for personal computers which enabled the move from specialized professional ("desktop") use to the home and consumers. As an early Mac user, Pekka Ala-Pietilä had first-hand experience of the emergence of the Mac as a consumer product. Similarly, Sony's Walkman had made listening to music mobile and personal, exactly what Nokia hoped to do for phone conversations.

Nokia's convictions were also shaped by the company's early experience in China. Faced with the need for rural telecommunication networks, the Chinese Communist Party had begun considering the possibility of leapfrogging costly fixed-line infrastructure by building a cellular phone network rather than a traditional one. Familiar with these developments through their efforts to sell network equipment in China and the contacts of their agents, Jorma Ollila, Matti Alahuhta, and Sari Baldauf, in particular, foresaw the huge potential emerging markets might offer.

One of my marketing colleagues at INSEAD, Christian Pinson, used to stress the innovative value of ignorance. This was exemplified by Richard Branson, the founder of Virgin Airlines and several other innovative ventures, telling the CEOs of incumbent airlines when launching his own, "I know nothing and this will be my strength. You believe your experience is a strong asset, but it is really your biggest liability—you are stuck in tradition" (Larreché, 2008). For Nokia, ignorance certainly was a virtue in the early days, as the management team, unencumbered by industry orthodoxies, could reimagine mobile telecommunications in an entirely new way.

In earlier research comparing Nokia to other ICT companies, Mikko Kosonen and I developed a construct we called strategic agility (Doz and Kosonen, 2010) to capture key differences between companies that seized new strategic opportunities flexibly and companies that remained stuck in their old ways. In essence, we argued that the strategic agility of successful companies was rooted in three key vectors—strategic sensitivity, resource fluidity, and collective commitment:

- Strategic sensitivity: the sharpness of perception, intensity of awareness, and attention to strategic developments.
- Resource fluidity: the internal capability to reconfigure capabilities and redeploy resources rapidly.
- Collective commitment: the ability of the top team to make bold, fast decisions, without being bogged down in top-level "win–lose" politics.

Below, Table 3.1 sketches the application of this strategic agility framework to Nokia and its most direct and strongest competitors in the early 1990s, Ericsson and Motorola.

One can clearly see from Table 3.1 why the two major incumbents neither forcefully responded to Nokia's entry nor perceived the full potential of the opportunity digital mobile phones offered. To Motorola, Nokia was a disruptor (Christensen, 1997). Initially, digital communication networks were of poorer quality than analog ones, but their cost was lower and, more importantly, they offered the remarkable potential for the accelerated cost reduction inherent to mass-produced digital electronics. By focusing on high-end analog phones for public service emergency users, Motorola was painting itself into a corner. Ericsson was a leader in GSM digital technologies, but its focus on incumbent national telephone service operators—some of which it had supplied for over a century—meant the Swedish firm failed to fully appreciate the growth opportunity offered by newly minted "mobile-only" operators. Nor did its main incumbent customers have a favorable view of the potential for the new fast-growing mobile operators.

Yet, without technological breakthroughs, providing a pocket-sized phone for the mass market would have been difficult to achieve. Yrjö Neuvo (who joined Nokia in 1993 to head mobile phone development) had worked on developing radio frequency communication and digital signal processors when he was a university professor prior to joining Nokia. His early work gave Finland, and Nokia, an advantage in the most important technologies for

Table 3.1. Nokia vs. Ericsson and Motorola in the early 1990s

	Nokia	Ericsson	Motorola
Strategic sensitivity	▪ Mobile phones seen as a separate consumer-driven business opportunity	▪ Infrastructure focus, 'terminals as extensions'	▪ Military/professional mobile radio heritage
	▪ A huge new opportunity to change the rules of the game	▪ Success of 'AXE' switch to be protected and nurtured	▪ 'Technical excellence'
	▪ New operators	▪ Incumbent telco customers	▪ Focus on Japanese competition
Resource fluidity	▪ Little legacy, focus on new operators	▪ Locally rooted multi-domestic management structure	▪ Public sector customers
	▪ 'Born global' (for the new global business opportunity)	▪ Focus on sales and support of traditional telcos	▪ US-driven autonomous business units
	▪ Cross-functional process organization with product programs		▪ Diversified electronics group
Collective commitment	▪ Integrated business ▪ Young, tightly knit top team ▪ Survival instinct (USSR crisis)	▪ Subunit advocacy ▪ Senior, very experienced top team	▪ Subunit advocacy ▪ Senior, very experienced top team

Source: Adapted from Doz and Kosonen (2008: 5).

mobile phones. Where other players had to rely on suppliers (such as Texas Instruments), Nokia was able to develop and integrate many of these critical technologies internally. Though for other technologies it worked with key partners, including Matsushita for batteries and ST Microelectronics for mixed-signal processors, to convert key presses (an analog signal) into digital signals. So, in-house, or via early collaborations, Nokia found itself mastering or accessing all of the technologies critical for mobile phones.

By 1989, the external planetary alignment had brought about digitalization and deregulation which had nurtured Nokia's growing perception of a potential mass-market opportunity through its first GSM orders from Radiolinja and export customers. Around the same time, the capability puzzle Nokia had built and assembled over many years clicked into place, allowing a breakthrough toward seizing the opportunity to grow in mobile phones.

The subsequent decision to focus on mobile communication, and its attendant global and high-tech nature, was of course courageous, but given the circumstances facing Nokia at the time, it was also natural: over the previous years it had become clear that not only would the consumer electronics and computers businesses fail to provide profitable growth opportunities for a small peripheral latecomer such as Nokia, but they would remain a cash drain; traditional businesses such as wood and rubber products which had benefited from the Soviet trade and Finland's geopolitical advantage were put into question with the end of the Soviet Union; and added to this, concerned with the losses and structural competitive disadvantage of Nokia's consumer electronics business, Ericsson had turned down the opportunity to acquire Nokia for a symbolic amount when Nokia's major bank shareholders had approached the Swedish company. Once CEOs Vuorilehto and then Ollila committed not to dissolve the whole company as a way out of the crisis, the idea of divesting the other businesses and remaining in telecommunications, which alone offered the prospect of a bright future, was an obvious choice.

Following deregulation, the newly licensed operators in various European countries were in many ways similar to the small local operators Nokia had been used to dealing with in Finland. They wanted state-of-the-art solutions, but had limited competencies. "End-to-end" turnkey offers, comprising handsets and network infrastructure, were well suited to their needs. Nokia's management anticipated that these entrepreneurial newcomers would provide a fast-growing set of customers.

In sum, there was no grand vision at the start of Nokia's commitment to mobile communications, but a rapidly growing confidence that a major opportunity would be there for the taking. This exemplifies the huge importance of how strategic opportunities and commitments are framed in an organization: Motorola's executives did not see how digitalization offered the possibility to transform the industry into a mass consumer business, and Ericsson's were proudly focused on fixed-line switches in which the firm excelled. This also shows how precedents and analogies can drive innovation: Nokia's leaders were familiar with how Apple had transformed the PC industry into a consumer-oriented "home computer" business with better user interfaces (which Nokia would offer consumers too) and an integral product (essentially "end-to-end" solutions with both networks and handsets which Nokia offered new operators).

Beyond the Apple precedent, it shows the immense value of diverse information and cognition in making sound strategic commitments. Between Apple's Californian product and marketing innovations and the Chinese Communist Party thinking around a cellular network to cover the country's rural areas, there was little if any *a priori* commonality, but both featured significantly in Nokia's decision. No other company was in a position to connect the proverbial "dots" that would provide crucial insights into the nature and potential of the mobile phone opportunity. Table 3.2 provides an overview of the various insights that Nokia's leaders gathered that allowed them to create and shape a new strategic frame, envisioning mobile phones as a mass-market consumer product.

Another critical factor shaping Nokia's trajectory for success was the decision to separate digital handsets from Nokia's network equipment business. In the late 1980s, when in charge of strategy, Baldauf had already been sensitive to the risk that handsets (considered by Ericsson as mere "terminals") may be resisted by defenders of analog phones within Nokia, a conflict that Motorola also fell prey to. Creating a separate unit provided focus and

Table 3.2. Toward a new strategic framework

Insight	Implication
Digital coding removes capacity barriers inherent to analog networks	Cellular networks with millions of customers are feasible
Cellular networks end natural monopoly character of telecoms networks. This should trigger deregulation and new competition	Foreign markets will come to resemble Finland's. Competition will drive service rates down
Digital technologies will drive massive cost reductions (following Moore's Law)	Particularly if we can use standard components. Radio loop technology is already mastered in Finland (technical university, the military)
Emerging countries may bypass fixed lines in rural areas and go direct to cellular networks	China will be an enormous market, India and others will follow
Apple turned PC into home / fun consumer products, why not for phones?	Outstanding design, user-friendly interface, branding are key (experience of consumer electronics may be valuable)

Source: Created by Yves Doz.

visibility to Nokia's efforts in handsets. In other words, the strategic context for handsets was able to emerge as complementary to, but also distinct from, that of network equipment. In Ericsson, and most other incumbent equipment suppliers, the core fixed-line switching business cast a long shadow over the new opportunity.

From the perspective of the CORE dimensions (Figure 3.1), perhaps the most remarkable enabler of Nokia's strategic breakthrough toward a mass consumer market in mobile phones was superior cognition—looking to the future rather than being framed by the past. Only Nokia was able not only to perceive clearly all the changes taking place in the industry (summarized in Table 3.2), but also meaningfully to "connect the dots" these provided. Legacy frames did not blind Nokia's cognition. As so often in innovation, Nokia's vision resulted from associative thinking (Dyer et al., 2011) between all these changes to create a new frame, inspired by consumer electronics more than traditional telecoms. Associative thinking in the absence of strong pre-existing frames also allowed Nokia to avoid the emergence of multiple conflicting frames put forward by different managers and organizational units as a function of past experience and parochial vested interests (Kaplan, 2008). The organizational set-up put in place at the end of the 1980s also allowed undivided and unconflicted attention on mobile handsets on the part of key executives such as Ala-Pietilä.

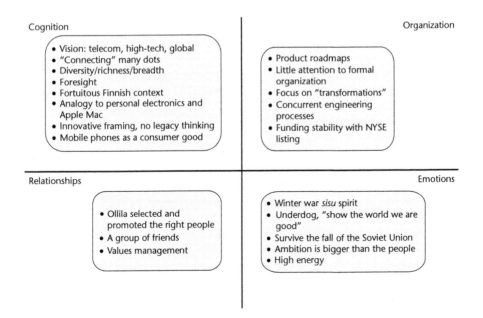

Figure 3.1. 1991–4 CORE profile

This clarity of focus also allowed a strong emotional commitment to take root among many Nokians. Granted, the alternatives were hardly attractive, so the vision of a focused, global, high-tech telecom firm was naturally compelling.

Lastly, and although the point is perhaps obvious, it is nonetheless worth-while stressing that Nokia was blessed to have the "dream team," a set of managers carefully selected by Ollila to bring social cohesion and complementary skills. All were young Finns, alumni of the same schools and with similar social and family backgrounds. Yet they brought deep and rich cognitive diversity. Except for Baldauf being a woman, they were not diverse in a demographic sense, and this allowed them to differ in their perspectives and priorities, but also to resolve their differences in a friendly way. Having witnessed how destructive giving free rein to self-interest could be (in the fight for Kairamo's succession) and been dismayed by this, the three operating managers also had promised each other to always work in the best interests of Nokia, and to surmount their possible divergence. Although competitive in individual sports (Ala-Pietilä in skiing, Alahuhta in basketball) they vowed never to compete against each other.

Note

1. For 1993 the average exchange rate was 1 Finnish markka (FIM) to 0.172 US dollars.

References

Kevin Brau, "Nokia" (CS First Boston, Equity Research, Europe, March 2, 1995).

Clayton M. Christensen, *The Innovator's Dilemma* (Harvard Business Review Press, Cambridge, MA, 1997).

Yves Doz and Mikko Kosonen, *Fast Strategy: How Strategic Agility Will Help You Stay Ahead of the Game* (Wharton School Publishing, Harlow, 2008).

Yves Doz and Mikko Kosonen, "Embedding Strategic Agility" (*Long Range Planning*, Vol. 43, 2010), pp. 370–82.

Jeffrey H. Dyer, Hal Gregersen, and Clayton M. Christensen, *The Innovator's DNA: Mastering the Five Skills of Disruptive Innovators* (Harvard Business Review Press, Cambridge, MA, 2011).

Sarah Kaplan, "Framing Contests: Strategy Making Under Uncertainty" (*Organization Science*, Vol. 19 Issue 5, September/October 2008), pp. 729–52.

Jean-Claude Larreché, *The Momentum Effect: How to Ignite Exceptional Growth* (Wharton School Publishing, Harlow, 2008).

Nikos Theodosopoulos, "Nokia Corporation: New Recommendation" (Bear Sterns Equity Research, November 15, 1994).

4

A Rising Star

As 1995 unfolded, Nokia's insatiable growth seemed to confirm the general consensus among analysts that the plucky Finnish firm was on course to play a leading role in the emerging mobile telecoms industry. Group operating profit was up 39 percent and revenues up 22 percent from the previous year. By the end of 1995, NTC's personnel count had increased 38 percent from the end of 1994, while to meet growing demand for mobile phones, which had more than doubled from the previous year to reach sales of eleven million units, the number of employees at NMP was up by a staggering 82 percent year-on-year. Just under three-quarters of all the new staff were based in Finland.

The atmosphere at Nokia was euphoric. Less than five years earlier, consultants had advised the group that its mobile telecoms businesses were too small to compete, and yet a bold vision, determination, and the Finnish *sisu*, can-do, tenacious spirit had brought them to the position of number two handset maker globally, behind Motorola, and kept them growing at breakneck speed. Then suddenly, toward the end of 1995, serious problems with Nokia's supply chains became apparent and they could no longer meet demand. In December the firm was forced to issue a profit warning and its share price immediately tumbled.

The Pitfalls of Rapid Growth

Although from 1991 Nokia had been a keen proponent of introducing concurrent engineering, and had adopted the approach in earnest, Nokia's practice was focused on the product development process and didn't fully integrate purchasing, manufacturing, and sales functions. At the same time, Nokia's prodigious growth in terms of volume and product variety between the beginning of the decade and 1995 meant the firm's IT and logistics systems, which had been set up in the early 1990s in line with projected volumes at the time, could no longer cope. And to make matters worse, thousands of new recruits received a baptism by fire, being thrown into operations with little to no training. The upshot of this frenetic growth was that Nokia began struggling to get the right volume of products to the right markets at the right time.

In the years leading up to 1995, NMP had begun to experience problems with component availability. According to Mikko Kosonen, things changed in 1995 as "difficulties with components quickly got worse and triggered a domino effect in the whole logistics pipeline." This was precipitated by a supplier of a critical part who was retooling a plant in Austria and consequently having problems with yields. The supplier was unable to deliver its component in anything close to the volume Nokia required, and this brought some assembly lines to a standstill while inventories of other components built up.

At the same time, without detailed real-time sales data or accurate forecasting models (actual sales now always exceeded forecasts and planned volumes), production managers were pushing ahead with supplying new products in as large a volume as they could, unaware that a slowdown in the US market was now leading to stockpiles of unsold products. "This complex multitude of interdependent supply chain weaknesses was given a simple name, the 'logistics crisis'," Kosonen explained. "We hadn't been able to develop the structures, systems, and competencies to keep pace with sales growth. It became painfully clear that the complexity, variety, and volume of our products in multiple production and distribution centers called for a new approach to be designed and implemented as quickly as possible."

Overcoming the Logistics Crisis

Nokia's top management team wasted no time responding to the logistics crisis. CEO Jorma Ollila was particularly vocal in stressing the need to avoid apportioning blame and instead reach a resolution by adhering to the Nokia Values of trust and teamwork. However, he did send his close and trusted lieutenant, Kallasvuo, to "help out" temporarily at NMP—although this wasn't universally appreciated in the business unit, as some felt this move represented Ollila asserting his control over NMP as Kallasvuo tended to observe more than help.

As the more senior managers had to focus on running the business, a young manager from northern Finland, Pertti Korhonen, was selected to head a cross-functional taskforce to re-engineer NMP's demand and supply chain. Korhonen had extensive R&D experience before moving into operations and running a key plant where Frank McGovern had identified and mentored him as one of the up-and-coming talented managers. Korhonen was given full authority to drive this critical, cross-organizational project.

Relishing the challenge and energized by the responsibility, Korhonen sought a vendor to supply a global transaction system to provide full transparency to Nokia's entire logistics activities, and finally selected SAP to design and install a globally integrated Enterprise Resource Planning (ERP) system. Innovative at the time, and SAP's first, this new build-to-order system was designed so that sales prompted production by linking every customer order with purchasing requirements, inventory management, manufacturing, and delivery.

Remarkably, the new ERP system was fully functional within six months. It gave NMP control of its supply chain and delivered significant efficiency gains: NMP's inventory and raw materials cycles were reduced from 154 to sixty-eight days and eighty-six to twenty-six days, respectively; inventory costs per mobile handset were halved; and the number of components purchased shrank from 900 to 200. At the group's main phone manufacturing facility in Salo, Finland, instead of taking months, a production line could now be established at full capacity in just four days.

But as importantly, the information generated by the new system was a valuable management tool, effectively providing real-time information covering Nokia's entire global logistics and supply chain. This enabled managers to respond quickly to shifting patterns of demand and ramp production up and scale it down accordingly. None of Nokia's competitors could come anywhere close to achieving this degree of speed and flexibility and over the coming years Nokia's unmatched prowess in supply chain, manufacturing, and distribution became a powerful strategic advantage.

Internally, the logistics crisis was officially seen as a consequence of rapid growth rather than a failure of NMP's management, and in the immediate aftermath not a single person lost their job over the episode. Instead, Nokia Values were reinforced by sending the message that, by pulling together, Nokia staff could overcome even the toughest problems and from adversity build strength. However, despite the official line from Ollila that individuals were not to blame, some managers who knew him well couldn't help but worry that they had failed in Ollila's eyes. Vital trust had been undermined and although censure might not be immediate, if and when it did come they feared it would be severe.

Just as fortuitous timing had played a role in enabling Nokia to list on the NYSE when it was in need of funding to internationalize, Ollila acknowledged that timing was also in Nokia's favor with the logistics crisis, "We were lucky that the really big growth came between 1996 and 2001. Had it come earlier, before the logistics crisis led us to put in place the organizational infrastructure, we would not have been able to grow. But after the logistics crisis we could accelerate again.... We had made the transition to enable us to play as a global company."

Finding New Growth through "Intellectual Leadership"

Prior to the logistics crisis and following on from previous years' themes around values and operations, at the beginning of 1995 Nokia had launched a new Annual Transformation around "intellectual leadership." This had been born of concern (though in our interviews with senior managers from the period, some went as far as to describe this as "paranoia") that Nokia's rapid growth would come to an end with inevitable market saturation. The company wanted to identify the next growth wave, or as they put it, "a third leg" to the existing handset and networks businesses. This became particularly important to Jorma Ollila in the aftermath of the logistics crisis, as he saw that too great a focus on a single business was a source of significant vulnerability.

To add rigor and bring reality to this particular Annual Transformation theme, Ala-Pietilä sought out leading experts on innovation and growth from around the world. In our discussions about this exercise he smiled, recalling an eventful journey to meet one such expert, Gary Hamel, in Boston for the first time, "A heavy snow storm had diverted my flight to New York and the only way to reach Boston was by taking a Greyhound bus. The bus had to make an unscheduled stop to throw out three guys who were smoking grass on the back seat. This was quite a different experience for me!" However, once he reached Boston and met Hamel, he recognized that Hamel's concepts of core competencies and strategic intent (which he had developed working with C. K. Prahalad) were just the framework Nokia needed to drive its search for a third leg and refocus on growth.

Ala-Pietilä engaged Hamel to run a core competency workshop in Finland, followed by a huge exercise involving over one hundred Nokia staff for around six months to identify and develop the ten most promising growth ideas for the firm. Even though there is now some disagreement about how useful this exercise really was, given Nokia's exclusive focus on telecoms, it certainly deepened and widened the strategic conversation within Nokia. Interestingly, it was during this exercise, in early 1995, that Nokia first recognized the potential for mobile communications to move beyond voice to include data and multimedia.

Although the intellectual leadership activities were slightly derailed by the logistics crisis at the end of 1995, by the middle of the following year Nokia's management saw even greater urgency in refocusing on future growth opportunities. The logistics crisis had made it very clear that the demands of rapid growth left little latitude for NMP and NTC to look at opportunities beyond their core businesses. And so Kosonen, who had recently become head of corporate development for Nokia Group, was asked to set up and run the New Venture Board (NVB), with a mandate to widen the firm's vision and interests.

The NVB inherited a number of fledlging ventures that had been initiated through the intellectual leadership exercise the previous year, and established a venturing process to evaluate the backlog of existing ventures and manage new ideas from conception to start-up. To undertake the final evaluation in this process and make the ultimate decision whether to fund or kill new venture projects, Ollila established the Strategy Panel—a new top management group from across Nokia's business units comprising the "dream team," members of the executive board plus Anssi Vanjoki, Yrjö Neuvo (Nokia's technology guru), and Juhani Kuusi (head of the Nokia Research Center). Later in 1998 this would be complemented by a New Business Development Forum, chaired by Ala-Pietilä, with participants from all business groups preparing the evaluations discussed by the Strategy Panel.

Despite great support and enthusiasm initially, the NVB struggled to gain traction within Nokia. A sense of speed and urgency resulting from the extraordinary growth of the core business permeated the organization and absorbed all management time and attention. Metrics in the firm were geared toward core business discipline and performance, and not the quest to find new ventures. When confronted with new venture ideas from the NVB, executives on the Strategy Panel often found the ideas too visionary and future-oriented to be able to assess whether they offered the complementary "third leg" that Nokia was seeking. It was also extremely difficult to find any idea that might offer the same growth potential as Nokia's core activities, making the search for a third leg self-defeating.

In fact, shunning the corporate-wide NVB activities, both NMP and NTC began their own internal venturing activities more closely aligned with shorter term, core business development. For example, in 1997, NMP formerly established the Mobile Data Unit as part of its Tampere R&D labs to address what they saw as the coming convergence between voice and data. (This unit became the official home of the "Communicator," which Nokia had launched the previous year and about which we shall hear more in Chapter 5.)

Internal Tensions and External Opportunities

A lack of commitment to the NVB process in favor of a business unit-initiated effort was symptomatic of an underlying problem that was beginning to manifest itself in other areas between Nokia's two major business groups. Where once Nokia gained advantage from close collaboration between NMP and NTC in delivering end-to-end solutions to customers, the strategies of the two businesses were increasingly being driven by different motivations as each pursued the best course for its own growth.

The crux of the divergence between the two business groups was that NTC operated in a buyer's market while NMP was in a seller's market. NTC had one customer group, the operators, and it was under a lot of pressure from operators to provide bundled infrastructure and handset deals. Being able to offer the very latest phones at a discount in their service offerings was critical to the operators' competitive position and they fought hard to try and secure a privileged supply of Nokia handsets by making this a condition of infrastructure procurement. A further point of difference by this time was that NTC was focusing on selling GSM infrastructure.

In contrast, NMP developed handsets for all 2G and 3G standards for the entire mobile market, with sales divided equally between independent distributors and operators (even with this group of customers it sold to many more operators than NTC). NMP had been very successful in repositioning the mobile handset as a consumer product. Not only was growth in units sold being driven by rapidly increasing market penetration around the world, but also through customers now regularly replacing their phones to take advantage of new standards and handset features. As such, NMP's products were a relatively scarce resource that it had to be seen to allocate with neutrality and fairness between its various customer groups. Priorities in serving customers thus diverged between the two business groups. Kosonen's brutal but fair analysis of the situation at the time was, "NMP needed NTC less and less." In 1997, NTC accounted for around 35 percent of group revenues in comparison to NMP's 51 percent (the balance being mainly the remnants of the consumer and industrial electronics businesses yet to be divested). And as much as members of the Strategy Panel discussed the divergence between the core businesses, they could not agree upon a resolution.

Frustrated by this impasse, still concerned about identifying the next growth area for Nokia, and increasingly worried about NMP's dominance and the vulnerability this entailed, toward the end of 1997 Jorma Ollila put together a task force to analyze the group's structural options in light of the growing strategic distance between the two core businesses and the need to identify possible new growth areas for Nokia. This task force comprised Ollila, CFO Kallasvuo, heads of businesses Ala-Pietilä, Alahuhta, and Baldauf plus Nokia's head of strategy, Kosonen.

With regard to strategic options, members of the task force were in agreement that the biggest potential threat to Nokia's current business came from data communications and the emerging corporate market. Even though at the time mobility within this arena wasn't much of a concern, the task force foresaw the convergence of the IT and telecoms industries down the line and recognized that the IT technology base, being driven by the likes of Cisco and Microsoft, would be of vital importance in the future. However, exactly how to counter this threat was less obvious—Nokia clearly didn't have the right competencies or channels to enter this market, nor, having grown organically, did it have the acquisition and post-merger integration skills for inorganic growth. Important though they felt the corporate market would be in the coming years, the task force concluded it would be too difficult a sector to enter.

In their discussions over Nokia's internal structural issues and about how best to address these challenges, the task force made little progress. Regardless of what proposals and ideas came up for discussion, none of the business heads was prepared to risk disrupting their own business to rebalance the firm.

This failure to find solutions for what he saw as a much-needed strategic and structural renewal weighed heavily on Ollila over the 1997 Christmas holidays. He knew that with complementary skills and characteristics Ala-Pietilä, Alahuhta, and Baldauf worked brilliantly together and that's exactly why they had earned the sobriquet the "dream team." But he felt they had all settled into their comfort zones, too entrenched in the thinking demanded by their current roles to the detriment of being able to recognize the need for change. And so, at the beginning of 1998, while keeping his top management team intact, he reorganized their roles in the hope that giving each of them a new perspective would enable Nokia to keep growing its core businesses in a complementary and cooperative fashion while also looking for future growth opportunities.

Alahuhta, who was strong on operational control, was moved from NTC to head Nokia's biggest and fastest growing business, NMP. Sari Baldauf took over from Alahuhta as head of NTC, which was shortly after renamed Nokia Networks (NET). At the request of the board, Ollila's own role as CEO was expanded to also take on the chairmanship of the board. And Pekka Ala-Pietilä, the most skilled strategist in Nokia's senior ranks, was appointed president of Nokia, with responsibility to build the elusive "third leg." While on paper this looked like a promotion positioning him as Ollila's number two and making him a full executive member of the board, in reality he had no responsibility for operations, no oversight role over NET or NMP, and had only 15 percent of Nokia's businesses reporting to him (many of which were earmarked for divestment).

Looking for New Growth Opportunities

With Ala-Pietilä at the helm, a new group, the Nokia Ventures Organization (NVO), was established to build a venture portfolio absorbing all of the ventures and projects that had been under the remit of the now defunct NVB. In addition, all of Nokia's remaining non-core businesses, including TV set-top boxes and display products were moved into NVO to be streamlined or divested.

Over the next three years NVO had a total of thirty-eight new ventures in its portfolio—some internal and some from the Silicon Valley-based Nokia Ventures Fund, which was given initial investment capital of US$150 million with a mandate to invest in firms developing disruptive technologies and capabilities.

With Nokia's remarkable growth and success had come a change in culture—speed was becoming paramount with a "now or never" rejection of anything that took time to develop. Although reflective and thoughtful by nature, Ala-Pietilä truly believed that NVO had to conform to this dominant culture. He felt compelled to show results and show them quickly and so introduced strict criteria for NVO's fledgling ventures. Rather than giving them time to develop, ventures had to become profitable and show significant growth potential within three years or be dismantled. He also recognized that for NVO to succeed, it had to be credible with NMP and NET and so would need to sponsor some ventures that were relevant to the core businesses in terms of technologies and business models.

NVO did prove successful in exploring new technologies and competencies that were directly relevant to NMP and NET. For example, under the guise of Nokia Internet Communications it nurtured a range of security-related products and capabilities which were transferred to the core businesses and proved critical for data communications when 3G standards were introduced. Longer term efforts were stifled however.

Ala-Pietilä also set up the "Insight-Foresight" unit within NVO. With a staff of around twenty-five, this group partnered with academics and thought leaders from around the world to explore new technologies and concepts, and each year it produced an analysis of world trends that provided a useful guide for anticipating near-term innovation requirements in the core businesses. Although a small team within the Insight-Foresight unit exclusively focused on new business models, organizing group-wide innovation days to explore potential future options, this activity, along with anything else that was deemed too future-oriented by the core businesses, tended to be overlooked and ultimately disregarded.

With both NMP and NET absorbed by the operational challenges of their own rapid growth, NVO struggled to find internal support or interest in its quest to find new growth opportunities for the group. In a company that had increased revenues by 128 percent in the three years to the end of 2000, operating profit by 132 percent, and headcount by 43 percent, the earlier concerns over how the group could counter stalling growth had dissipated—particularly as beyond the top management group, few staff in Nokia ever really understood the role NVO had been mandated to fulfill. As a result, none of the ventures NVO managed became Nokia's "third leg."

Focusing on the Core Business

In June 1998, Nokia had overtaken Motorola to become the world's number one handset producer. "This changed everything," according to head of business planning at the time, Juha Putkiranta. "Everyone would now have us in their crosshairs and so Ollila and Ala-Pietilä created market share targets, so we would not rest on our laurels." In a further move to tighten control of the core businesses, 1998 had also seen the rollout of common support platforms for IT, finance and accounting, and HR (human resources) designed to increase transparency as well as economies of scale across Nokia's growing international operations.

Although the infrastructure business was growing year-on-year, and despite Ollila's attempts to rebalance the two core businesses, NMP was racing ahead, growing at a much faster rate than NET—in 1998 it accounted for 60 percent of group revenues (this would rise to 72 percent in 2000). But with very high penetration in key markets, maintaining growth momentum in NMP called for more than Nokia's world-class supply chain, cool design, and innovative technologies—Nokia estimated that within a few years between 70 and 80 percent of all sales would be for replacement phones. NMP had after all successfully turned the mobile handset "terminal" into a consumer product, and now needed to find a better way to sell more of these to its customers in 130 countries.

To meet this challenge, in 1998 NMP began segmenting the market based on customer lifestyles—the idea being that different types of user groups would be drawn to phones with features, styling, and price points that met their specific requirements. Not only would some user groups upgrade their phones more frequently to get the latest features, but others would buy new phones as they migrated from one user group to another, and some customers would have more than one phone for different uses—for example one phone for business and one for personal use.

As well as selling more phones, NMP wanted to find a way to reduce the bargaining power of the major network operators, who essentially controlled the relationship with end users. So to interact directly with end users and build loyalty, NMP ramped up an initiative called Club Nokia that Ala-Pietilä and Vanjoki had launched in 1997. To quote Nokia's 2000 annual report, "Club Nokia is all about information, support and fun." Anyone with a Nokia phone could join Club Nokia via a website and gain access to a range of multichannel content services including customer support, special offers, games, customized picture sharing, the ability to compose individual ringtones, new software, and digital services.

While shrewder marketing approaches and Club Nokia were aimed at gaining and maintaining the loyalty of end-user customers to the Nokia brand in the near-term, technology advances were ushering in a new 3G standard that Nokia, along with all of its competitors, believed would result in a surge of new demand for both infrastructure and phones by 2002. 3G brought data services to mobile communications, and Nokia's R&D community as well as top management viewed this new mobile Internet as a complementary architectural layer to its core telecom businesses and not a disruptive technology. In Kosonen's words, this framing "gave a strong feeling of confidence that Nokia's business models in NET and NMP could continue growing on the same trajectory forever."

Leading up to the millennium, Nokia was riding very high. In 1999 and 2000 it was ranked the eighth most valuable company globally, and a number of articles in leading business papers lauded CEO Ollila as one of the most influential business leaders in the world. This success brought even greater drive and energy to the firm. But it also inflated market expectations, and the management team knew that even with 3G around the corner, meeting these wouldn't be easy.

Commentary

The logistics crisis was a key formative event in Nokia's history. *Ex post*, it can be seen as a simple problem of supply chain imbalance stemming from product diversification coupled with very fast and unexpected growth. In the early 1990s, Nokia's growth in mobile phones outstripped its management's expectations by a widening margin each year. The firm's success exceeded any plans management made. The origin of the logistics crisis was the inability of a particular supplier to meet rapidly rising orders, and this became the catalyst throwing the whole supply system into disarray. This was compounded by the fact that Nokia was focused on building phones as fast as it could, without always paying attention to the ability of its production lines' output to match supply with demand for particular models, various regions, or specific standards. Its product range had also started to widen significantly, making the whole supply system more heterogeneous and more complex.

In substance, the handling of the logistics crisis by management was both simple and effective. After a few months of fire fighting, putting the supply chain back in order, and catching up with delayed deliveries, the core of the crisis was solved with the introduction of a SAP single-instance ERP system. This allowed a shift to a "build-to-order" process, where customer orders pulled the whole supply system. The registering of every sales contract and delivery schedule into the ERP allowed all actions, up to detailed volume planning by component suppliers, to be coordinated and scheduled effectively. This system was scalable and could support the astounding growth of Nokia in the latter 1990s.

Despite a simple and effective solution being found, the logistics crisis remained a very traumatic event, and memories of it were fraught with emotion. Its consequences were important. At that point in time, NMP might not just have faltered, but fallen beyond recovery and lost everything at the very moment the mobile phone market was exploding! Nokia had been very close to catastrophe.

With the immediate stress receding, Ollila drew strong lessons on at least two levels. First, beyond concurrent engineering being extended to the whole value chain (from suppliers to customers, including, most critically, machine and other manufacturing equipment suppliers), the need for greater management discipline became a strong concern. Second, the vulnerability of having a dominant business, rather than a wider and more balanced portfolio, revived the yearning for renewal and diversification, despite the astounding success of NMP.

The emphasis on management discipline, the exploding growth of Nokia's sales, and the relative maturing of mobile phones toward a Nokia-led dominant design (Abernathy and Utterback, 1978) incrementally led to more conservative approaches in product development and tighter operational control.

Responding to Ollila's second concern proved more difficult. The development of NVO was meant to address the need for renewal and diversification. But, although it may not have been fully clear at the time, NVO and new ventures were victims of contradictions set up for them by Nokia's leadership, both in terms of strategy and metrics. The initial ambition to look for new growth opportunities beyond the short- to mid-term time horizon of NET and NMP, and to build on the growth areas identified in the intellectual leadership exercise, was laudable. But the yearning for a "third leg" was unrealistic, in particular given the extraordinary growth of the core businesses, and of NMP in particular. One can understand Ollila's concern with the risk of overreliance on two businesses (or, as NMP's growth and profits now dwarfed NET's, perhaps only one)—and the need therefore to rediversify the group. But "the next big thing" (as Steve Jobs used to say) would have to be really big, and Nokia really successful at capturing it!

Obviously, the challenge was that Nokia's distinctive competence base was rather narrow. Mass manufacturing of small electronic devices was imitable, and so was radio frequency innovation—in fact, as the business matured Samsung would finally take leadership. The advantage of "end-to-end" network equipment and handset sales, a strong differentiator in the early 1990s, became less and less important and even turned into a disadvantage as new operators consolidated into very large multinational companies such as Vodafone, or were gobbled up by the old incumbents. These larger and more competent customers saw little benefit in bundled sales except by extracting Nokia's commitment to deliver newly introduced handsets, still in short supply, in exchange for commitments to network equipment purchases. This tie-in was not satisfactory for NMP, the customer base of which was wider than NET's: NMP wished to satisfy its most important handset customers first, irrespective of whether they also procured NET's equipment. So to discover potentially very large growth opportunities that would leverage Nokia's narrow and less distinctive competence base, and avoid creating further potentially conflicting interdependencies between the businesses, was extremely difficult.

Nokia's exclusive focus and commitment to telecoms also started to contradict the search for new growth opportunities, many of which, if they were to draw on Nokia's competencies, would not necessarily be found in telecoms. As an example, Gary Hamel, who had just led a major exercise with Strategos to identify Nokia's core competencies, quipped in a conversation in 1996, "Nokia should really make microwave ovens!" Perhaps Nokia could also have made them connected and remote controlled, anticipating the Internet of things. Silly as this may sound, this hypothetical example denotes the difficulty Nokia had in finding opportunities beyond mobile phones that would leverage its key competencies.

Many opportunities NVO identified were too far ahead of their time to lend themselves to the creation of new ventures. For instance, Nokia did indeed correctly identify what is now becoming the "Internet of things" as an opportunity that would fit its capabilities and be of significant size. But as this has only recently begun to materialize as a business, they were nearly twenty years too early. The same was true in health care and wellness where, long before it became mainstream, Nokia identified remote monitoring and interactive multimedia health management as a growth area. Many of NVO's projects were too visionary, and too long term to gain traction. Some are still under development today, albeit under a different roof!

New ventures at Nokia also fell into a trap we observed in many other companies: while the vision is long term, the context within which the venture is developed is short-term oriented and this is reflected in demanding metrics. In other words, even if they do not have to fit into existing organizational structures, ventures still have to conform to heuristics and metrics prevalent in more mature businesses. To get funded they need to comply with existing rules and criteria, and this leads to their failure (Gilbert, 2005). Nokia had an implicit tradition of tight financial control. In this light it is symptomatic that, in one of our conversations, Ala-Pietilä stated he felt compelled to have individual ventures be profitable after three years. When this was met with a surprised reaction, given the clearly long-term nature of most venture projects, he explained that setting up ventures and making them profitable was the way to gain credibility and be self-sufficient. So ventures would have to succeed after three years, and this set many up to "fail," even before the dotcom crisis.

In retrospect, one can see that the closeness of the Nokia Research Center to the business groups, and its lack of a strong independent research and innovation agenda, combined with Nokia's desire to give ventures business unit status, with profit and loss reporting, as quickly as possible, led to several ventures being set up prematurely—before the markets or technologies vital for a profitable business opportunity were in place. A longer gestation period, typical when innovation projects are developed in a central corporate research center, plus a more patient and discriminating approach to transforming innovation projects into ventures, would have given NVO's projects a better chance of success. So would a clearer differentiation between managing early-stage projects and established ventures (Keil et al., 2009; Harreld et al., 2007; O'Reilly et al., 2009).

By the mid-1990s the Nokia culture had become one centered on speed. Nokia managers saw themselves as pacing the market and thriving on its extremely fast development. This focus on, and pride in, being fast came to permeate the whole organization. The slower ripening of an emerging strategic opportunity and its patient nurturing over longer periods, slowly resolving ambiguities and removing uncertainties, as was needed for new ventures, became all but impossible in Nokia.

Further, throughout Nokia's venturing program there was some ambiguity between two quite different overall strategic roles for ventures. One was to generate several options of sufficient magnitude to become a "third leg." The second was to scout for NMP and NET, so that their tighter operational focus post-1995 did not lead Nokia to underinvest in their longer term future. In neither role did NVO succeed. There simply was no "next big thing" of a magnitude required in telecom to provide the third leg in any foreseeable time frame. At the same time, most new ventures' activities were really too far out to be of direct, shorter term interest to the business groups. There was a logical complementarity between the business groups' own renewal efforts—for instance around data-enabled phones and data networks—and NVO's efforts, but these remained of limited perceived importance to core businesses preoccupied with their own continued growth along existing trajectories.

So rather than creating renewal options, or even complementing the business groups' innovative activities, the contribution of ventures is perhaps best seen from a different perspective—that of improving the quality of strategy dialogs (Tukiainen, 2004; McGrath et al., 2006). The venturing effort did, for example, contribute to alerting Nokia's leadership to impending disruptive changes—such as Internet telephony—and widened their angle of vision, for instance toward multimedia opportunities.

The Venture Board, Strategy Panel, and the Insight-Foresight staff group also contributed to stretching and deepening the strategy conversations in Nokia. These provided a series of future-oriented circles for strategic dialogs which involved a larger group of senior and middle managers in these conversations, and resulted in many Nokians developing a greater strategic awareness. This was somewhat countercultural in a now very successful firm where decisiveness, fast commitments, and quick aggressive debate were increasingly valued, and the patience needed for dialogs was in short supply.

The withering of Nokia ventures reduced the intensity of longer term and wider scope strategy dialogs. Together with the growing focus on lifestyle market segmentation, which was driving greater fragmentation, the degree of attention to strategy post-2001 was seriously eroded. The development over time of a bloated corporate strategy staff, increasingly distant from line operating managers in the businesses, and its staffing with a mix of outsiders recruited from consulting companies and insiders who had not made it as line managers, further weakened the quality of strategic reflection among business managers.

The end of NVO may also have ultimately contributed to making Ollila's succession more delicate. Although Ala-Pietilä (the widely tipped successor as CEO) had not been blamed for the logistics crisis, and had even been praised along with Korhonen and others for its prompt and effective resolution, he was now associated with a second set of difficulties: that of ventures. This made him appear a weaker candidate to Ollila's succession in 2001, and led the board to ask Ollila to stay on rather than appoint Ala-Pietilä as CEO.

The logistics crisis had also revealed an incipient divergence in management. Although Ollila had been quick not to apportion blame but focus on a problem-solving approach to resolve the crisis, he nonetheless detached Kallasvuo to NMP for a few months ostensibly to assist Ala-Pietilä. Not surprisingly, the distinction between assisting, watching, and controlling became lost on NMP managers, who felt they were not trusted and saw little value in closer corporate attention. (Kallasvuo was a "numbers man" whose skills in finance perhaps did not equip him to contribute most effectively to addressing a supply chain logistics challenge anyway.) Although the recovery was quick and successful, and created the basis for future growth—to the credit of NMP's leadership—one cannot help consider that Ollila's support and leniency created a sense of obligation on the part of the NMP leadership. In addition, his handling of the crisis contributed to the emergence of a clear distinction in roles in the top team between the operating line managers (Pekka, Matti, and Sari) and the corporate officers (mainly Jorma and Olli-Pekka). The "dream team" was now becoming a team of three + two, not five!

So, back to the CORE dimensions. Nokia's *Cognition* in the mid-1990s was characterized by a form of ambidexterity (O'Reilly and Tushman, 2008) between exploiting the extraordinary growth mobile phones offered and (with its leaders keenly aware this would not last forever, and was exposed to possible crises such as the one they had faced in logistics) exploring new growth options. At the time, Geoff Moore's ideas about high growth in technology markets, summarized in his book *Inside the Tornado* (Moore, 1995), were popular among Nokians and they found themselves exercising all their energy just riding the tornado! This formidable runaway success more than vindicated the courageous decisions Ollila and his team made at the beginning of the 1990s, when consultants and investors had been warning against such choices.

Taking a leaf from C. K. Prahalad and Gary Hamel's bestseller, *Competing for the Future* (Hamel and Prahalad, 1994), Nokia engaged them to help search for "intellectual leadership" in the telecoms industry (their argument being that the highest level of competition in an industry is for its intellectual leadership, i.e. for developing the best and smartest foresight-driven strategy to build future advantage). But beyond seeing data and multimedia messaging opportunities on the horizon and fruitlessly dreaming of discovering a big, fast-growing "third leg" that would provide balance to Nokia and lessen its deepening dependence on mobile phones, developing intellectual leadership proved difficult. Not surprisingly, finding a third leg was elusive and the unrealistic growth expectations put on new ventures were dashed. Ventures remained peripheral and were easy targets when their credibility was further shattered by the dotcom crash. By 2002 most had been abandoned or divested. Strategic deliberation arenas that were set up around ventures with the participation of core business strategists did sharpen strategic thinking in the company, and diffused it beyond the few at the top, but these were not to survive the failure of the venture effort in the early 2000s.

The mid-1990s can be characterized more by the effort to build a professionally run *Organization* than by new cognition and effective strategic thinking. The greatest contribution to future success and adaptability was the introduction of a highly effective ERP platform and the tight and efficient management of the complex supply chain system it enabled. This allowed fast scaling-up, and could accommodate constantly increasing product variety and effective and efficient sourcing and manufacturing worldwide. This was one of Nokia's most critical success factors, but one that drove an emphasis on operational scale, efficiency, and speed at the cost of innovation. Nearly all the executives interviewed stressed that through the second half of the 1990s, NMP became more conservative. Of course, basic voice communication was now a mass-market reality, SMS (Short Message Service) had come as a windfall, and other applications such as email were still in their infancy, so it is natural that innovation in the industry would slow down, irrespective of Nokia's actions. However, the logistics crisis had seriously scarred Nokia—the experience of being so close to potential collapse resulted in a greater professionalism in management, which translated into more conservative decisions and some forms of risk avoidance. Cost discipline also became more critical, with price reduction pressures leading to tighter control.

From a *Relational* standpoint, the first cracks had started to appear in the "dream team." In essence, Ollila's "no blame, these are growing pains not management shortcomings" perspective was seen by many as almost too good to be true, and hence not entirely believable. The temporary secondment of Kallasvuo to NMP also started to draw a sharper line between corporate and operating unit managers.

Emotionally, some of the elation and enthusiasm that had characterized the courageous and uplifting strategic choices, the definition of values, and the articulation of a simple but energizing vision in the early 1990s, started to wane. The emotional engagement became less intense. These elements are summarized graphically in Figure 4.1.

In closing, it is important to note that NMP was not only becoming very large very quickly (in fact at an unprecedented pace for an industrial manufacturer), but it was still a very new organization—barely an adolescent—led by a relatively inexperienced group of executives, most of whom had never held senior roles in more mature global companies. This left them to learn to run by themselves with no prior experience, and do it rapidly. The speed at which

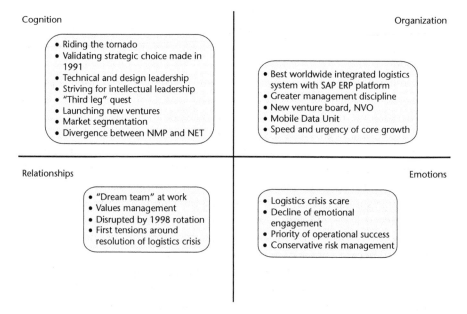

Figure 4.1. 1995–8 CORE profile

they learned to build and run a global giant is impressive. Of course, though, their business model was very simple, scalable, and extremely focused: design, engineer, make, and sell mobile phones. Although it also sold to independent distributors, network operators were Nokia's major customers and they provided phones to end users as part of service subscriptions. This left Nokia building a leading brand based on product excellence more than shrewd marketing. However, the development of smartphones and the ushering in of the Internet era were about to challenge Nokia's simple business model.

References

William Abernathy and James Utterback, "Patterns of Industrial Innovation" (*Technology Review*, Vol. 80 Issue 7, June/July 1978), pp. 41–7.

J. Bruce Harreld, Charles A. O'Reilly, and Michael L. Tushman, "Dynamic Capabilities at IBM: Driving Strategy Into Action" (*California Management Review*, Vol. 49 Issue 4, Summer 2007), pp. 21–43.

Clark Gilbert, "Unbundling the Structure of Inertia: Resource Versus Routine Rigidity" (*Academy of Management Journal*, Vol. 45 Issue 5, October 2005), pp. 741–63.

Gary Hamel and C. K. Prahalad, *Competing for the Future* (Harvard Business School Press, Cambridge, MA, 1994).

Thomas Keil, Rita G. McGrath, and Taina Tukiainen, "Gems from the Ashes: Capability Creation and Transformation in Internal Corporate Venturing" (*Organization Science*, Vol. 20 Issue 3, May/Jun 2009), pp. 601–20.

Rita G. McGrath, Thomas Keil, and Taina Tukiainen, "Extracting Value from Corporate Venturing" (*MIT Sloan Management Review*, Vol. 48 Issue 1, Fall 2006), pp. 50–6.

Geoffrey Moore, *Inside the Tornado: Marketing Strategies from Silicon Valley's Cutting Edge* (HarperCollins, New York, 1995).

Charles A. O'Reilly, J. Bruce Harreld, and Michael L. Tushman, "Organisational Ambidexterity: IBM and Emerging Business Opportunities" (*California Management Review*, Vol. 51 Issue 4, Summer 2009), pp. 75–99.

Charles A. O'Reilly and Michael L. Tushman, "Ambidexterity as a Dynamic Capability: Resolving the Innovator's Dilemma" (*Research in Organizational Behavior*, Vol. 28, 2008), pp. 185–206.

Taina Tukiainen, "The Unexpected Benefits of Internal Corporate Ventures: An Empirical Examination of the Consequences of Investment in Corporate Ventures" (doctoral dissertation series, Helsinki University of Technology, laboratory of industrial management, 2004).

5

Attracting the Planets

As the new millennium got underway, Nokia was much better placed than many of its competitors to roll out new 3G data communications technologies. Much as it had shaped the mobile voice industry in the early 1990s, later in the decade—while NMP's main mobile phone centers focused on core voice phones—the Mobile Data Unit in Tampere was busy with a raft of product innovations.

As early as 1992, at the initiative of its director, Reijo Paajanen, Nokia's Tampere R&D center had started a "skunk works"-type project to develop a mobile data-optimized phone, which for lack of a better name was called the Communicator. Both Ala-Pietilä and Vanjoki firmly believed that digital convergence between mobile phones, personal digital assistants (PDAs), and personal computers would lead to the type of pocket computer envisaged by Paajanen and so provided "air cover" for the entrepreneurial activity.

They also perceived a competitive threat for this type of hybrid data phone. Apple (with its Newton) and IBM (with its own Communicator) had both launched non-voice mobile devices in the past. Even though neither had been successful, Ala-Pietilä and Vanjoki assumed that both firms would try to enter the mobile communications industry again. Perhaps of more immediate concern, Microsoft was known to be seeking collaborations with operators and device manufacturers to introduce a version of its Windows OS for mobiles. If it were successful in extending and replicating the success of its "Windows" OS to data-enabled phones, it could capture a very large share of Nokia's value—much as it had done in PCs with IBM, Hewlett-Packard (HP), and Dell—reducing the firm to a mere hardware supplier unable to generate much profit.

Developing the Communicator had proved a significant challenge. On the one hand, the project faced strong internal resistance from NMP's main phone development center in Oulu, where engineers working on traditional mobile phones failed to see the need for a new data-enabled product and were unhappy about the growing resources the Communicator seemed to be attracting.

On the other hand, the Communicator proved a bigger departure from traditional phone development than had initially been supposed. Nokia's strong competence lay in developing the product hardware and an underlying simple OS to support voice functions that could be sold as a "global product" with minor adaptations for local markets. The Communicator took Nokia into entirely new and much more complex territory. Software and wider ecosystems became much more important, as downstream the Communicator required user interfaces, application software, and content, while upstream it needed tools to support applications and their development, differing network operators' standards, and specific OS software.

Microsoft's Windows domination of the PC market had made NMP's management team fully aware that the OS providing the user interface layer was critical in the world of data, and that depending upon an external source to provide this was a dangerous strategy. Yet Nokia didn't have the capabilities internally to develop a new OS for the Communicator within the time frame they had in mind to bring this innovative product to market. And so they turned to California-based Geoworks, developer of the Palm Pilot PDA OS to provide an OS for the Communicator.

The Smartphone and Symbian OS

The first Communicator smartphone was launched in 1996. Although sales volumes were low, this breakthrough product with a folding hinged design which featured a large horizontal screen and full miniature keyboard received much critical acclaim. Even though the Geoworks OS had significant limitations, being both power- and memory-hungry, work was nevertheless begun on a second-generation product.

With development underway, toward the end of 1996 Nokia switched to an alternative OS developed by UK-based Psion, which provided not only lower power and memory consumption but also supported color screens—a huge step forward at the time. Psion had developed the OS for its handheld "palmtop" computing devices, and as it was keen to position it as the de facto mobile OS had decided to license it to other companies, the first licensees being Nokia, Ericsson, and Motorola.

Experience had taught Nokia (and its competitors) that collaboration and open standards were the surest way to speed up the development and adoption of new technologies, and so in June 1998 Nokia and Ericsson joined Psion in setting up a new joint company called Symbian to create an "open" mobile OS for the industry (Motorola signaled its intention to join the consortium and over time they and many more companies joined). There was a degree of urgency, as Microsoft was developing a mobile Windows OS and the Symbian partners wanted to prevent the Seattle giant locking in key partners in the value chain and dominating the fledlging mobile data industry.

The principle behind Symbian was that each firm licensing the OS would pay the same fees and no single company would own the specifications. Third-party software developers and device creators (such as video camera makers) would easily be able to "plug in" to the OS and so work with the same platform across different manufacturers' handsets. Operators would be able to create proprietary services which could be ported across different manufacturers' phones. And consumers would gain from having a much wider and broader range of functions and applications on their phones.

The Symbian partners had agreed that while they would share the OS, each would develop their own proprietary user interface. Nokia was the first to release a Symbian OS phone, when toward the end of 2000 it launched its third-generation Communicator (the 9210), with a color screen and expandable memory slot. The following year, NMP began developing a new user interface for the Symbian OS, the Series 60 (later renamed S60). The Series 60 was a platform which included all of the basic options needed for a data-enabled phone—personal information management, messaging, applications, a browser, and a modifiable user interface.

The Series 60 attracted a lot of interest from other partners, and as a result Nokia decided to license the source code to enable other manufacturers to adopt the interface and create proprietary extensions. As Matti Alahuhta recalled, "With early smartphones we were worried that Microsoft would try to take over the smartphone software-business. Opening up S60 and making it available to all other companies was a tactical move: it made it hard for Microsoft to expand." Siemens, Matsushita, and Samsung all licensed Nokia's Series 60, and a wide range of companies including ARM, Borland, Metrowerks, and Texas Instruments joined a Product Creation Community set up by Nokia for the design, manufacture, and integration of hardware and software for Series 60-equipped phones.

Setting Standards for the Mobile Data Era

Just as Nokia had previously collaborated with partners and rivals in both the NMT and GSM consortia to create common industry standards at crucial transformation points in the development of mobile voice communications, in 1997 it had entered into a coalition called the Wireless Access Protocol (WAP) Forum, with its two biggest competitors Ericsson and Motorola along with US technology firm Unwired Planet, to define a set of industry standards for accessing the Internet from mobile devices. Membership of the WAP Forum quickly grew into a broad church of over 200 companies, including major network operators and technology firms.

Not for the first time, Japanese companies presented a competitive threat. NTT DoCoMo had launched its own wireless protocol, i-mode, in February 1999. Not only was this some months ahead of the launch of the first WAP service, but with customized handsets, a user-friendly content portal, a wide range of third-party services, and ease of use for content developers, i-mode was widely seen as superior to WAP. In fact a number of operators in Europe, Australia, and East Asia adopted i-mode, although ultimately the Japanese standard struggled to gain traction against the breadth and size of WAP.

Even though i-mode didn't prove a competitive threat outside Japan, it provided managers at NMP with a critical insight: key to the success of mobile data would be a compelling range of applications and services for users. Acting on this, over the course of 1999 and 2000 NMP entered a number of alliances to develop services with Internet companies, including AOL, e-commerce firms such as Amazon, telecom operators, and several European banks. However, managers in NMP struggled to see how Nokia could extract any real value from these alliances and services, as being an open platform, anything they developed on WAP was available to all other consortia members.

The conclusion NMP drew from this experience was that in the new world of data, the only way Nokia could differentiate itself from its competitors was to focus on what it did and understood best—producing a better range of well-designed, high-quality, innovative products and getting them to market faster than their competitors.

Reinforcing the Focus on Products: Nokia's Camera Phone

Shortly after the Communicator had been launched, Vanjoki, Erik Anderson (who was leading the GSM product line in NMP), and Christian Lindholm (in charge of user interface) had begun thinking about the next major innovation and started playing with the idea of a phone with an integrated digital camera. Over the next couple of years, NMP's engineers in Tampere developed a feasible product architecture.

In February 1999, at the GSM World Congress in Cannes (an annual industry gathering), Vanjoki presented Nokia's plans for camera phones with "rich" (or "multimedia") messaging. Here, for the first time, the idea of using mobiles to send more than text was mooted. When interviewed a few years later in 2003, Ala-Pietilä summarized the thinking and events that had led to Vanjoki's announcement in Cannes, "In 1998 there were a series of convergent enablers for something new: the open OS platform—Symbian; the Communicator experience; the idea of a device that could be held and operated in one hand; the SMS precedent; wide color displays; reduced power consumption with ARM; and the idea of 'presence'—by this we meant seeing, not just hearing, as part of the customer experience."

In other words, everything was aligned for Nokia to move from mobile voice to multimedia, with consumers creating their own content. Well, almost everything. What NMP was lacking was a dedicated, entrepreneurial business group with the old "can-do" spirit that had defined Nokia's earlier days, to drive all of its data-related activities. In 2000, this was rectified with the creation of the Digital Convergence Unit (DCU). Based in Tampere and born from the Mobile Data Unit, head of the new DCU was NMP's visionary and enthusiastic supporter of the opportunities afforded by a data-rich future, Anssi Vanjoki.

Tampere's developers had faced strong skepticism from the traditional mobile phone community within NMP during the development of the Communicator, and Vanjoki expected the same reaction to the camera phone project—codenamed Calypso. Even though this time the fact that the project would sit within the new DCU which would not only shield it to some extent but also give firm-wide legitimacy, Vanjoki knew that selecting a team who could deal with distrust from the core would be key, and recalled, "We chose Mikko Moilanen to lead the project. He was well organized, conservative, prudent in his thought process, and suspicious of what might go wrong."

The Calypso project rapidly grew to involve around 500 people and sixteen sites around the world, as far apart geographically and culturally as Tampere, Tokyo, Dallas, Beijing, and Budapest. It was NMP's first truly global innovation project. Multiple suppliers and technology partners were brought into the project, ranging from software specialists to a Japanese firm to develop the imaging module. Speaking to Moilanen about the experience of heading Calypso, he told me, "The mainstream thinking was set against camera phones, and you had a project that kept growing and growing and always needed more and more resources. If we had tried to establish that program in the main phone development process, I doubt we would ever have completed it." It was clear that the divide between the innovative and experimental approach of the DCU in Tampere and the core phone business was becoming ever greater.

Nokia's first camera phone (the 7650) was released in the summer of 2002. Setting the standards for camera phones, it featured an integrated camera, multimedia messaging, large display, fast processor, a big memory and was much lauded for its ease of use, proving an instant success with critics and users alike. Even though it was described in 2013 in a retrospective of camera phones by *Techradar* as "arguably one of the most important phones ever," Nokia's 7650 wasn't in fact the first camera phone on the market. That accolade had gone to Sharp eighteen months earlier, when it had launched the J-SH04—the first true camera phone capable of taking and sending pictures (though the J-SH04 was only available in Japan and had poor image resolution in comparison to the 7650).

A Slowdown in the Mobile Telecoms Market

Nokia's efforts around Symbian, the S60 interface, and development of the camera phone, had been taking place against a backdrop of a slowdown and tough market conditions for the industry in 2001. Between 2000 and 2001, governments in Europe, Asia, Australia, and New Zealand had auctioned off 3G licenses for vast sums (these auctions were particularly frenzied in the UK, where thirteen operators bid for five licenses, ultimately spending US$34 billion, and in Germany where operators spent US$45 billion). Ripple effects from overspends on 3G licenses in Europe, combined with the dotcom crash, meant the surge in growth from new data communications services anticipated by the industry failed to materialize. In its stead, the industry as a whole was left with overcapacity and significant debt.

Handset manufacturers were hard hit, as to keep their own businesses afloat operators not only cut the subsidies they had been paying on handsets but also began selling SIM-only packages—which obviously reduced demand for new phones and stimulated a market in used phones. According to analysis from Gartner Dataquest, sales in mobile phones decreased for the first time in the industry's history in 2001, to just below 400 million units, down from almost 413 million the previous year. While a 3.2 percent decline may not seem too drastic, this has to be taken in the context of the phenomenal growth rates of previous years: 51 percent in 1998, 65 percent in 1999, and 46 percent in 2000.

NMP weathered the storm relatively well, seeing its global market share increase in 2001 to 35 percent (Motorola, the next largest manufacturer, was way behind with 14.9 percent) and operating profits only slightly down from the previous year at 4,521 million euros. However, Nokia's share price fell from a high of US$56 in 2000 to US$15.66 in September 2001. Not only was poor performance from NET (which made a loss in 2001) behind this, but with traditional phones still dominating NMP and no clear signs of a data strategy, investors had begun to question Nokia's ability to respond effectively to the digital convergence challenge between mobile communications, computing, and consumer electronics.

A Response to Digital Convergence and Commoditization

Until the telecoms slowdown in 2001, NMP had been growing so rapidly that there had been little time or attention focused on renewal of the core business. Between 1996 and 2000, NMP's headcount had increased 150 percent to 27,353, while revenues over the same five-year period were up 503 percent, and operating profit increased by a staggering 1,924 percent. Yet, with data services becoming ever-more important and basic phones becoming a commodity thanks to increasing numbers of new entrants to the sector (including at least twelve mobile phone manufacturers in China alone), senior managers were aware they would have to explore new ways to grow.

What seemed like an obvious route to increasing growth was for NMP, like its competitors, to find ways to encourage users to upgrade their phones more regularly. Back in 1998, NMP had begun segmenting the market based on lifestyles. Its four broad categories included basic and premium phones for both personal and business users. In the wake of the events of 2001, this approach was extended and deepened with a strategy of micro-segmenting the market. NMP created a product matrix with six categories of phone style and five types of application: voice, entertainment, media, business, and imaging.

By adopting this matrix product segmentation, NMP planned to meet specific design and feature requirements of much narrower user groups, providing what would feel like products tailored to individual needs. Better still, from a marketing perspective, not only might customers have more than one phone for different uses (business and leisure for example), but they would be more likely to upgrade to premium phones to gain the specific features they valued.

Hand in hand with the matrix product segmentation strategy, in the spring of 2002, NMP announced a new structure organized around nine value domains. In a conversation a couple of years later, Alahuhta explained, "The shift to 'value domains' reflected our realization that to enter new market areas we needed more than just a product. We needed to work downstream to make real market and business models, and learn about the requirements of other parts of the business system. Establishing value domains was a way to shift the language to reflect this."

The value domains included traditional core phone activities such as GSM and Code Division Multiple Access (CDMA), as well as low-end basic phones to accelerate market expansion in developing countries and newer opportunities within the remit of DCU. Each would be responsible for setting their own growth strategy but would share common technology platforms, as well as a range of support services including regional sales and marketing, logistics, and sourcing. A new horizontal business unit was also established to license open software, such as the Symbian OS and NMP's S60 interface, to third parties—the idea behind this being to create a widely available smartphone middleware alternative to Microsoft.

Still with the threat of Microsoft in mind, and specifically in relation to business users, toward the end of 2002 Ala-Pietilä launched an NMP-wide strategic analysis of the enterprise market. It's also noteworthy that although Canadian firm Research in Motion (RIM) had released its first mobile device allowing enterprise users to connect to corporate email servers back in 1999, it wasn't until March 2002 with the introduction of its first BlackBerry smart-phone with voice capabilities that Nokia recognized the entrepreneurial firm as a potential threat to its own business customer offerings.

The findings of the strategic review presented to Nokia's Strategy Panel in March 2003 concluded that mobile data would be critical to enterprise customers, Internet-based communication would present a major disruption to mobile voice services (and therefore threaten the profitability of Nokia's major customers), and enterprise customers would demand solutions as well as products that offered continuity and security—the very opposite of the more fashion-driven consumer world at the core of NMP's success.

It was clear to Nokia's senior managers that although the enterprise market presented a threat to Nokia's existing businesses, it also represented a huge opportunity. Members of the Strategy Panel agreed that Nokia had to be more involved in the enterprise space, and in May that year announced that NMP would establish a new business group called Enterprise Solutions. While Enterprise Solutions would absorb NMP's existing enterprise-related activities, the head of the new unit would be recruited externally from the IT industry, and in a major departure for Nokia, Enterprise Solutions would be headquartered in the US—the world's leading enterprise market.

Working with Wider Ecosystems

The nature of the mobile communications industry was changing more rapidly than almost any other industry in history. Even though Nokia's huge core phone business was becoming increasingly sclerotic and cost-focused, there appeared to be enough awareness of the need for product innovation (with the Communicator and camera phone), a strong OS, and new business areas (with Enterprise Solutions) to give the impression that Nokia understood the changes needed to compete in mobile data.

Yet in many respects, while NMP's managers saw what needed to be done at a high level, in reality the firm lacked the skills and deep understanding to be effective. Nowhere was this clearer than in NMP's engagement with and involvement in the ecosystem way of working—and a project to develop visual radio which began in 2003 provides a clear illustration of how NMP underestimated what their contribution would be to the development.

The Nokia Research Center (NRC) had come up with the idea of combining FM radio broadcasts with relevant visual services on the screen of a mobile phone—such as song lyrics, the libretto of an opera, biographical information on the artist, information about their forthcoming concerts, and links to purchase tickets for these events. Early consumer market research was positive about this concept of "visual radio."

However, the business case for visual radio was imprecise, and the ecosystem required to deliver it was more varied than anything NMP had engaged in before. As the head of the visual radio project, Tomi Mustonen, explained, "We understood the key drivers at the beginning as being end-to-end solutions and the quality of experience for the consumers. We also knew we had various categories of players to bring together to create the ecosystem: advertisers, radio stations, telecom operators, copyright owners and other content providers, and technology developers—for hardware, software, applications, and tools. But Nokia didn't have the practical capabilities to make this work. We didn't understand how radio stations operated, the service and hosting of IT applications, or even how to sell value-added services via operators."

As a business concept began to take shape in early 2003, it also became clear that a deployment partner with global reach outside the telecoms industry would be critical to provide IT services, hosting capacity for new offerings, deploying new IT applications globally, and providing marketing and sales support. Several potential partners made it to the shortlist but only HP had an interest in building an entertainment-oriented consumer business—and HP had already sold IT systems to radio stations. According to Mustonen, "HP was the best partner, the most interested, and easiest to interact with. They met our criteria, we had good interpersonal chemistry, and simple terms." Toward the end of 2003, HP and Nokia reached an agreement to create a non-equity, equal revenue-sharing alliance to develop the visual radio opportunity.

While it seemed clear on paper what each of the partners would contribute to the building of the visual radio system, once work got underway significant differences in approaches and expectations emerged. As one of the HP executives put it, "How to measure success was clear, but not how to achieve success. Nokia did not bring us a business model. They brought a piece of hardware and took a production ramp-up perspective. It was as if they had a turnkey project and needed HP just as a go-to-market channel." Product thinking was so entrenched in Nokia that it was struggling to understand the intricacies of the contributions from other players in the ecosystem. Consequently, the burden of work fell on HP.

Many commentators have attributed Nokia's seeming inability to work effectively in the new type of ecosystems critical for mobile data to an arrogance stemming from having been so dominant in the old paradigm. Yet according to Juha Äkräs, who at the time was general manager of IP Networks and would later become Nokia's head of HR, "What people saw as arrogance was actually ignorance, not NIH [not invented here], but NUH [not understood here]. Strategy aside, Nokia had never been externally oriented and just didn't know how to do this. Management didn't see that as everything was changing, the company needed to be managed differently." In achieving spectacular growth over the last decade, Nokia had lost its agility, flexibility, and entrepreneurialism and was instead viewing the future through the lens of its present success.

Commentary

At the start of the 2000s, Ala-Pietilä, Kosonen, and a few other senior managers at Nokia began to argue using the simple diagram shown in Figure 5.1, that their industry was moving to the right, as a way to illustrate to their colleagues Nokia's looming strategic predicament: the world was changing, and the Internet was shifting from being a sub-area of the mobile (and fixed-line) telecommunications industry to being a central force into which mobile communication would be absorbed. Convergence would take place in favor of the new Internet businesses, not the incumbent telecoms industry. The impending reality proposed by Ala-Pietilä and Kosonen was too far removed from the realm of experience and familiarity to be meaningful to most Nokians and many either did not want to see, or accept, the implications of the diagram. They saw the Internet as being just a small component in the wider mobile communication world they knew so well (perhaps with some new connectivity and access protocols, but little more). Yet as the narrative of this chapter has shown, the world was indeed changing for Nokia, and these changes brought significant challenges.

For many within Nokia, the implications of the sea change they were about to face were hard to comprehend and easy to deny. To be fair, there were few external threats at this time to really challenge the orthodoxies prevalent in Nokia's main development centers. Attempts at introducing tablet computers had been unsuccessful (witness the well-publicized failure of Apple's "Newton"), email was still a recent phenomenon, and RIM was focusing on pagers, at best a "push to talk" device largely inferior to a regular mobile

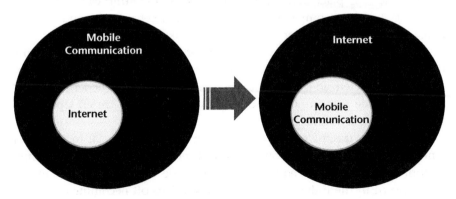

Figure 5.1. Industry service-centric view

phone. None of Nokia's key competitors such as Ericsson and Motorola, or main followers such as Siemens, Philips, or Alcatel, was doing data-enabled phones for the general market. What's more, there was no sense of urgency to move toward data from Nokia's operator customers, who obviously wanted to avoid the possibility of struggling to find new business models which could monetize data communication and Internet voice calls, and were keen not to cannibalize their highly lucrative voice traffic.

In justice to the doubting Thomases at Nokia, the market for data-enabled phones had not been ready when Tampere introduced the Communicator in 1996—this had enjoyed only limited sales and reinforced the perception that betting on data-enabled phones was of limited importance.

To a large extent, Nokia's strategy had insulated it from external threats. Nokia's alliances in the late 1990s had very deftly moved competition to areas where Nokia could win, and neutralized it in areas where it might not. By collaborating on standardization in the 1990s with the other two leading suppliers of mobile phones (Ericsson and Motorola), Nokia played a classical game of "desegmentation." Through adopting common standards for access protocols and operating systems, for example, Nokia managed to bring competition to bear on areas in which it excelled (product design, manufacturing, and logistics) and where its large industrial scale paidoff. In other words, Nokia was smartly leveraging the strategic assets it had built up in the 1990s. It secured broad-based industry-wide value creation around software and captured value from superior, lower cost hardware.

Nokia had always looked to the PC industry for broad strategic lessons, and something important it had learned was that "vertical" integration from hardware to software and services was not sustainable for leading companies. Large firms prospered when the "horizontalization" of an industry prevailed, with different competitors contributing different "layers" to value creation. This had been shown in the PC industry, where competition for market share and volume took place between separate companies within each horizontal layer (e.g. between companies providing software, hardware, and applications). And competition for value capture took place between layers. The best place to play was in layers where network effects were high, generating increasing returns to adoption for customers, and in layers providing differentiation characterized by strong economies of scale and experience—in the PC industry the software (Microsoft) and microprocessor (Intel) layers took the lion's share of value.

Applying the lessons of horizontalization proved beneficial to Nokia for a number of years. When Psion started to license its OS, Nokia was prompt to form an alliance of "equals" to create a de facto emerging standard OS. Concern in the industry over the risk of Microsoft becoming dominant with a mobile OS led to the involvement in the Symbian OS joint venture of

Nokia's major competitors. Nokia, however, was "more equal than others" in Symbian and this proved a significant advantage. As the largest investor and Symbian's largest customer, Nokia was able to draw the attention of Symbian's management to its own product roadmaps and timings. Symbian would be sensitive to Nokia's needs first, and that conferred an advantage on Nokia. Just as the dominance of Microsoft and Intel in their respective horizontal layers enabled them to pace innovations in the PC industry, Nokia's position in the mobile industry allowed it to do the same. This development reinforced the belief in Nokia's unassailable strength within the core phone business.

The "rules of the game" in the future of the telecom industry were about to change, however, with several sources of added complexity (see Figure 5.2) coming into play.

Particularly noteworthy were two key changes. First, the nature of mobile phones was changing from being a global product to a cultural good. In essence, whereas mobile communications had been about products which were essentially the same across the world except for variance in technical standards, a change was underway in which content access, social media, and culturally determined patterns of interaction and phone use which varied around the world were becoming more important. This called for a deeper understanding of contextual and complex knowledge, and a shift in innovation from a focus on technology improvement to a more market-driven approach sensitive to multiple usage patterns.

The second key change saw a shift from the primacy of hardware products to that of software platforms. From design to manufacturing, Nokia had built a very strong competence in hardware and their competitive advantage had flowed from this for many years. Although Nokia employed thousands of software engineers to develop Symbian, their role was to write code to support hardware innovations. With a genuine lack of software industry expertise

Product business		*Ecosystem business*
Success criteria: products sold, profits from sales	←——→	Platform adoption, number of transactions on platform, transaction commissions
Customers: one type of key customer—telecom operators	←——→	Multiple types of customers: end users, context providers, distributors, etc.
Business development: product-oriented, specifications, design, etc., largely in-house, autonomous	←——→	Business model innovation-oriented, constant attention to all complements in alliance web

Figure 5.2. Challenge in moving to ecosystem model

within Nokia, it was difficult to see how software or platform innovation could gain strategic prominence.

So, as Nokia faced serious challenges in adapting to a changing industry, an indirect consequence of the tightening of Nokia's management after the logistics crisis meant that new, innovative initiatives would be more difficult to pursue. A more systematic and formal product development process, combined with tighter metrics, resulted in a lower tolerance for innovation projects that departed from routine product policy. Like the Communicator, the Calypso camera phone went against mainstream priorities and so had to be developed out of sight, with extensive personal support from both Vanjoki and Ala-Pietilä. As obvious as it is today, when almost every phone comes with a high-quality miniature camera, putting a decent camera in a mobile phone with the corresponding picture storing and sharing software was far from an obvious proposition back in the late 1990s. Nokia's product specification process went through several iterations before zeroing in on the 7650, and its development was more costly and demanding than expected. Yet picture phones provided a "bridging" (Zhu and Furr, 2016) application and technology between traditional and multimedia phones, and by relying on user-provided content neatly circumvented what would become a key challenge for multimedia phones: content provision and management.

Nokia had to confront that challenge head-on with visual radio. To be implemented, visual radio required collaboration from many parties including radio stations, content providers, advertisers, operating companies, and an IT deployment partner. Visual radio faced all the usual challenges of innovation adoption and ecosystems: the ecosystem participants had to commit and each would only do it insofar as its financial objectives and strategic goals could be met (Adner, 2012). Yet even with a concept as complex as this, Nokia still framed the challenge in product terms (equipping the radio receiver function in its phones with a digital graphic receptor chip), and underestimated how difficult it would be for all other parties to join and deliver their contributions effectively. Nokia's failure to understand the visual radio ecosystem was particularly noteworthy, as this was a precursor to many other ecosystem opportunities such as music and video distribution on mobile phones.

In terms of our CORE framework, one can grasp the magnitude of the challenge brought by the transformation of the mobile phone industry. In terms of *Cognition*, while as far back as the 1990s Nokia's most senior executives, including Alahuhta, Vanjoki, Ollila, and Ala-Pietilä, had anticipated the changes now taking place—with phones going beyond the voice function—and had sharpened their awareness with the 2003 review of the enterprise market opportunities, this recognition did not seep into the beliefs, attitudes, and behavior of Nokia's management. The hardware product mindset was still dominant and the intricacies of ecosystem collaboration and competition were not fully appreciated among middle managers—as I discovered through teaching numerous strategic alliance management seminars at Nokia. The readiness of most of these managers to embrace new ecosystem business models appeared limited.

There also emerged progressively over time among these managers what Mikko Kosonen and I called in our earlier research a "dominance mindset" (Doz and Kosonen, 2008). In short this led to a "my way or no way" attitude to collaboration. And even when agreeing to the need for "win–win" alliances, a quiet arrogance at Nokia resulted in an implicit "I win big, and I deserve it, and you win small" approach, which was unhelpful in eliciting true and sincere commitment to the ecosystem building efforts Nokia undertook. Concerns for value capture and securing "control points" (a term Nokia managers were particularly fond of) would sometimes cloud the need for value creation and wholehearted collaboration. Even in Symbian the other key partners, Motorola and Ericsson, would be concerned and irritated with Nokia's leadership undermining their own commitment. In other words, the rank and file of Nokia's management were not quite ready for the transformation that was about to affect them.

How the *Organization* evolved within Nokia did not help. Rather than fade over time, the boundaries and rivalries between the Tampere site (originator of the smartphone efforts) and the Oulu main phone development center became more ingrained in attitudes and beliefs. Of course, the support of the most articulate and visible strategic leaders for smartphones also contributed to make the rest of the organization passively more defensive.

The strain of maintaining a 30–40 percent global market share and the value of one of the world's top brands would lead any executive to think twice before embarking on a potentially risky move away from the core business, even without the organizational difficulties Nokia faced. So, given Nokia's situation, it is not surprising the innovative drive of the organization was dampened. As this happened progressively and manifested itself in the myriad decisions around product definitions, roadmaps, technical choices on particular features and components, marketing actions, and relationships with customers, it was not obviously visible.

The fact that the core technologies and architectures of mobile phones had matured and perhaps offered less room for significant innovation also contributed to conservatism. One can see that project leaders of major new innovative undertakings, like Mikko Moilanen for Calypso, would at least express doubts *ex post* about the ability of the "regular" organization to develop such innovations. This sense of a growing conservatism in Nokia's mainstream organization was already felt after the logistics crisis of 1995, and continued despite the leaders' rotations undertaken in 1998. This led to a growing concern on the part of Jorma Ollila in particular, that properly addressing the multimedia and enterprise communication opportunities would require dedicated and differentiated efforts outside the main phone development organization.

In *Relational* terms, except for the tension between smartphone and regular phone developers, and following the 1998 rotations, there was no major evolution. Alahuhta imposed his mark on NMP and Ala-Pietilä pursued new growth opportunities, with limited success.

The main phone development center in Oulu had long been reticent about data-enabled phones (the development of which largely took place in the innovative Tampere center). Many Nokians were *Emotionally* committed to the voice communication reality they understood, in which Nokia was the undisputed leader. Before the Tampere center had developed the Communicator, integrating voice and data communication in one device for the first time, engineers in Oulu had adopted such a narrow product definition of a phone being a device to merely make and receive calls, that they had relegated data communication to a separate plug-in "data module" which required a separate power unit and plug. They saw data as belonging to the world of PDAs: agenda keeping devices that were not even "connected."

A fatal confluence of *Emotional* elements evolved during this period that widened divisions within the firm between those looking to the future and those locked in the past and present. A growing self-confidence throughout the firm pushed those in the core businesses closer toward arrogance and

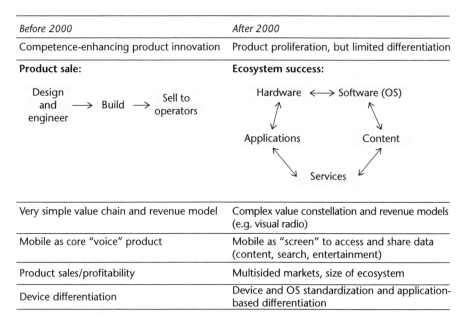

Before 2000	After 2000
Competence-enhancing product innovation	Product proliferation, but limited differentiation
Product sale:	**Ecosystem success:**
Design and engineer → Build → Sell to operators	Hardware ⟷ Software (OS) / Applications / Content / Services
Very simple value chain and revenue model	Complex value constellation and revenue models (e.g. visual radio)
Mobile as core "voice" product	Mobile as "screen" to access and share data (content, search, entertainment)
Product sales/profitability	Multisided markets, size of ecosystem
Device differentiation	Device and OS standardization and application-based differentiation

Figure 5.3. Transformation challenge

hubris. As in many other organizations, managers overattributed success to their own skills (and Nokians had achieved some remarkable feats indeed) at the same time as downplaying risks and emerging challenges (the nature of this is summarized in Figure 5.3). Yet this hubris was tainted by fear—both of a future that most in the main phone development unit did not understand, and of conceding ground to their colleagues in Tampere. A long-standing rivalry between the traditional phone development center in Oulu and the innovative data-focused Tampere development center deepened, reducing the chances of Nokia leveraging internal expertise and foresight from Tampere to position itself more effectively for the newly emerging reality. The CORE dimensions for this period are summarized in Figure 5.4.

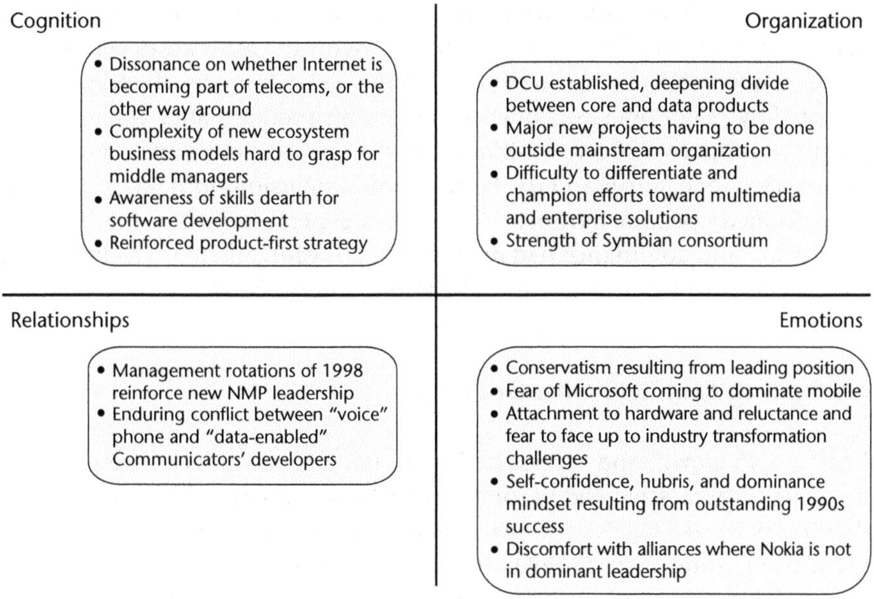

Cognition

- Dissonance on whether Internet is becoming part of telecoms, or the other way around
- Complexity of new ecosystem business models hard to grasp for middle managers
- Awareness of skills dearth for software development
- Reinforced product-first strategy

Organization

- DCU established, deepening divide between core and data products
- Major new projects having to be done outside mainstream organization
- Difficulty to differentiate and champion efforts toward multimedia and enterprise solutions
- Strength of Symbian consortium

Relationships

- Management rotations of 1998 reinforce new NMP leadership
- Enduring conflict between "voice" phone and "data-enabled" Communicators' developers

Emotions

- Conservatism resulting from leading position
- Fear of Microsoft coming to dominate mobile
- Attachment to hardware and reluctance and fear to face up to industry transformation challenges
- Self-confidence, hubris, and dominance mindset resulting from outstanding 1990s success
- Discomfort with alliances where Nokia is not in dominant leadership

Figure 5.4. 1996–2003 CORE profile

References

Ron Adner, *The Wide Lens: A New Strategy for Innovation* (Penguin, Harmondsworth, 2012).

Yves Doz and Mikko Kosonen, *Fast Strategy: How Strategic Agility Will Help You Stay Ahead of the Game* (Wharton School Publishing, Harlow, 2008).

Feng Zhu and Nathan Furr, "Products to Platforms: Making the Leap" (*Harvard Business Review*, Vol. 94 Issue 4, April 2016) pp. 72–8.

6

A Supernova

In April 2004, Nokia announced that first-quarter revenues were down and it had lost market share in Europe and the US. While the root causes behind this were complex and varied, the sudden slump in performance had been precipitated by major operators boycotting Nokia's products after voicing complaints in February 2004 at the Mobile World Congress in Cannes about gaps in Nokia's phone ranges and the Finnish firm's incursions into services which were deemed operator territory. There was a general feeling in the industry that its size and dominance had made Nokia arrogant, and in severely cutting back orders the operators had found a way to punish Nokia.

Navigating Conflicts with Operators

NMP's rapid growth and success had come at a price: in order to keep increasing market share, scale had become a priority over the speed and innovation that had defined Nokia's early years. In an interview with Tero Ojanperä, who spent twenty-one years at Nokia in various roles including CTO (chief technology officer), head of the Nokia Research Center, and chief strategy officer, he put the issue rather clearly when he explained, "A mantra *'since we are the biggest we don't need to be the first'* began to spread and so scale rather than speed became the dominant paradigm." It seemed that being late to market with every innovation became the accepted way of doing things. Nokia would now wait until components for new technologies were available in high volumes from suppliers before coming to market "en force" as a second or third mover.

In reality though, Nokia's products became so increasingly late to launch that "en force" wasn't enough and it was losing ground to its rivals. To take just a few examples of how slow Nokia had become, Ericsson released the first full-color graphic display toward the end of 2001, and it wasn't until the final quarter of the following year that Nokia launched its first phone with a color display (the 3510i). With its 7650 camera phone released in mid-2002, Nokia had been a year and a half behind Sharp's camera phone. In introducing phones with GPRS capability to enable wireless data services, Nokia's first GPRS phone (3510) came to market in 2002 after Ericsson's first GPRS phone launch in April 2001 and Motorola's a few months later in August.

Operating companies were not only angered over how late Nokia was releasing new technologies and features, but also over omissions in its product range too, chief of which was a clamshell, flip phone to compete against Motorola's RAZR range. Launched in July 2003, the RAZR offered customers something visibly new with an ultra-thin, flip phone in a metal casing. Even though it was priced at the high end of the market, demand for this new type of design was strong (130 million RAZR phones were sold in the four years to 2007).

Key managers at Nokia, including Nokia's CTO at the time, Yrjö Neuvo, and Anssi Vanjoki, did not believe clamshell designs were anything more than a fad and argued that developing a similar product would wrongly signal to the market that Motorola had captured design leadership over its Finnish rival. There were also more pragmatic technical reasons behind Nokia's reluctance to introduce a clamshell design: the circuits Nokia used were too thick for a slim clamshell phone and redesigning these would be a costly and slow process, and the hinge was a key component that Nokia neither had the knowledge to develop quickly and build internally nor would wish to subcontract. Furthermore, Nokia was already preparing for the introduction of thin phones with a curved sliding cover that it saw as a superior design to clamshells.

The list of operator grievances continued over Nokia's reluctance to supply either operator-branded phones or phones extensively customized to individual operator requirements. In recent years, large operators that had emerged as winners in the industry, like Vodafone and T-Mobile, had been carving out a wider role for themselves and using their size to make new demands of phone manufacturers. Senior managers at NMP, however, unanimously agreed not to dilute the power of the Nokia brand by starting to manufacture "white label" devices (based on Interbrand ratings, in 2003 Nokia was the world's sixth most valuable brand, behind Coca Cola, Microsoft, IBM, General Electric, and Intel). Nor did it make economic sense for NMP to retool its manufacturing lines for smaller runs of phones customized with different features for different operators.

The final touchpaper for the operators was Nokia's incursions once again into services. Matti Alahuhta explained how this had come about, "Collaborating with operators had been easy in the 1990s as the whole industry was growing fast. However, the slowdown in 2000–1 hit the operators on the back of them bidding for 3G licenses. By 2003 they began to react—it was a value chain gain issue and most thought Nokia had become too strong."

But this wasn't the first time the operators and Nokia failed to see eye to eye: back in 1997 when NMP had launched its Club Nokia user portal, many operators had been very unhappy and warned Nokia to keep clear of competing with them on services. However, instead of retrenching, NMP had begun to offer a wider range of Nokia-branded digital services as part of its Club Nokia strategy, arguing that the services it offered would also benefit operators by increasing network traffic. The operators disagreed.

With its share price in decline, Nokia had to act quickly to resolve the disputes with operating companies. Harking back to the Nokia of the 1990s that had prided itself on listening to its customers, NMP's senior managers spent long periods in face-to-face meetings with key customers to try and understand their needs and concerns. The upshot of these meetings was a series of tough strategic decisions reversing earlier policies. These were implemented between April and May in 2004: Nokia closed down Club Nokia and announced it would stop developing Nokia-branded multimedia services. It updated the product roadmap to include clamshell designs (although, as many in Nokia had predicted, this design ultimately proved to be a fad). And to placate the operators further, Nokia agreed to start co-branding phones with its large customers and customizing these devices in line with individual operator needs. These changes meant that Nokia's strategy was becoming increasingly co-dependent with those of major European operators.

By reacting quickly and being sensitive to the operators' concerns, the purchasing boycott was lifted and Nokia's competitive position rapidly improved. By the end of the year sales were up and it had regained its market share in Europe. There were also signs of strong growth from emerging markets, which renewed managers' confidence in the core phone business.

The only region in which Nokia continued to struggle was the US. The TDMA market in which it had been strong had almost completely disappeared by 2004 to be replaced by CDMA—a technology in which Nokia's phones proved to lack competitiveness. Further adding to Nokia's US woes was regulation which meant only network operators could put forward new phone models for certification and registration with the FCC. As the US market was consolidating around a handful of operators who expected close strategic relationships with their suppliers, Nokia's stance of treating its customers equally put it at a disadvantage. In this important market, where most phones were sold as part of a service subscription, NMP found its phones increasingly confined to niche GSM networks and being sold through small independent distributors.

Nokia had shown its "can-do" spirit to the full in facing and resolving the conflicts with operators so quickly and effectively. But as Vanjoki later reflected, "In 2004 the downshift in our business was attributed to not having clamshells and being late with GPRS and color screens. But the underlying problem was that we were internally oriented and short-term focused." At the same time as Nokia faced the operators' boycott it was in fact undergoing a much more serious internal challenge and reorganization that it was hoped would reshape the firm for the better.

The Matrix Reorganization

The tensions between NMP and NET which had resulted in the 1998 management reorganization (discussed in Chapter 4) did not abate over the early years of the new millennium. While NET had been hit hard by the global telecoms slowdown in 2001, posting losses in each of the three years to 2003 and undergoing a 31 percent reduction in headcount over the same period, NMP in contrast had been flying ever higher. Between 2001 and 2003 its operating profit had increased 21 percent to 5,483 million euros, representing 134 percent of group operating profit in 2001 and 109 percent for the following two years. By 2003, NMP had also grown to account for 80 percent of group revenues. (To put this into perspective, back in 1997, leading up to the management reorganization, NET and NMP had contributed almost equally to group revenues).

There were feelings in some parts of Nokia that by 2003 NMP had grown too powerful. Its overwhelming size and strong management had all but negated a role for corporate management. Corporate executives could not "see through" NMP's hierarchies to gain a nuanced, detailed, and substantive understanding of its performance drivers, and it seemed as if the group's strategic leadership also increasingly rested with NMP. Take the example of strategy development: by 2002, NMP had sixty people working in this function, compared to just six within the corporate strategy group. It is perhaps worth noting at this point that although Ollila had been due to relinquish his role as CEO of Nokia in 2001, a combination of the slowing market and Ollila riding high on his reputation as the "genius architect" of Nokia's spectacular rise, had led the board to ask him to stay on as CEO for another five years (recall that since the beginning of 1998, he had also been chairman of the board).

Although Ollila as CEO of Nokia and Alahuhta as head of NMP had complementary roles, with Ollila focusing on finance and shareholder and government relations, and Alahuhta on the operational leadership of NMP, the two men had such different working styles and interpersonal skills they were unable to develop a close working relationship. Symptomatically, whereas Ollila met one-on-one with Kallasvuo at least daily and with Ala-Pietilä several times a week, his meetings with Alahuhta were much less frequent. By 2003, to many in the outside world, as head of the formidable NMP, Alahuhta was increasingly being seen as the de facto CEO of Nokia.

Ollila himself had also begun to express frustration that in growing so large, so fast, NMP had lost the agility, innovativeness, and entrepreneurial spirit that had defined its early years. He felt that if Nokia were to continue driving the agenda in emerging areas such as multimedia and enterprise, and stave off threats from competitors as varied as Microsoft and RIM as well as its traditional mobile phone rivals, the group would need to be reorganized into smaller, more flexible, and more agile business units. Benchmarking against other leading ICT companies had pointed to a matrix being a better structure for developing innovative businesses.

In September 2003, Ollila announced that early the following year Nokia would be restructured into a matrix organization. As Alahuhta explained, "We needed to separate M [Multimedia] and ES [Enterprise Solutions] from mobile phones, emphasizing the vertical dimensions and bringing differentiated capabilities closer to customers. These used common technology platforms. Also, NMP had developed into a 24 billion euros unit and it wasn't good to have such a huge unitary core business. Splitting up NMP into M, ES and MP [Mobile Phones], each having their own leaders and more vertical control was a way to achieve more balance." However, many people saw the reorganization as a way to stem Alahuhta's growing influence—one manager suggested that Ollila was putting into practice one of his management principles that "lieutenants should not turn into barons."

Within the new matrix organization were four vertical business groups. The products from NMP's nine value domains were clustered into three new groups: Mobile Phones, Multimedia, and Enterprise Solutions. While the Mobile Phones group absorbed all of NMP's familiar core activities in both developed and developing markets, Multimedia incorporated DCU and Mobile Data to focus on the new areas of mobile imaging, gaming, TV, and digital services. The Enterprise Solutions group similarly had a more exploratory mandate to grow Nokia's offerings for business customers. An unchanged NET was the fourth vertical business group.

The central objective in adopting the new organization was to allow strategic differentiation between Mobile Phones, Multimedia, and Enterprise Solutions while at the same time benefiting from resource integration across these three business groups. To this end, they would share common marketing, sales, logistics, sourcing, and technology platforms, a policy already successfully implemented for "business infrastructure" processes and information systems as well as other corporate support functions. Each business group would also use the central research function for basic technology and advanced product engineering. Symbian would be used as the common software platform across the three phone groups, though each would be able to develop and adapt it to meet their specific requirements. NET retained a high degree of independence in the matrix as it was not tightly integrated via the horizontal functions that bound the three NMP legacy businesses.

When the new matrix structure was put in place in January 2004, the biggest surprises were around some of the new leadership roles. Kallasvuo moved from his long-time corporate role as CFO to head the Mobile Phones group. As the champion of many of NMP's forays into new and leading-edge areas, Vanjoki was given the new Multimedia group. Enterprise Solutions, which would be unique in being headquartered outside Finland closer to major corporate customers in the US, would look to the IT industry to recruit a new head—a few months later Mary McDowell took on this role after sixteen years at Compaq and HP. Mid-level managers, often with backgrounds in sales, marketing, and logistics, were selected to head the product lines within each of the vertical business groups.

At the helm of the horizontal support functions were Pertti Korhonen leading technology platforms, along with Nokia's two big hitters, Ala-Pietilä as head of customer and market operations, and Alahuhta taking on research, strategy, and business infrastructure.

The new structure restored the corporate role and created a clearer divide between corporate and business line responsibilities. Power and authority would unquestionably now rest with corporate, not business groups, and Nokia could once again be run (almost) like a financial conglomerate with the corporate group imposing tough performance demands and "managing by numbers."

The Matrix: Creating More Problems than it Solved

In March 2004, I was invited to speak to Nokia's senior managers about the advantages and perils of matrix organizations. Among the risks I highlighted were paralysis stemming from infighting and slow decision making, the growth of a "tournament culture" where small wins and defeating internal rivals drive behavior, decentralized mutual selection that reinforces the already strong and powerful over the new and innovative, and the primacy of subunit performance over joint interdependent success. At the end of the presentation, Alahuhta turned to his colleagues and said, "We need to be sensitive to these issues."

However, events overtook Nokia and it wasn't long before problems with the new matrix structure began to arise.

Leadership Vacuum

Nokia's "dream team" members, Ala-Pietilä, Alahuhta, and Baldauf, had not only led autonomous business groups successfully through years of exceptional growth, but as Korhonen explained, "The close relationship between Matti, Pekka, and Sari enabled them to utilize cross-company synergies, link operational strategy, and get things done." In other words, they had always played a strong integrative role between Nokia's businesses. Yet, without much consultation, Ollila moved two of these experienced business leaders to run support functions, and in doing so removed a highly successful informal integration mechanism without stepping into that role himself (paradoxically though, by 2004 he held the combined roles of chairman and CEO, and was the de facto COO).

Very rapidly, the business groups (and product lines within them) began to compete with each other. Ollila's desire to give autonomy and accountability to the business groups, and his high visibility in Europe, "hero" status in Finland, and stellar reputation in the IT industry, all conspired to draw him to focus more on external issues—government relations, corporate communications, and European policies for the technology sector—rather than overseeing the company's internal management and strategic needs. Never having been a technologist, and without an up-to-date, deep understanding of technological and industry challenges, Ollila was reluctant and unable to provide the arbitration required to settle competing claims from the business groups.

Many of Nokia's more seasoned senior and middle managers had done very well financially in the early 2000s from stock options which had been issued in the 1990s. Even though they had become financially independent, the majority of these managers enjoyed working at Nokia and so had remained committed to the firm after receiving their financial windfall. However, many were demotivated by the implementation difficulties and conflicts in the new matrix structure, and hundreds resigned between 2004 and 2005.

Dissatisfaction grew even with the most senior executives. At the end of 2004, and in a move which came as a surprise even to his closest colleagues, Alahuhta was the first of the "dream team" to resign. He moved to Kone Corporation as CEO (he had for some time wanted to lead a major company). A few days later, Baldauf announced her resignation. Feeling Nokia was in need of new blood and new competencies, she had decided to leave in the summer of 2004 and had spent time working on a smooth and effective handover to her successor. She later elaborated on why she felt it was time to leave, explaining, "I didn't appreciate the undercurrents any longer and I never wanted my career to define my identity. I'd been at Nokia twenty-two years and I knew it was time to move on."

Shortly after, with succession on his mind, Ollila approached Ala-Pietilä about taking over as the next CEO. When we talked about this some years later, Ala-Pietilä reflected, "I was never after the power. To me life is a learning journey—doing things where I can learn and go beyond my current skills, and can develop myself as a person and a professional. In Nokia, as funny as it may sound, I didn't see that becoming CEO would have brought the next level of learning." Ala-Pietilä resigned in August 2005. Other high-profile departures at around the same time included technology guru Yrjö Neuvo, and the following year Nokia's CTO and head of technology platforms, Pertti Korhonen.

Nokia's big strategy and technology thinkers had all resigned within a year, and with them Nokia lost a huge amount of strategic competence. Ala-Pietilä in particular had long been seen as the industry visionary in Nokia—as the CEO of one of Nokia's key partners put it, he was "the real brains behind Nokia's success in the 1990s." To a large extent, Vanjoki had shown the vision, foresight, and understanding to step into the breach, but his passion, flamboyance, strong opinions, and lack of diplomacy made him a controversial figure not only within Nokia but also with customers. On a purely practical level, his hands were too full building the new Multimedia group to have time to think about broader group strategy.

Slowing of Decision Making

Many of Nokia's managers had difficulty adapting to working in the new matrix structure. For a start, the idea of a general manager with line responsibility was a new thing within the firm, as prior to the matrix NMP had been run as a big unitary organization with functional managers and specialized subunits. Culturally the matrix presented a problem too: the close interdependencies needed for the matrix to work effectively were anathema in a firm which was used to decentralized initiatives, "can-do" problem solving, and where individual and small-team prowess was highly valued.

In the new structure, strategic decisions and resource commitments had to be negotiated between the business groups and the heads of the horizontal resource groups. Proposals could be put forward by either side, based on market knowledge or functional and technical knowledge. In theory, a matrix dialog would then see the proposals refined before a decision was made whether to run with them. In practice, however, a lack of clear strategic vision resulted in middle managers negotiating resource allocation via committees. And with multiple product lines within the Mobile Phones, Multimedia, and Enterprise Solutions groups all chasing similar resources, access became a source of intense rivalry between the vertical groups, and the committees became a forum in which self-serving cliques developed.

Product line managers, under intense pressure to deliver short-term results and faced with demanding product development schedules, began to resort to underhand tactics to sway resource allocation decisions. It was not uncommon for junior managers with no authority to be sent to resource allocation committee meetings so that "unfavorable" decisions could be stalled. Meanwhile, decision making became slower and slower.

Alberto Torres, who had first worked with Nokia in 2001 as a consultant from McKinsey and in January 2004 was hired as the group's head of strategy, expressed strong feelings about how the poor implementation of the new structure was impacting Nokia: "A matrix is not good for speed. In high-speed, high-complexity contexts like the mobile industry, you need very fast decisions and in Nokia's matrix, decisions were negotiated extremely slowly." The growing bureaucratization of processes stemming from the matrix structure resulted in many Nokians spending more and more time in committee meetings and less time actually working.

Many of the rivalries between the business groups that slowed down decision making had arisen because of a lack of clarification around the scope of roles when the new structure was put in place. For example, one unit was responsible for phones based on Qualcomm's CDMA standard and another for camera phones. But it was never clear which would take the lead with CDMA camera phones. This type of blurred boundary led to a surge in product proliferation, with around fifty new products being released each year. Despite this growing number of product introductions there was a corresponding decrease in differentiation across the vertical business groups.

To make matters worse, a lack of coordination between the business units meant a common technical product architecture, especially in critically important software, was not adhered to, with each new product team creating different specifications and requirements for the software platform. "The different demands from those different businesses put a huge strain on the platform organization," Korhonen recalled when talking about his last few months at Nokia. "We had to start to fulfill a huge number of different and conflicting requirements coming from a vast number of different products, which overloaded and suffocated the resources in the platform development. The new game [platform for apps and services] would have required a huge amount of commonality, disciplined standardization and coherence to make Nokia an attractive platform for the developer community and the ecosystem at large. All business units wanted to manage their products independently and a proposal to establish cross-Nokia product management to deal with this problem was rejected."

It was clear that far from alleviating the problems of fragmentation and distance between the different businesses, the matrix structure was taking Nokia down the opposite route.

Growing Issues with Symbian

Limitations with the Symbian OS had begun to emerge a couple of years prior to the matrix reorganization, but the events of 2004 exacerbated these problems. Symbian had its origins as an OS for a single standalone product (the Psion PDA), which had an integrated software-hardware architecture—the advantages of decoupling software platform development from hardware development not having been anticipated in Symbian's early days. So, as NMP widened its product line in the early 2000s, the integrated nature of the Symbian OS required extensive software development and code rewriting for each new device.

Recognizing the matrix structure (and performance metrics) would likely result in further product proliferation and as a result even greater difficulties with Symbian, Vanjoki and Korhonen tried to establish a governance platform for the OS to create standard software that was not device-related. Quarterly meetings were established in which representatives from Mobile Phones, Multimedia, and Enterprise Solutions would get together with the software platform group to decide which features should be included in the standard Symbian. But, as Vanjoki explained, "We all needed different things. Multimedia needed better features such as touchscreens, Enterprise needed strong security, and Mobile Phones wanted the simplest, cheapest platform possible. So, we came to the meetings fighting, we fought some more and in the end nothing could be agreed."

The upshot of failing to establish a shared view on Symbian was that each product group went ahead in developing and adapting its own version of the Symbian OS software to suit its own devices. The new head of Mobile Phones, Kallasvuo, remarked, "By 2004 Symbian was archaic. It had become too complex over time trying to address disparate needs that went well beyond what it had been originally designed for." (By 2009, Nokia would be using fifty-seven different and incompatible versions.) Having so many different versions of Symbian had two major consequences: first, the reliability of software applications became increasingly unpredictable; and second, rewriting code for each new product line swallowed up both time and resources. Agile, lean development was no longer possible within Nokia's three vertical device groups.

Reinforcing the Dominance of Hardware

Symbian had been allowed to get out of hand, with different versions for different products, because the matrix reorganization had done nothing to question the primacy of the product units. Nokia had always been first and foremost a product company. At all levels within the firm, the majority of managers came from a hardware telecoms engineering background, and as Mikko Terho, a veteran of Nokia Data and leading proponent of software innovation within Nokia told me, "The product developers did not understand software. For them, it was just one item, among 250 in a bill of materials. Nobody respected the importance of software, or recognized it was the 'soul' of the product." So even though Symbian's limitations were widely known, the concept and value of a "platform" through which to deliver applications and services was yet to be acknowledged.

Believing that hardware lay at the core of competitive advantage in the industry, few of Nokia's product managers recognized that software was in fact becoming the key differentiator. The culture and understanding within Nokia was based on a hardware-first approach (although some years later Kallasvuo would describe this to me as a "hardware-only" approach), and basic business economics seemed to support this: hardware came with a bill of materials and high unit costs—margins were easy to understand. The software needed for phones on the other hand was costly to develop, seemed to have little intrinsic value, yet could be copied at no cost.

The reluctance to recognize the value and importance of platforms and software also had deep roots in long-standing internal divisions within Nokia. The majority of managers came from Nokia's main mobile phone development and manufacturing centers in Oulu and Salo. These traditional product development sites had never seen eye to eye with Nokia's Tampere site (home of the Communicator), which had been born out of Nokia Data and was home to engineers and managers from a software development background. People from what had always been Nokia's dominant and mainstream development hubs not only lacked an understanding of software but were not about to concede the controlling drivers of development to what they saw as the "fringe" software activities at Tampere.

Fear and self-preservation also played a role in preventing a shift from a hardware- to software-first approach in mobile phones within Nokia. Had the new organization structure emphasized a shift to the primacy of software, this would have led more or less to the announcement that the existing skills of many thousands of Nokia employees were about to be made obsolete. In a small country like Finland, in which Nokia was the largest employer of highly skilled staff, and about the only private sector one in secondary cities such as Oulu, this was neither desirable nor palatable.

Compounding the problem of hardware dominance was a new "software factory" approach Nokia had adopted within the new matrix structure. This relied on product program managers, who rarely had a strong competence in software development, splitting up the coding work and assigning small modules to software development specialists working in huge teams. Each software specialist would work on multiple development programs simultaneously. Confused overall software architecture, poor documentation, and incompatibility between modules became a real problem, and as Torres saw the situation, "Not only did we have thousands of people doing things we could have bought off the shelf but we weren't able to integrate what we were doing in-house." Correcting errors became a major source of delay and extra work.

The software platform group tried to bring greater discipline by introducing new processes to software development. However, these not only dampened morale but resulted in higher costs, as in the words of one newcomer at the time, "For every person who writes code there seems to be another forty-nine who observe, check, control, and correct." The inefficiencies of Nokia's software development activities only served to reinforce the dominant hardware-first perspective in the company.

Cost Savings and New Metrics

Concerned about Nokia's escalating R&D costs, which by 2004 were well above those of its competitors—owing in part to the idiosyncrasies of Symbian—Ollila introduced a new cap on R&D spending of 10 percent of sales. At the same time he put in place a set of metrics to drive new product development in each of the three vertical business groups.

Targets were set for the number of annual product introductions, quickly leading to excessive proliferation and an even greater lack of differentiation between the offerings of various product groups; unit costs were strictly controlled through the bill of materials—further emphasizing the focus on hardware rather than software; and product development team rewards were to be based on first-quarter sales of new product introductions. Beyond the obvious orientation toward short-term success, the immediate result of this was an increase in internal competition—leaving many customers bemused as Nokia product executives openly competed to promote their own products, rendering key account executives frustrated that their credibility was being so blatantly undermined.

In addition, Ollila stipulated that product roadmaps and schedules should be strictly adhered to. The "product roadmap" which had helped Ala-Pietilä drive innovation in NMP's early years now became a straightjacket, allowing room for little more than incremental innovation in order to meet strict product launch dates. Bottlenecks in software and feature development functions meant product line managers regularly found launch dates slipping. To avoid missing their targets, it became common practice to drop the features that were causing delays (even though they had been announced) in favor of releasing incomplete, downgraded new products on time.

Although in theory the matrix structure was supposed to deliver greater differentiation between products, in reality cost-saving pressures led to a reduction in differentiation. The user interface was a particular casualty of this problem. After the initial success of its Series 60 (by now renamed S60) Symbian user interface, Nokia had developed a simpler S40 version for the lower end of the market, and the S90, with a sensitive touchscreen, for the top end (it's worth noting that the finger-stroke touchscreen technology Nokia developed for the S90, which was released in November 2004 on the Nokia 7710 smartphone, was a precursor to the touchscreen on Apple's iPhone released over two and half years later). But the 7710 was the only phone ever to use S90, as shortly after its release a decision was made to save costs by using one interface for all Nokia phones, the S60—and this did not readily accommodate touch-sensitive screens.

Similarly, the focus on unit cost reduction led to a decision to use cheaper yet lower power processors and smaller memories in the high-end phones being developed by Multimedia and Enterprise Solutions. As a result, phones were unable to support high-speed data downloads, interactive gaming, or video-streaming applications. Still frustrated by this some years later, Tehro explained: "All phones were now measured in the same way so the high end looked too costly. We had forgotten how much 'high-end' flagships contribute to IPR [intellectual property rights] and brand value." In a vicious circle, the lack of differentiation exacerbated rivalry between product line executives—for technical resources, for sales volumes, and for sales-force attention. Competition between Nokia's product groups was gaining more focus and gathering more strength than competition with the outside world.

Delivering Results

Any disruption caused by the matrix reorganization was yet to have an impact on the firm's performance. On the contrary, Nokia's device-based businesses looked stronger than ever. Revenues continued to rise, up 20 percent between 2004 and 2005, and then 22 percent to 33,677 million euros in 2006, and still accounted for around 80 percent of group revenues. Similarly, operating profit from the device businesses increased 11 percent in the year to 2005 and 24 percent to 5,161 million euros in 2006, by which point it contributed 94 percent of group operating profit.

In the midst of working through the reorganization pains, when interviewed in November 2005, Anssi Vanjoki summed up Nokia's situation, "We know what needs to be done and we have the organization in place, now it is very much up to whether we have the courage to move to a 'mobile computer all IP [intellectual property]' company and take our customers through this transformation."

Commentary

The period immediately following the adoption of the matrix organization proved pivotal, and if one had to identify a watershed point in Nokia's history in mobile phones this would be it. From success the company went into decline. Of course, although it is easy to understand this with the benefit of hindsight, it was hardly apparent at the time and only a few senior executives saw the challenges that lay ahead (including Kosonen, who shared his deep concerns about the sustainability of Nokia's amazing success—concerns which were part of his motivation for our research on restoring strategic agility in ICT companies). Nokia would continue to appear successful for some time, with 2007 being its strongest year financially. It wasn't until 2010 that a deep crisis would set in.

To understand these challenges to the sustainability of Nokia's success one has to go back to the choice of Symbian as an OS. This decision triggered what Ala-Pietilä, reflecting on that period later on, called "creeping commitments" and strategy academics usually refer to as "path dependency." As we discussed in Chapter 5, committing to Symbian had been an expedient and effective approach to developing a second-generation Communicator and staving off the threat of Microsoft coming to dominate the mobile communications industry in a replay of its success in the PC market.

Given the need to address that particular threat, combined with the technical superiority of the Psion design and ARM architecture over what Geoworks could offer, Symbian was a good choice at the time. Once Symbian was chosen, it was only natural to use it as a common OS for further products. Rallying almost the whole telecom equipment industry around Symbian obviously also deepened and widened Nokia's commitment to it. As Symbian grew in importance, so did the number of software development staff dedicated to it, the majority of whom were based in Oulu in northern Finland. As time passed and Symbian became entrenched, a degree of inertia set in within the development community in Oulu—which itself was becoming more and more like a Nokia company town.

The incompatibility of a product proliferation strategy which relied on Symbian as a common OS only became visible over time. The fact that Symbian's lack of modularity resulted in extensive integral software rewriting necessary for each new phone type, and that testing could not be carried out until the whole development was complete (a slow and expensive approach), had not been anticipated. Development costs were ballooning and delays became more and more of a problem.

The platform organization felt the brunt of the conflicting commitments and, with limited resources, soon found itself stretched too thin. The decision to limit R&D expenditure to 10 percent of sales, a sound decision in the face of escalating costs, actually made the problem worse: the platform organization was in fire-fighting emergency mode and product lines started to cut back on the features their new products incorporated, sometimes after these features had been announced to customers and end users.

At the root of the challenges becoming visible in 2004 was a series of decisions taken over time. Each was rational and each had been made in good faith, yet these decisions had also been made within a frame that not only ignored key interdependencies but also rapidly became obsolete. Choosing Symbian for a single product, the Communicator, had made perfect sense in 1998–9, but staying with Symbian in a strategy of product differentiation and proliferation did not. By then though, "creeping" and increasingly irreversible commitments to Symbian had been made. Although each new phone model developed using Symbian slightly increased tensions, this seemed a more palatable and manageable problem than the type of major discontinuity and enormous resource commitment which would have resulted from a decision to move away from Symbian. Developers also expressed concern about shifting OS or user interface because of the growing installed base and user community. In the absence of a shared view of the integrated structural context, it became easy to make decisions and commitments in a fragmented way as a reaction to problems only when they arose. In other industries, such as airlines, an approach that does not integrate interdependent decisions has been shown to lead to "normal accidents," with tragic consequences (Perrow, 1984; Weick, 1990).

The divergence between relying on Symbian and pursuing a product differentiation and proliferation strategy was made worse by Nokia's adoption of a matrix organization for mobile phones. In shifting from NMP to a more complex matrix organizational form—with business groups and a horizontal platforms organization—Nokia did not develop adequate new management systems and processes to help managers operate effectively in the new structure. It failed to build what Joseph Bower (as early as 1970) called "structural context"—i.e. a consistent set of principles, decision rules and processes, measurement yardsticks, and incentives to guide middle managers in decision making, in particular relating to resource allocation commitments, and in assessing the results of these decisions. Ghoshal and Bartlett (1994) enriched the concept of context beyond Bower's social and political process conceptualization, by focusing on additional dimensions in the quality of management, in particular discipline, stretch, trust, and support.

Matrix organizations usually run into trouble because of poor implementation and insufficient attention to process rather than structure. Jay Galbraith, who devoted a lifetime to researching matrix organizations, stresses, "Organization structures do not fail; management fails at implementing them" (Galbraith, 2008: 6).

During Nokia's wildly successful growth of the 1990s, the management team had largely operated as a "band of friends," a small group of strong complementary personalities, each with natural charisma and leadership skills. Although they would intellectually agree in principle with the need for a stronger management process, the realization that in the new structure strategy would result from a series of middle-management commitments made as a function of a guiding structural context did not immediately gain prominence. Alahuhta had been anticipating the need to build a structural context for the different and less centralized form of leadership needed in the three new groups replacing NMP, and to prepare middle managers for more sophisticated management processes. Alahuhta—strong, proud, ambitious, and image-conscious—was keen to lead a major corporation, but worried about his chances of becoming CEO of Nokia due to the board perhaps blaming him for the operators' boycott and for NMP's product policy choices. The offer of the CEO role at Kone triggered his departure from Nokia leaving no one with the experience or foresight to recognize the true importance of developing such a context and preparing middle managers.

As for the remaining senior management team, Kallasvuo, who replaced Alahuhta as head of the Mobile Phones group, came from a legal and financial background which together with his previous roles did not equip him to recognize the importance of structural context in the new organizational architecture, where many more decisions would have to be negotiated between middle managers. While Kallasvuo was sensitive to the measurement and financial control dimensions of the new organization, the need for guiding rules, principles, and processes for collaboration was less apparent. Vanjoki was an entrepreneur and innovator at heart, keen on the substance of strategic choices, but not on process. The Multimedia group he was now heading was a new venture and entrepreneurial effort, where issues of matrix negotiations were muted or handled by Vanjoki himself and a small team of lieutenants. Mary McDowell had developed a healthy dislike of bureaucratic processes at Compaq and HP, and had little patience for the inherent negotiation complexity in Nokia, in particular on a terrain and in a culture she was not familiar with.

The new middle managers themselves were ill-prepared. They mostly came from functional roles within NMP, in which they had had little exposure to the work of a general manager. And NMP had been a very large functional organization, tightly run by Alahuhta, through simple but strong management principles and hierarchical processes and a strong personal presence and leadership. It had offered few opportunities to develop general managers and prepare them for the complex interfaces they now faced.

Unsurprisingly, the newly appointed product line managers were an uneven crop. Nokia had grown so fast that it had found itself recruiting very large numbers of staff without thorough selection and screening processes, and without the time to devote much attention to training, coaching, and development. And so, at Nokia like elsewhere, fast growth and outstanding success had masked underlying managerial weaknesses and led to overconfidence.

Added to this, the *sisu* "can-do" spirit from which Nokia had greatly benefited when facing a simpler set of challenges in its early days, now resulted in excessive trust being placed in the abilities of untrained people to do well.

Exacerbating this situation, Nokia's HR function was also trailing rather than leading the growth of the company and its managerial ranks. It wasn't until 1998 that a senior HR executive was brought in from HP to develop and lead the function. As it happened, creating a systematic HR management process to fit Nokia's culture required time and the result was not perfect.

The senior middle managers who were in charge of product lines or product families were not quite general managers, but their role was even more demanding: they were accountable for profit and loss results and other performance parameters of their units. But these "units" lacked full direct control to a limited percentage of the value created, of the costs incurred, and of the work required to develop and launch a new phone. In this highly interdependent and integrative structure, nearly everything had to be negotiated with horizontal platforms, and this required a quantum leap in their managerial skills.

Muddying the waters further, the messages and incentives given to product unit managers from the top implied that they were fully responsible for the performance of the market segments, product lines, and families they were managing. So, inadvertently, a structural context of sorts did emerge through the measurement of product unit performance. While this provided discipline, it did not encourage the cognitive and resource allocation shifts that new external demands required and matrix processes were supposed to enable. Performance was not assessed against a more balanced set of measurements and collaboration inducements that would have encouraged an integrative "win–win" approach to negotiations. Galbraith stresses that within a matrix structure, reward systems should be based around collaborative process, as "when a collaboration matrix structure conflicted with a reward system that promoted individual rather than group efforts, the reward system won every time" (Galbraith, 2008: 12). In adaptive theory terms, the internal "selection environment" that Nokia's metrics created was no longer consistent with the external market "selection environment" for products (Burgelman, 1991, 1994). In more concrete terms, what internal incentives encouraged managers to do no longer met external needs.

In the context of giving autonomy and power to product line managers, I vividly recall the phrase used by the CEO of a major chemical company I interviewed in the 1970s when I was a doctoral student. He was facing rather similar matrix collaboration issues with his business unit managers, "Once they have tasted blood there is no reining them in anymore." By 2005–6, the push to segmentation had become stronger, partly because "once they had tasted blood," product line executives kept emphasizing the market differentiation that gave them autonomy and power in the organization even when such differentiation was hard to ground in true market demands.

"Re-integration" in an organization is more difficult than "de-integration," i.e. to rally ambitions around a big common project and increase collaboration and teamwork around that project is much harder than to delegate a large number of small projects to autonomous managers. And for several years Nokia had been on a "de-integration" path. In early 2014, having dinner with Kallasvuo, I compared his predicament in the 2006–10 period to "having become like 3M—a proliferation of separate product development programs recombining Nokia's core competencies—you are now trying to become like Boeing, making a multibillion 'bet the company' commitment every few years." He acquiesced and I added, "this is extremely difficult . . . perhaps even impossible." He nodded wearily. And, indeed, for Nokia there was no coming back.

Up to the late 1990s, Nokia had focused on a very simple and narrow set of functionalities: voice calls later complemented by SMS, and then with the Communicator, email and Internet access. From a market-fit standpoint, product specifications became progressively less sharp and differentiation between products in the Nokia range often became blurred. Although differentiation was now achieved based on styling (undermining the unity of Nokia's brand image), rampant product proliferation made individual products hard to differentiate, particularly once S60 became the sole user interface. As a result the competitiveness of Nokia's products declined. The twin desires for greater product differentiation and lower unit costs proved increasingly incompatible.

Strategy, as a guiding framework and a "tie-breaker" for product policy and resource allocation choices that might have alleviated the contradiction between low cost and high differentiation, fell into disrepair. In his own book, Ollila refers to strategy making as "very mundane work" and states that "a strategy should pretty much update itself automatically," suggesting he did not feel he had to devote much attention at all to the strategy process. What's more, Ollila hadn't been engaged in product policy matters since the early 1990s and had no inclination to reinvolve himself. Having wanted to step down as CEO in 2001 and been asked by the board to stay on, Ollila was looking to his succession rather than deep involvement in the management of the businesses. He wanted to give Kallasvuo and the newly appointed managers the best possible chance to succeed and stave off suspicion he would still be running the show. So he was careful not to let his sometimes overbearing personality influence the choices made by Nokia's management, limit their decision-making autonomy, or stifle their entrepreneurship. He also needed to maintain some distance, as is normal for a board chairman.

Ala-Pietilä, who had been the main strategic architect in Mobile Phones, removed himself from the CEO succession race in 2005, and left Nokia in

October that year, leaving a void in strategy making. He had been an intellectual leader in the 1990s, but when charged with finding new growth areas found himself with few real options for Nokia beyond a push toward emerging markets as the dramatic growth of the core businesses left precious little opportunity to reallocate resources. Furthermore, the declining relevance from 1999 to 2004 of the Strategy Panel, and the discontinuation of the New Business Development Forum chaired by Ala-Pietilä, contributed in no small way to the decline in strategic thinking among senior executives.

Vanjoki, who had significantly contributed to product policy in NMP over the years, would partially step into the shoes of Ala-Pietilä as the key strategist, but he never had a clear mandate, and was too deeply different from Kallasvuo for the two of them to collaborate. Vanjoki was passionate and visionary, but was not perhaps analytical or dispassionate enough in substance. One of his former colleagues summarized this difficulty, noting that "he had a tendency to sometimes present his convictions as if they were facts."

A matrix organization requires lateral integration between its multiple dimensions, at one level or another. At the top, many CEOs or business group heads have used matrix organizations to bring different perspectives on key issues and choices to their attention, as a way to ensure that different voices express themselves and are heard before making decisions and encouraging a "fair process" in reaching these decisions (Kim and Mauborgne, 1997). This presupposes some substantive and decisive strategic leadership in the context of technology roadmaps at the top to make such decisions, something always difficult as product–market diversity increases. In Nokia in 2005 the matrix was left largely unmanaged, and strategy became hostage to an organization going in an uncertain direction.

It is quite natural in a matrix for decision making and responsibility to be "delegated upwards," with only top management being accountable and leaving little room for the development and commitment of mid-level executives. Aware of these pitfalls, and to enable speedy decision making when arbitration at the top becomes a bottleneck, many matrix leaders simply push decisions back to middle managers, expecting them to reach common commitments. This type of pushback to middle management is what Nokia attempted to do. However, this requires collaborative skills, a careful balance of self-interest and collective interest, and as we have stressed, a structural context to match. As Nokia found out to its cost, when these three enablers are absent, conflicts and delays result and poor decisions are made. Negotiating with mutual interests in mind (seeking the proverbial "win–win") and from a relational perspective is not easy, in particular under high performance pressures. A matrix can also be run from the bottom, with entrepreneurial customer-facing executives (such as key account managers) pulling support and commitment from the rest of the organization. This is better suited to a service business than to a product business where resource allocation trade-offs may be more difficult. Figure 6.1 sketches a summary of the alternative ways to run a matrix, and highlights the approaches required.

In sum, and taking a wider reflective perspective, Nokia was unable to make an effective transition from personal "hands on" (the "dream team" of the

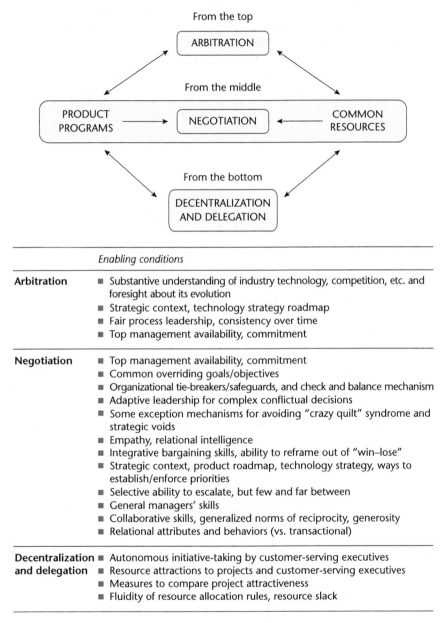

	Enabling conditions
Arbitration	■ Substantive understanding of industry technology, competition, etc. and foresight about its evolution ■ Strategic context, technology strategy roadmap ■ Fair process leadership, consistency over time ■ Top management availability, commitment
Negotiation	■ Top management availability, commitment ■ Common overriding goals/objectives ■ Organizational tie-breakers/safeguards, and check and balance mechanism ■ Adaptive leadership for complex conflictual decisions ■ Some exception mechanisms for avoiding "crazy quilt" syndrome and strategic voids ■ Empathy, relational intelligence ■ Integrative bargaining skills, ability to reframe out of "win–lose" ■ Strategic context, product roadmap, technology strategy, ways to establish/enforce priorities ■ Selective ability to escalate, but few and far between ■ General managers' skills ■ Collaborative skills, generalized norms of reciprocity, generosity ■ Relational attributes and behaviors (vs. transactional)
Decentralization and delegation	■ Autonomous initiative-taking by customer-serving executives ■ Resource attractions to projects and customer-serving executives ■ Measures to compare project attractiveness ■ Fluidity of resource allocation rules, resource slack

Figure 6.1. Three ways to run a matrix

1990s) to institutional and contextual leadership (a set of management systems and processes that provide guidance, discipline, stretch, trust, and support). To redirect strategy, top management needs either to set up a rich structural context, and reset and trim this context when required by technology, market, and competitive changes (so the internal selection environment for strategic initiatives remains aligned with external demands), or to remain actively involved in decision making relating to substantive matters. Post-2004, Nokia's leadership did neither.

The quality of role integration and differentiation informally achieved in the "dream team" could not be extended or reproduced once the key members had left. Furthermore—as is often the case with well-functioning teams and remarkable people whose true importance is only fully apparent once they are no longer present—it was only after the fact, when its loss began to be painfully felt, that Ollila's and Nokia's good fortune with the "dream team" became apparent. By then it was too late.

Transitions to institutional leadership tend to be slow, and often go through lapses and recovery (it took decades and several attempts for IBM to achieve this (Gerstner, 2002; Carroll, 1993; Doz and Kosonen, 2008), and HP did not quite get there (Burgelman et al., 2016; House and Price, 2009)). They also require CEOs and key executives who are institution builders and structural context developers (for examples one can read Sloan (1964) to explore the building of General Motors, and Chandler (1962) and Chandler and Salsbury (1971) for that of DuPont and other companies). The transition from personal to institutional leadership often gets waylaid by creeping bureaucracy, as it did to an extent at Nokia and also at HP.

Turning to our four CORE enablers, from a *Cognitive* and strategic perspective the key difficulty of this period was a growing divergence and the resulting inconsistency between various strategic choices made by Nokia. The original ambition of achieving both low cost and differentiation called for walking a tightrope, and Nokia was unable to maintain the balance this required. The lifestyle-based market segmentation scheme may have made sense, but it was not implemented successfully. Nokia progressively fell on the side of cost optimization—driven by a core mobile phone "dominant logic" (see Prahalad and Bettis (1986) and (1995) for a development of this concept)— and failed to differentiate its products sufficiently to create value that end users with various lifestyles would appreciate.

In the 1990s, Nokia had won the competitive battle for mobile phones against Motorola and Ericsson, but then let that success slip from its hands. Given Symbian's limitations and Nokia's dominant cost-containment logic, it was simply unable to continue to provide the high-quality, innovative products its loyal customers had grown accustomed to. The introduction of Motorola's innovative RAZR phone provided a shot across Nokia's bow, but

Motorola failed to retain the upper hand as its new CEO, Ed Zander, had different priorities and restricted R&D. The fact that Motorola's innovative leadership was short-lived comforted Nokia's executives and reinforced their belief that Nokia was still the leader in product design and engineering. Yet they chose to overlook the fact that the clarity of product specifications, quality, and the timeliness of product introductions had all started to decline around the same time.

As Nokia was letting victory slip in the war for mobile phone leadership, a new war, on a different terrain, was about to start: traditional mobile phones were about to be superseded by smartphones. Since the development of the Communicator in the early 1990s, Nokia had been the leader in smartphones, but somehow middle managers who made key product policy decisions did not recognize and respond to the fundamental changes smartphones would make to the competitive game. Rather than hardware features, the range of software applications an end user would install would now be the key differentiator. This heralded a shift from market segmentation to mass customization. Every single end user would now configure an application suite to meet his or her own personalized needs.

Mobile communication thus became what economists call a two-sided market: end users would choose a particular phone-provider based on how many applications were available on that phone's OS; and application developers would develop applications for the operating systems that attracted the most end users. Network economics would now apply, and phone makers would need to attract not just customers but application developers too.

It would be wrong to assume that no one in Nokia had recognized the advent of this shift nor understood the implications of such a deep transformation. Indeed, as we saw in Chapter 5, in the 1990s Ollila and Ala-Pietilä had already developed a keen sense of the transformation of the industry they would face in the 2000s. However, top management's understanding did not result in effective middle-management action. Why, exactly, is hard to figure out. Of course, a strategic vacuum had developed in top management after 2004, and the product line managers were exclusively focused on the very short-term success of their own products (timely introduction and initial quarter sales). The tensions between traditional phone developers, focused on hardware, and smartphone developers, who saw how critical software now was, remained high and made the commitment to the new reality of platforms and applications more difficult.

Nokia may also have been a victim of what some academics (Barnett and Hansen, 1996) have called a "Red Queen" effect. This refers to the well-known exchange in Lewis Carroll's classic novel, *Through the Looking Glass* between Alice and the Red Queen, about having to run faster and faster just to stay in the same place. This is indeed how the world must have felt to many Nokians following the amazing growth they had achieved since the mid-1990s. In strategic management terms the basic argument about the "Red Queen" effect is that a period of sustained competition for a market with the same set of rivals leads to excessive attention being focused on these well-known competitors, and to a corresponding lack of attention to new and different competitors. The argument gained relevance and importance in studying how incumbents in oligopolistic markets failed to see the threat posed by new (often disruptive) entrants in their markets. For instance, Xerox was focused on Kodak's and IBM's entry into copiers—neighbors in Rochester, New York—and neglected Canon, Savin, and other Japanese competitors. The same was true of the initial disdain of Detroit's "big three" carmakers toward the Japanese, or of how the Scottish cashmere sweater industry underestimated Chinese entrants (Porac et al., 1989).

The fact that in the late 1990s a lot of Nokia's strategic deliberations had somehow been "hosted" by new venture-related forums (the New Business Development Forum in particular), and that these were abandoned in the early 2000s, also contributed to the impoverishment of strategic foresight and to a less inclusive strategy process. Middle managers were now less involved in strategy dialogs, and strategy increasingly became the purview of strategy staff.

So, in sum, the intensity of the cognitive dimensions declined. Nokia's management was now less strategic in its reflections than it had been in the late 1990s and at the beginning of the 2000s.

On the *Organizational* dimension, the matrix organization did not help. Negotiation skills and collaborative attitudes were wanting, and were not encouraged by an organization that gave responsibility and accountability to product line managers but left them dependent on horizontal platforms for key scarce resources. The idea of adopting a matrix organization was, in principle, sensible, but it was poorly implemented and the product and platform perspectives were not integrated effectively.

With the departure of key figures in the "dream team," *Relationships* became simpler but also less effective. Part of the difficulties stemmed from a preference for trust over skills, consistent with the Nokia "can-do" spirit. This led to a continued reliance on executives from mobile phone operations, most of whom were very competent but also steeped in a hardware voice product tradition. When faced with cost-reduction pressures for mid-range phones in both developed and emerging markets, these managers focused more on unit cost reduction than value enhancement. In other words, the "willingness to pay" (what customers are willing to pay based on what value they find in the product) of end users was decreasing, often stimulated by competition, but also because customers did not find enough value in new products (they started keeping their phones for longer before replacing them, and more of a second-hand market also developed).

Thus, Multimedia and Enterprise Solutions were the standard-bearers of a value-enhancing perspective, but their efforts were often stifled by pressure to reduce hardware unit costs for screens, processors, memory sizes, etc., which were becoming increasingly inconsistent with providing the value consumers now wanted. Containing hardware cost became a severe constraint on the type and variety of applications one could effectively use on a Nokia phone.

On the *Emotional* side, morale declined. Matrix conflicts were abrasive and Ala-Pietilä (with his quiet but clear intellect and trusting mind) and Alahuhta (with his practical, action-oriented authority and charisma) no longer provided reassurance. Yet, the company was still remarkably successful and it had built a strong reservoir of trust with its employees. Even when many would observe "I am not sure what's going on ... " they would be prompted to add " ... but I am sure someone must know." So, despite some concerns, growing confusion, and worrying evidence of a decline in key competitive factors, there was still a climate of trust and emotional commitment. Figure 6.2 provides a summary of the key elements of each CORE dimension for this period.

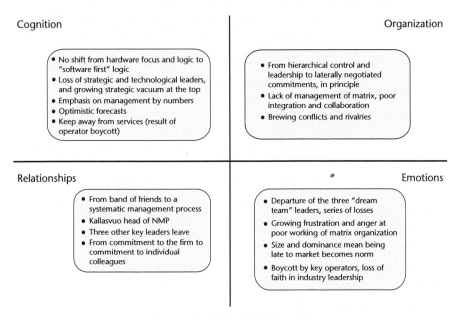

Figure 6.2. 2003–6 CORE profile

References

William Barnett and Morten Hansen, "The Red Queen in Organizational Evolution" (*Strategic Management Journal*, Vol. 17, Summer 1996) pp. 139–57.

Joseph Bower, *Managing the Resource Allocation Process* (Harvard Business School Press, Cambridge, MA, 1970).

Robert Burgelman, "Intraorganizational Ecology of Strategy-Making and Organizational Adaptation: Theory and Field Research" (*Organization Science*, Vol. 2 Issue 3, August 1991) pp. 239–62.

Robert Burgelman, "Fading Memories: A Process Theory of Strategic Business Exit in Dynamic Environments" (*Administrative Science Quarterly*, Vol. 39 Issue 1, March 1994) pp. 24–56.

Robert Burgelman, Webb McKinney, and Philip Meza, *Becoming Hewlett-Packard: Why Strategic Leadership Matters* (Oxford University Press, New York, 2016).

Paul Carroll, *Big Blues: The Unmaking of IBM* (Crown Publisher, New York, 1993).

Alfred Chandler, *Strategy and Structure: Chapters in the History of the Industrial Enterprise*, (MIT Press, Cambridge, MA, 1962).

Alfred Chandler and Stephen Salsbury, *Pierre S. du Pont and the Making of the Modern Corporation* (Harper & Row, New York, 1971).

Yves Doz and Mikko Kosonen, "The Dancing Elephant," in *Fast Strategy: How Strategic Agility Will Help You Stay Ahead of the Game* (Wharton School Publishing, Harlow, 2008) pp. 36–52.

Jay R. Galbraith, *Designing Matrix Organizations that Actually Work: How IBM, Procter & Gamble and Others Design for Success* (John Wiley & Sons, San Francisco, 2008).

Lou Gerstner, *Who Says Elephants Can't Dance: Inside IBM's Historic Turnaround* (Harper Collins, New York, 2002).

Sumantra Ghoshal and Christopher Bartlett, "Linking Organizational Context and Managerial Action: The Dimensions of Quality of Management" (*Strategic Management Journal*, Vol. 15, Summer 1994) pp. 91–112.

Charles House and Raymond Price, *The HP Phenomenon: Innovation and Business Transformation* (Stanford University Press, Stanford, 2009).

Chan Kim and Renée Mauborgne, "Fair Process: Managing in the Knowledge Economy" (*Harvard Business Review*, Vol. 75 Issue 4, July/August 1997) pp. 65–75.

Charles Perrow, *Normal Accidents: Living with High-Risk Technologies* (Princeton University Press, Princeton, 1984).

Joseph Porac, Howard Thomas, and Charles Baden-Fuller, "Competitive Groups as Cognitive Communities: The Case of Scottish Knitwear Manufacturers Revisited" (*Journal of Management Studies*, Vol. 48 Issue 3, May 2011, original article published in 1989) pp. 646–64.

C. K. Prahalad and Richard Bettis, "The Dominant Logic: A New Linkage Between Diversity and Performance" (*Strategic Management Journal*, Vol. 7 Issue 6 November/December 1986) pp. 485–501.

C. K. Prahalad and Richard Bettis, "The Dominant Logic: Retrospective and Extension" (*Strategic Management Journal*, Vol. 16 Issue 1, January 1995) pp. 5–14.

Alfred Sloan, *My Years with General Motors* (Macfadden-Bartell, New York, 1964).

Karl Weick, "*The Vulnerable System: An Analysis of the Tenerife Air Disaster*" (*Journal of Management*, Vol. 16 Issue 3, September 1990) pp. 571–94.

7

A Fading Star

When Ala-Pietilä had turned down the CEO role in 2005, Ollila then looked to his trusted lieutenant and new head of Mobile Phones, Kallasvuo, to replace him. With Nokia facing an internal struggle to adapt to the new matrix structure and ever greater external pressures, many saw the CEO role as a poisoned chalice. But the softly spoken Kallasvuo agreed, and in October 2005 was put in charge of operations in preparation for becoming the next CEO of Nokia in June the following year. Ollila retained not only his role but also a certain degree of control, as chairman of the board.

Kallasvuo, a lawyer by training, had spent most of his career in Nokia in legal affairs and finance. For almost the last decade and a half he had been Ollila's right-hand man and an exceptional CFO. But these roles hadn't required him to develop an in-depth strategic or technological understanding of the industry, and there was doubt in some quarters within Nokia as to whether he had the right background and skills to guide the firm through the changes the industry was facing. He was, however, widely seen as a good operational manager, not just a finance expert, who understood shareholders and analysts and was extremely sensitive to what was needed to please them—and when Kallasvuo took over as CEO, they had every reason to be happy as Nokia's growing internal problems had yet to have an impact on its performance.

Nokia could still rely on a loyal customer base and had the best retention rates in the industry—53 percent of Nokia customers replaced their phones with new Nokia products in 2006, compared with rates of 32 percent for Sony Ericsson, 30 percent for Samsung, and 29 percent for both Motorola and LG. And while most manufacturers were suffering from a double whammy of slowing mainstream markets and falling handset prices (which dropped from an average of US$120 in 2004 to US$40 by 2008), Nokia continued to grow due to its dominant position and strong demand in emerging markets. Against this backdrop, a strategy of "more of the same" looked liked the least risky route for Kallasvuo and his senior management team.

Despite the combined phone businesses posting strong results in both 2006 and 2007 (with revenues up 12 percent to 37,691 million euros in 2007, and operating profit at 5,161 million euros in 2006 and 7,931 million euros the following year) all was not well within Nokia. The problems brought about by the new matrix structure remained, and as time passed had become entrenched as barriers to innovation and decision making. Anonymous feedback from an internal survey I was asked to conduct in 2006, investigating obstacles and weaknesses, revealed a general consensus that the matrix wasn't working. One respondent commented that "The matrix structure encourages silos." Another noted, "The matrix demands that we are more internally focused. We now prefer not to make decisions but to share responsibility and we hide behind processes." And in a rather bleak analysis, someone said, "In the matrix nobody owns anything and nobody is responsible for anything."

Ollila had brought in the matrix structure to try and reinvigorate innovation, but by 2006 it was clearly dysfunctional. When we met in the summer of 2016, he explained how this had happened, recalling, "Matti Alahuhta had been aware of the challenge of differentiation and integration and had planned a series of actions, training, new incentives and working groups to make the matrix work. But he left and his plans weren't pursued. There was no one to arbitrate between the product lines, and middle managers lacked collaboration and negotiation skills. We were just too slow to learn." Faced with challenging environments both internally and externally, Kallasvuo began thinking about how to overcome the matrix problems.

A Reorganization for Better Integration

In 2007, Kallasvuo brought his top team together in New York for a two-day meeting to try and find solutions to the deepening fragmentation between Mobile Phones, Multimedia, and Enterprise Solutions and the product lines within them. He explained, "We came to the conclusion that we needed to run as an integrated company where phones, operating systems, and services would be developed in an integrated fashion." To achieve this, Kallasvuo announced that from January 1, 2008 Nokia would adopt a new organizational structure designed to bring about harmonized roadmaps across the various product lines and eliminate overlaps in R&D, sales, and marketing.

In the new structure, NET's network activities, which had merged with Siemens in June 2006 to create Nokia Siemens Networks, would remain a separate business. The existing vertical phone-based businesses were all merged, along with the horizontal software functions, to create a single business group named Devices and Services. This new business group comprised three business units: Devices, covering all hardware products (regrouped into five business units) and headed by Kai Öistämö, who since 2006 had taken over from Kallasvuo as head of the Mobile Phones group; Services and Software, responsible for the technology platform under Niklas Savander, who had run platforms in R&D; and finally Markets, under Anssi Vanjoki. Other moves saw Mary McDowell, previously head of Enterprise Solutions, becoming the chief development officer, and Tero Ojanperä, head of strategy and CTO, taking charge of services in Savander's group.

The appointment of Vanjoki, who was regarded as one of Nokia's few remaining technology visionaries, in a new markets organization was the only surprise in the reorganization. The relationship between the mild-mannered Kallasvuo and confrontational Vanjoki had never been good, and Kallasvuo explained, there were several motives in appointing Vanjoki to oversee sales and marketing, "I didn't want to lose him but neither could I let him dominate the product side—he had a very strong vision and priorities for where he thought Nokia should be," and so this new role both utilized his skills but reduced his (often domineering) influence.

Unfortunately, the reorganization did little to alleviate the fragmentation, internal conflicts, and inefficiencies within Nokia, and in his own words Kallasvuo admitted that, "By reversing the logic of 2004 we created huge additional complexity with many more interface and articulation points." The heads of the new business units were too focused on reaching their own performance targets to put any priority on collaboration, and with very different approaches and visions they weren't well suited to working as an integrated whole as the "dream team" had done so successfully in the past.

Neither had the reorganization changed anything at the product line level, and so even though these groups were now under the same Devices umbrella, they continued to compete for resources from the Services and Software units. This put Services and Software under unrealistic pressure trying to respond to multiple demands and priorities—which inevitably couldn't all be met. So, just as in previous years, whenever software and service development delays looked likely, product line managers regularly dropped features from their phones in order to meet product release schedules. Not only did this result in much wasted effort internally, but in this new ecosystem environment in which multiple partners were critical to success, Nokia lost credibility with content and application providers.

While the world was changing around Nokia, continuing with a strategy that had middle-market mobile phones at its core reflected a lack of technology leadership in the firm. Ironically for a company whose success had been dependent upon technology breakthroughs, Nokia had a poor record when it came to appointing visionary CTOs after Neuvo left, relying instead upon its individual businesses and research centers to drive the technology agenda. In fact, between 2005 and 2008, when the industry was in the grips of a massive technology shift, Nokia didn't even have a dedicated CTO—Tero Ojanperä had taken on the role in 2006 but this was in addition to being head of strategy (which is where both his heart and head had been focused). What's more, Nokia's board proved ineffective in providing much-needed guidance.

With his reorganization, Kallasvuo also tried to improve Nokia's technology vision with an infusion of fresh blood in the CTO role. In 2008, Bob Ianucci from HP was appointed head of the NRC and as the unofficial CTO. However, his desire to create an independent corporate research center modeled on HP Labs did not go down well in Nokia, nor did the fact that he remained based in Palo Alto. After eight months, he left. He was followed by Charles Davies from Psion and the Symbian alliance, and then Richard Green from Sun Microsystems, but neither stayed long as CTO in Nokia.

The Changing Nature of the Industry

Without a thorough grasp of platform software, ecosystems, and applications, Nokia's senior management team lacked a strategic understanding of where the industry was heading. It was a case of trying to deal with "unknown unknowns," and the default response to this became delay and procrastination. When in doubt, decision making was delegated to committees, but this tended to lead to stalemates and further delays. Exacerbating the lack of technology competence in the top team was a widespread superficial veneer of understanding elsewhere in the management ranks. When reflecting on this, on more than one occasion Kallasvuo has expressed his frustration that too often Nokians "Used all of the right words—they learned to 'speak Internet' and gave the impression they knew what they were talking about. They had quasi knowledge and it was easy to be misled by articulate people using the right language masking a lack of the right skills."

When Apple had launched its first iPhone in 2007, viewing it from a product perspective, its poor voice quality and reliance on 2.5 GPRS connectivity made it easy for Nokia to dismiss. Just over a year later, Google released its Linux-based mobile OS, Android. Both platforms offered customers a good range of applications and both supported user-friendly touchscreen interfaces. In comparison, Nokia's range of smartphones based on the Symbian OS had what now felt like old-fashioned keypads and drop-down menus. By this time Nokia was using fifty-seven different versions of its Symbian OS, which made it not only time-consuming for developers to create apps but meant the portability of apps across different phone models was extremely difficult. Consequently Nokia's own app store, called Ovi, offered a fraction of the apps available from its competitors (around 8 percent of the number available from Apple's App Store and 19 percent of the total apps on the Android Market).

The game was clearly changing, and for Kallasvuo this realization only hit home in late 2008 in a meeting he had with Steve Jobs. Summarizing the conversation, Kallasvuo recalled, "Steve Jobs told me he didn't regard Nokia as a competitor as we weren't a platform company. When I argued that we were investing in platforms he looked at me and said he'd been investing in a platform and OS for forty years and so he wasn't worried by our recent effort." Nokia's CEO came away from that encounter realizing that the change wasn't just about technology, it was a complete shift from one business to another.

In June 2009, almost two years after Apple launched the first iPhone (and the day of the introduction of Apple's third-generation iPhone), Nokia released the N97, its first smartphone with a touchscreen interface. However, hardware limitations due to the use of cheap components, combined with software limitations from the Symbian OS, did little to win over consumers. By 2010, sales of the iPhone, RIM's BlackBerry, and Android-based smartphones were chipping away at Nokia's dominant market share, and shareholders and analysts were beginning to question Nokia's ability to compete in the smartphone market.

An Alternative OS to Symbian

It was becoming ever-more clear that in the world of smartphones, having a good, accessible OS platform was key, and with its multiple versions and complexity, questions about Symbian's suitability could not be avoided. Although it had invested heavily in Symbian, both financially and in terms of commitment, Nokia had developed an alternative OS. In 2002, frustrated with the limitations imposed by Symbian, and aware that any alternative would be met with stiff resistance from the thousands of Nokian's working on it, Vanjoki had begun a "skunk works" project based in Tampere (and codenamed OSSO—Open Source Software Operations) to create an alternative open source Linux-based OS.

The entire effort was funded under the radar by Vanjoki, and even though the small OSSO team, headed by Ari Jaaksi, had limited resources they worked quickly and development was fast. The new Linux-based OS was renamed Maemo in 2007. Jaaksi's team had been focusing on developing a touchscreen smartphone, but as Maemo became a more visible threat to Symbian they were forced to scale back their plans. And so in 2007, what had been planned as the first Maemo smartphone was actually launched as the N800 Internet tablet—in other words, a smartphone without voice capabilities!

Internal resistance to Maemo was strong. There was a large camp within Nokia that was loathe to accept any project initiated by Vanjoki because of personal feelings, regardless of how good the outcome may be. On a more practical level, migrating to a new OS would be difficult and disruptive for customers and app developers, not to mention the thousands of software developers working on Symbian within Nokia.

Failing to see any real sense of urgency in moving to a new OS, Nokia's senior managers allowed Symbian development to continue and dominate while encouraging the two platforms to find common ground. In January 2008, Nokia acquired Norwegian firm Trolltech, hoping it had found a solution to bringing Maemo and Symbian closer together. Trolltech's main product, Qt was a cross-platform application layer that allowed developers to write applications in just one source code that could then be used on different OS platforms. Rivalries between the Symbian and Maemo teams led to each developing their own (and incompatible) Qt user interface tools, and so the hoped-for collaboration didn't happen.

Prior to Kallasvuo's 2008 reorganization, the small Maemo team had managed to maintain a degree of autonomy from the main phone development activities. However, under the new structure Maemo joined Symbian as part of the Devices group. This caused much disquiet with a number of senior managers, who felt that by putting Maemo with Symbian it would no longer be able to grow independently and risked being penetrated by the culture of a large company. Their concerns were realized as the Maemo team rapidly grew to over 1,000 engineers and in doing so lost its agility and flexibility.

Partnership with Intel

No matter how compelling an alternative it provided, Maemo continued to struggle to gain traction within Nokia. Then, in 2010, a possible tie-up with Intel offered an opportunity to expand Maemo. Since abandoning its successful Xscale range of processors in 2006 (which had been popular in early smartphones and PDAs), Intel had been unable to compete against ARM which dominated GSM standards, and Qualcomm with CDMA architectures. By combining its own Linux-based Moblin OS with Nokia's Maemo, Intel saw an opportunity to expand its presence in mobile and Nokia recognized a route to legitimize Maemo.

The two firms announced a partnership at the Mobile World Congress in Barcelona in early 2010, renaming the new joint OS MeeGo. Unlike the fifty-plus annual Symbian product launches, MeeGo announced it would focus on releasing one flagship phone each year.

However, the MeeGo alliance immediately encountered problems. Combining the two development teams was difficult, and Moblin and Maemo had very different modular architectures which proved arduous to merge and impossible to test until the entire OS was completed. This resulted in frustrating delays at a time when the sense of urgency for a new platform was increasing.

The Wimax access technology Intel had developed not only proved slow and unreliable, but only a few months into the alliance it became apparent that most operators were adopting the alternative LTE (long-term evolution) technology. Further delays were encountered while integrated LTE support was developed.

Smartphone Strategy Options

The onslaught from Apple, RIM, and Google in the smartphone arena, stiffer competition from new producers in emerging markets, and continuing internal wrangling over operating systems had really begun to take their toll by 2010. Nokia still had one of the strongest patent portfolios in the industry, a valuable global brand, and an installed base that was second to none. But this was no longer enough, and so the management team outlined the different strategy options open to them.

One obvious route was to join Android. However, mobile carriers including AT&T and Verizon in the US, and Orange, T-Mobile, and Telefonica in Europe, were wary of an Apple iOS–Google Android duopoly taking over the industry, as this would reduce their own power and ability to innovate. They let it be known that they would support the emergence of a third platform ecosystem and Nokia's further two options catered to that: it could strengthen its own Symbian and MeeGo platforms, or join forces with Microsoft.

Join the Android Platform

When Apple released its first iPhone, Google was already working on Android, a Linux-based OS. Initially only T-Mobile and HTC used Android, but in 2010 the ecosystem expanded as it was adopted by Verizon and Motorola in the US, and by Samsung for its Galaxy range of phones. Joining the Android platform was a relatively attractive proposition for Nokia: integrating the Android OS would be a fast and easy option and the Qualcomm chipset used by Nokia was already designed for Android. Nokia would also gain access to a vast range of apps and app developers, instantly countering one of the biggest criticisms it currently faced. There was also the possibility that the combined might of Google and Nokia could create a real competitive threat to Apple and the emerging Asian players.

Yet the flipside of the low-risk choice was an equally low reward. Moving to Android would remove some differentiation in Nokia's offerings, and for a firm that had always controlled its OS platforms this was a genuine concern. Customers that had long been loyal to Nokia would easily be able to switch to any other manufacturer in the Android ecosystem, and a large number of

Nokians felt Samsung had already established itself as the dominant device player in the grouping, which would leave Nokia on the back foot from the outset. Nokia's CFO at the time, Timo Ihamuotila, highlighted another potential problem of joining Android, "There was a conflict between our Navteq mapping business and Google Maps." The highly successful Navteq provided the mapping services to Google's competitors Microsoft and Yahoo, and it was difficult to see how the two competing map providers could coexist on the Android platform.

A Combination of MeeGo and Symbian

Although Symbian was unwieldy and unloved by apps developers, Nokia had made progress on rationalizing its OS. As Kallasvuo explained, "Lots of work had been done to merge and standardize the various versions. We were 'pruning' the incredible Symbian tree." With such a huge investment in terms of skills, knowledge, and resources in Symbian (by 2010 there were around 6,200 engineers working on it), dropping the OS entirely did not seem feasible. As an alternative it was envisaged that mid- and low-end phones could retain the Symbian OS, while high-end smartphones could migrate to MeeGo. According to Alberto Torres, head of MeeGo by this time, "Symbian needed to be discontinued but Qt would have prolonged its life a bit and made the transition to MeeGo easier" by providing a path to developers from Symbian to MeeGo.

MeeGo seemed to offer Nokia the opportunity to compete head-on with Apple and Android and create a third ecosystem, which being Linux-based would offer developers and consumers easy portability. It also offered the opportunity to extend beyond smartphones to support a wider range of devices including tablets, netbooks, Internet-enabled televisions, and in-car entertainment systems. On the downside, Nokia continued to experience problems working with Intel, and overtures to Sony Ericsson, Samsung, and LG in 2010 to join a MeeGo ecosystem had all been rejected.

Ally with Microsoft

Microsoft had been slow to recognize that mobility would be the future driving force of the industry, and seriously lagged behind the competition with only a 1 percent market share. Access to a global hardware brand would instantly boost its presence in the mobile communications sector, and so Microsoft was eager to join forces with Nokia.

From Nokia's perspective, Microsoft wasn't an entirely unknown quantity, as the previous year the two firms had formed an alliance to enable Nokia to offer Microsoft Office Mobile on its enterprise-targeted phones. Building further on this partnership to work with Microsoft on a Windows Mobile OS would enable Nokia to make serious inroads into RIM's 75 million BlackBerry business subscribers by offering full, seamless mobile access to Microsoft Office via the Windows Phone OS, as well as offering a distinct alternative to Apple and Android. Microsoft was also very bullish about how quickly it could deliver the new platform.

The benefits of moving to a Microsoft OS were not clear-cut though. As Erkki Ormala, Nokia's head of technology policy, explained: "By moving to the Windows Mobile OS we would have to lose some of the most advanced features on Symbian. Of course this had to be balanced with the connectivity to the Office suite and business systems that Microsoft offered." Neither Nokia nor Microsoft had a strong record in content and applications and so would need to attract content providers to the alliance, and this might not be straightforward as both firms had poor reputations as partners: a combination of Finnish cultural traits and years of dominance in the industry meant that Nokia could seem aloof and arrogant, while Microsoft was well known for being a ruthless partner (Nokia's own board investigated whether Microsoft would benefit disproportionately from a potential alliance).

Another Reorganization

In just over two years since the 2008 reorganization, the much hoped for closer integration had not been achieved. Nokia's share price had dropped around 60 percent and delays to new phone launches had become a more regular feature. While grappling with decisions about which smartphone strategy to pursue, in May 2010 Kallasvuo undertook another reorganization designed to simplify Nokia's structure and at the same time strengthen the group's smartphone operations.

A new Mobile Solutions group, including smartphone devices and all related software and services, was created. Anssi Vanjoki was moved from his markets role to head this critical new group. All of Nokia's traditional middle- to low-end phones were put into the Mobile Phones group led by Mary McDowell, while Niklas Savander moved from services to run the Markets group.

Without a bold vision for the future or any concrete announcement about how Nokia was going to compete in Internet services, shareholders and analysts were unimpressed by the latest reorganization, and at the AGM later that month became very vocal in pushing for a new CEO. However, these calls were quashed by Ollila and the board, which gave Kallasvuo a vote of confidence.

A New Leader for a New Strategy

Less than two months later, Ollila and the board were forced to acquiesce to shareholder demands. In a statement announcing that the search for a new CEO was underway, Ollila said, "The time is right to accelerate the company's renewal; to bring in new executive leadership with different skills and strengths in order to drive company success." More and more criticisms had been leveled at Nokia for being overrun with managers who lacked vision and made too many financial-based decisions. Many outside observers suggested that to stand a chance of fighting back against the iPhone and Android, Nokia should hire a tech-savvy visionary with strong consumer electronics experience.

The board instructed search agents that potential candidates should have a background in Internet and software development in large, complex, multinational firms. But the relatively low remuneration package on offer, combined with the geographic remoteness of Finland and the prevailing Finnish culture within Nokia, resulted in only two names being put forward to replace Kallasvuo—one from inside Nokia and one external candidate.

The internal candidate was Anssi Vanjoki. Widely admired in the industry as the visionary who turned the mobile phone into a consumer product, he had supported the development of the Communicator in the 1990s and more recently been responsible for the Maemo OS. He had long been tipped to be Nokia's next CEO. He knew Nokia inside-out and had not been shy to voice his disagreement with Nokia's leadership and their strategic decisions. Of course, his passion, outspokenness, and lack of diplomacy during his nineteen years at Nokia hadn't endeared Vanjoki to everyone.

When approached by Ollila to see if he would be interested in the CEO position, Vanjoki explained, "I knew Nokia was in trouble and so spent the summer of 2010 developing a rescue plan. I visited all our R&D centers to understand what each was doing, what skills they had and how they could be used to turn around the company." Vanjoki's grueling schedule paid dividends, and by the end of the summer he had developed a new strategy to accelerate the development of MeeGo for high-end smartphones that would be ready for introduction in October that year.

The external candidate was Canadian national Stephen Elop. As president of Microsoft's Business division, he had been working with Nokia for almost a year on the alliance to provide Microsoft's Office suite on Nokia's enterprise smartphones. Prior to Microsoft, Elop, an engineer by training, had worked for a number of firms including Macromedia and Juniper Networks.

Elop certainly wasn't the high-profile tech visionary investors hoped for, but he represented what many believed was an urgent infusion of new blood into Nokia's leadership. A quiet and thoughtful manager, Elop didn't display the more demonstrative traits often associated with North American leaders.

He was considered a good cultural fit, and the importance of this in a firm that had always been headed by Finns, and which despite being a global company maintained a strong Finnish culture, cannot be underestimated. There were internal detractors to Elop who questioned whether, if chosen as CEO, he would retain his allegiance to Microsoft and simply position Nokia as the Seattle firm's largest licensee.

Nokia's board met on September 21, 2010 and reached the decision to appoint Stephen Elop as Nokia's new CEO. They believed that Elop could lead the transformation of Nokia from a hardware to software company needed to compete against the iPhone and Android. They also felt he was better placed than a Finnish national to steer the firm to a stronger position in the US, where it was now languishing with around an 8 percent market share. Prior to the meeting, Ollila had warned Vanjoki which way the board was likely to vote—in response to which Vanjoki recalled saying, "If you appoint Elop, I will leave that day." True to his word, just after the announcement Vanjoki resigned.

Commentary

By 2006, when Ollila relinquished the CEO role, Kallasvuo was the last of the original "dream team" remaining at Nokia. His appointment was not a great surprise, as since he had been appointed to head the Mobile Phones group in 2004, it had been assumed he was being groomed for the top job. The company was still financially successful, and he was trusted by Ollila and many others at the firm, but not everyone viewed his appointment with great confidence: he lacked the charisma and decisiveness of previous leaders. Years later, Kallasvuo himself would tell me that he, too, realized that he was not the perfect candidate, but that he accepted his appointment out of a sense of duty to both Nokia and to Finland, suggesting that he saw that times ahead would be difficult, but wanted to protect the company and its employees. Laudable as this attitude was, it did not put him on the right path for facing a difficult future.

By 2008, Nokia was first and foremost confronting the full intensity of rapid convergence between industries, and becoming a victim of that convergence (it is important to note that disruption was not, as some observers mistakenly argue, affecting Nokia at this point, but would only come into play later when much cheaper and better quality Korean and then Chinese phones began to dominate in the mid-range market). Convergence is not a balanced or symmetrical process, where pre-existing industries simply fuse and become one in a "merger of equals." When industries converge, one may dissolve into the other much as an acquired company is absorbed and dissolved into its acquirer.

It turns out that in the late 2000s mobiles phone dissolved into computers. What had been the lifestyle-changing telecommunications innovation of voice calls and MMS on the move became just one function, or feature, of a new breed of pocket computers which were somewhat inaccurately called "smartphones," as if to imply the phone was still central. In the same way that telecom services dissolved into Internet communication with Voice over Internet Protocol (VoIP), Wi-Fi, and "over the top" (OTT) service providers, the telephone handset industry dissolved into the personal computer industry. The imbalance in convergence leads to the migration path of the "converged" industry being much steeper and shorter than that of the "converging" side. This was captured by the dismissive comment made by Steve Jobs to Kallasvuo, "You are not a competitor of ours, you are a device company now having to develop platforms."

Nokia was a victim of convergence largely because its new competitors saw themselves as platform businesses. For them, mobile phones were indeed just a type of screen, not dissimilar from TV monitors or personal computers, through which consumers could access their core products: applications and content downloads via iTunes for Apple and advertising messages triggered by information search for Google. The platform approach of these competitors was being deployed across a whole range of access channels, and mobile phones just happened to be winning the race as one of the most prominent channels. What had for many years been a distinct and simple telecoms platform was now being enveloped and dissolved into much larger platforms (Eisenmann et al., 2011).

In terms of *Cognition*, this was new and uncomfortable territory for Nokia and its senior managers struggled to respond. Becoming an Internet platform company would be very hard. The migration from software to include hardware does seem easier than migrating from hardware to software. Beyond the obvious skill gaps and the difficulty of filling these from Finland, combined with a social capital deficit with the media and content industries, even deeper issues blocked Nokia's path. Researchers familiar with the industry and the plight of incumbents trying to "reinvent" themselves, or to use a popular phrasing, "re-engineer their DNA," suggest the deeper challenges are identity related (e.g. Altman and Tripsas, 2015). Trying to change corporate identity is akin to an individual changing their personality—an unlikely mutation.

The possibilities open to Nokia to transform itself were limited, and by 2010 none of Nokia's options was particularly attractive. The collaboration with Intel for MeeGo proved to be more difficult than expected. Technical differences, such as the structure of software modules in the architecture of Maemo and Moblin, made their combination difficult and meant that individual modules could not be tested separately—somewhat reminiscent to problems with Symbian. As both Nokia and Intel were incumbent leaders in their respective fields, development was slow and arduous as the process of collaboration between the two large incumbents proved difficult. And with its broader gauged focus on tablets and laptops, Intel had failed to find a successful approach to mobile communications.

Yet Nokia was now facing considerable urgency. It had done its best to make Symbian an industry-wide platform and open it fully (in particular after Psion cashed in and Symbian was transformed into an open source platform). However, beyond its product development inefficiency, Symbian was also proving unattractive to independent application developers—as a development environment, it took much longer for developers to master and had fewer software development kits to help them than either iOS or Android offered (Figure 7.1). As a result, Nokia suffered both in hardware, with inferior products, and software, with fewer applications sold in smaller volumes (Figure 7.2).

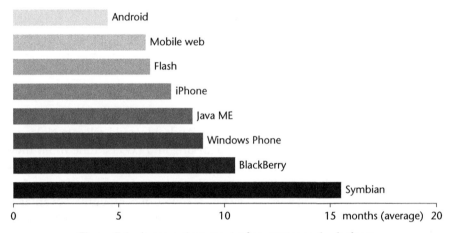

Figure 7.1. Average time required to master each platform

Post-2008, some ex-Nokians have argued that there was a lack of support for MeeGo's development. This is open to debate. MeeGo's development team had been substantially increased, and with around 1,000 people was large by any standards. Software development specialists tend to argue that large teams (for which they put the threshold as low as sixty to a hundred professionals) are grossly inefficient and ineffective, unless the development project is very clearly divided into modular sub-projects and these are very well specified and integrated. This would suggest that the issue facing MeeGo was not one of quantity but quality. Nokia suffered from a dearth of software system architects and project managers—talented software system architects are a scarce resource and project management in software development requires complex knowledge that is acquired through practice. Exactly how limited Nokia's software architecture definition and management capabilities were remains debatable.

Yet the alternatives to MeeGo were not particularly attractive. Joining the Android club had obvious advantages: Android was an open platform and

125

	Apple Store	Android Market	Ovi Store	BlackBerry App World
Fundamentals				
Owner	Apple	Google	Nokia	RIM
Distribution model	Via App Store on iPhone and iPod Touch	Via Market on Android devices (closed source)	Via download, and pre-loaded from 4Q09	?
Platforms	OSX	Android	Symbian, S40	BlackBerry
Key figures				
Sales base since launch (2010 est.)	90 million	68 million	400 million	125 million
Downloads per month as of end of 2010 (est.)	510 million	270 million	90 million	60 million
Cumulative downloads since launch as of end of 2010 (est.)	10 billion	2.5 billion	N/A	N/A
Applications to end of 2010 (est.)	300,000	130,000	25,000	18,000
Revenue model	70% to developer	70% to developer 30% optional to operator	70% to developer (less w/ carrier billing)	70% to developer

Figure 7.2. Mobile application stores 2010

poised for potential leadership across a broad range of phones, from basic ones to smartphones. On the downside, joining Android would relegate Nokia to the role of hardware supplier, just like Samsung and LG at a time when they were facing an onslaught from a host of lower cost emerging Chinese competitors. In a world where its traditional sources of advantage were fast eroding, Nokia would also lose the key future source of competitive advantage: mastery of its own OS. Its supply chain excellence was no longer a unique advantage, particularly against the Apple-FoxConn duo, and in light of Apple's policy of only having one phone model—the iPhone—which made its logistics and supply system much simpler than Nokia's.

What had been an advantage for hardware feature-based differentiation turned into a disadvantage for software application-based mass customization. Despite all its efforts at cutting costs, it was difficult to envision Nokia winning a cost-reduction race against China and Korea. In Korea, Samsung gained a growing advantage in hardware optimization as it improved the quality of collaboration between its various businesses, in particular semiconductors and mobile phones (Song et al., 2016). The supplier partnerships that Jean-François Baril (as head of purchasing) and others had built for Nokia were losing their unique value as the industry matured, not just against integrated companies like Samsung but against phone assemblers who could rely on a wide network of suppliers. And Nokia had missed the opportunity to become a strategic partner of Google years earlier when Google informally sounded out senior executives at Nokia and was rebuffed. By 2010, Google was only willing to offer Nokia regular membership in Android, with no special advantages. Key executives at Nokia, committed to Symbian or dazzled with the potential they saw in MeeGo, had failed to take sufficient notice of Google's ambitions.

The option of allying with Microsoft was, given what Nokia's executives knew at the time, not an unreasonable option. Although the Gartner Group (a well-respected source of industry forecasts) did not expect Windows Mobile to succeed, other industry analysts predicted Microsoft would gain market share leadership in mobile operating systems by 2016, and some even contemplated Samsung dropping Android in favor of Microsoft. Yet, as with MeeGo, pushing Windows Mobile would be an uphill battle to develop a new, credible ecosystem from a late start—not an enviable undertaking. Within Microsoft itself, there was disagreement about the role of hardware in its future development, with some arguing for Microsoft's exit from all hardware businesses while others pushed for an acquisition of Nokia. Although Microsoft had been remarkably successful, from a market development and market share point of view it had had little success in creating a profitable business from game consoles, its one major hardware product. In 2010, the features offered by Microsoft Windows Mobile lagged behind those of Symbian, but Microsoft engineers were confident they would quickly catch up and create a superior platform. Microsoft proved willing to subsidize Nokia's development of Windows phones (the exact amount was not officially announced, but was rumored to be US$250 million per quarter), providing a welcome cash injection into Nokia's ailing business.

When discussing the options of MeeGo, Android, and Microsoft with a small group of the most senior executives at Nokia just prior to 2010, one of them jumped to a flipchart in the room and drew the diagram in Figure 7.3, intimating that, although no option was perfect, Microsoft was the worst with high risks and low returns.

When I teach the Nokia alliance case (Doz and Wilson, 2016) in executive seminars on alliances I run at INSEAD, the participating managers from a range of companies and industries are usually quick to point out that although no single option was perfect for Nokia, a mix perhaps could have been. They suggest that joining Android could have been a "stopgap" measure, to prevent Nokia from being dependent on an increasingly obsolete Symbian platform. Accelerating the development of MeeGo (as far as the alliance with Intel allowed) and making it compatible with Android—enabling end users to migrate to MeeGo as a "better Android" in the future—would have allowed Nokia to piggyback on the application developers and installed base of Android, while regaining strong differentiation once MeeGo was introduced.

The *Organizational* dimension was also problematic for Nokia. Day to day, the reorganization of 2007 had not resolved any conflicts. The three business groups that had been set up in 2004 were abandoned, but within the new integrated Devices and Services group, apart from the removal of a layer of senior management, nothing much had changed: Devices (products) still had

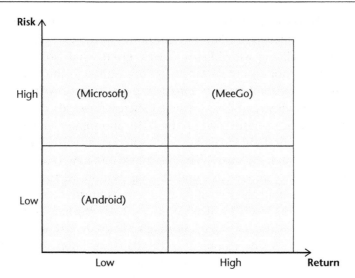

Figure 7.3. Comparative alliance options

to interact and negotiate with Services and Software (including technology platforms) and Markets. Multimedia and Enterprise Solutions phones were folded back into a common entity with Mobile Phones. This was almost a return to pre-2004 NMP. Now, the pull of core mobile phones toward the middle range became even stronger.

To many, the reorganization acknowledged the failure of the product differentiation and market segmentation strategies pursued since 2001. It was not necessarily that these strategies had been unfounded or unwise from a market standpoint, but they were poorly implemented and so did not have a real chance of success. Traditional mobile phones, bolstered by Nokia's huge success in emerging markets, still accounted for nearly all mobile phone sales. Smartphone sales were increasing, but not all that fast, and multimedia products beyond camera phones (a feature which was now adopted in mass-market phones as well) had not met with real success. Nokia's foray into mobile gaming consoles, again a victim of hardware capacity compromises and questionable design, had failed to capture users' imagination. And Enterprise Solutions had not really taken off, partly because Nokia lacked expertise in corporate networks and communication architectures, and had not developed the encryption software that secure communication would have required.

The Services group would, to an extent, replace Multimedia, making multimedia features, software, and content more widely available through the whole product range. However, the challenge would remain for Nokia to establish itself as a distributor of media content, without again entering into conflicts with the network operators (themselves seen by new media entrepreneurs as mere providers of the "pipes," a commodity), a significant challenge for a firm which was now seen as a legacy hardware manufacturer by leading new media types. One media group executive commented, "The problem with Nokia was they didn't even have the credibility any longer to meet the right people."

Once again, it would seem that the approach taken toward the workings of the organization under the new structure was schematic, and to an extent simplistic: organization charts and reporting relationships were redrawn without addressing increasingly problematic behavior issues. Conflicts were now eroding the basic substance of Nokia's culture. In essence, the challenges Nokia now faced could not be solved by changing the firm's structure. As Kallasvuo himself later noted, there were simply too many interdependencies and these were not amenable to an organizational design approach. In very simple terms, the creation of three business groups whose tasks and performance remained interdependent—via the horizontal platforms—created a strong imperative for coordination and collaboration across these units (Zhou, 2013). But that imperative was not met.

Relationships deteriorated further. As one former Nokia leader put it, allegiances had shifted from loyalty toward Nokia and its success, to personal loyalty toward particular individuals or "brotherhoods." This change in loyalties was most visible in the ongoing conflict between Kallasvuo and Vanjoki. Their interpersonal differences were starting to gain precedence over sound, substantive decision making and were leading to consequences of some magnitude: the strategic need to develop a new OS was for many conflated with taking sides in an interpersonal conflict. For example, rivalry between the core phone and smartphone developers reached fever pitch, and resulted in the wings of the smartphone team being clipped to the extent that they were confined to developing tablets (just when the smartphone market was beginning to take off).

The conflict between Kallasvuo and Vanjoki became increasingly acrimonious, partly because they embodied very different views—prudent evolution on Kallasvuo's part and radical change on Vanjoki's—and partly because their personalities and management styles were very different. The fact that Vanjoki was now the last senior leader with a strong view of the industry, and the technologies and strategies its evolution required, was disquieting to Kallasvuo, who was often placed in the position of having to agree or disagree with a forcefully argued position, the basis for which he did not fully grasp. That made him uncomfortable and resulted in a tendency to procrastinate. In retrospect, one can see that having Kallasvuo and Vanjoki coexist in the two most senior roles from 2008 to 2010 became a major source of difficulties. Some people close to Nokia have argued that these tensions could have possibly been diffused to an extent by Ollila, who as chairman of Nokia was still influential, even though by then he devoted most of his time and attention to his role as chairman of the board at Royal Dutch Shell.

Beyond the toll of interpersonal rivalries, there were serious *Emotional* consequences post-2006 resulting from the underdevelopment of Nokia's structural context and the seeming lack of attention to this on the part of Nokia's CEO. A function of a strong structural context in a company is to connect the external performance demands from financial markets with internal measurement and reward systems, so choices can be guided to meet external needs, but not in a simple mechanistic transmission mode. What a well-developed structural context provides is not alignment but buffering. It should protect and shield middle managers from the full force of external pressures, with corporate management absorbing some of those pressures. Yet Kallasvuo did not shield the operating management or middle managers from stock market pressures. Years later, when reflecting on how hard it had been for him to lead Nokia, and asked what his main mistake had been, Kallasvuo responded that rather than do everything to meet market expectations, he should have decreased shareholder returns for two years, and accepted a stock price decline to allow resources to be directed toward sustainable performance rather than current results. This fits with a more general observation researchers have made about shareholders and boards generally contributing to the renewal difficulties incumbent firms face (Benner, 2010).

Over many years the Nokia assessment and reward system, based on trust and transparency, had put considerable emphasis on informal and subjective evaluation by line managers. It's worth noting that within this system Nokians had a high degree of job security, as a poor performance assessment led to a "personal development plan" to improve skills, never termination. In keeping with Nokia Values and a strong team spirit, considerable emphasis in the assessments had been put on how results were achieved (for a detailed analysis see Kolehmainen, 2010). Yet, at the same time, the system became vulnerable to a shift in emphasis to merely "meeting the numbers," and also to a loss of interpersonal trust and a decline in communication. In turn, the integrity of the management control process was compromised, and interactions—including at the top—took a theatrical rather than authentic character. Success in past years having bred "natural optimists," a true, sober assessment of situations was replaced by exceedingly optimistic reports and a denial of rising difficulties.

Success had also led to an ethos of "doing a lot with limited means." Nokia's leaders had inherited a conviction from the firm's heyday that more could actually be done with less, as in the 1990s when targets had been routinely exceeded. During the 2000s, this resulted in a culture in which resourcing was no longer commensurate with expected results. Doing more (and more) with less (and less) was being attempted. In the late 2000s, Nokia's top management found it difficult selectively to connect external demands with internal commitments to enable internal efforts to bear fruit. As the extent of the challenge posed by the iPhone and then Android had not been fully grasped, management's internal demands for ever-greater performance were essentially around "more of the same," only faster and with fewer resources.

A consequence of this "more performance with fewer resources" approach was that Nokia's leaders saw themselves, retrospectively, as having been profligate and lenient in the years of munificence. A form of hubristic self-confidence developed. Ironically, even though performance demands were increasing, poor performance was no longer tolerated and managers who failed to meet targets were openly chastised.

The quality of dialog between top managers and the managerial ranks declined. Some of this was the result of decision overload, while some was a consequence of top managers finding it difficult to engage in substantive dialogs about the specifics of projects. This is a common tendency in maturing, self-confident organizations, and is characterized by a shift from dialogs of substance to theatrically scripted style conversations. In that context, "speaking the truth to power" (Wildavsky, 1987) became increasingly difficult. The forceful personality and temperament of Ollila also became a barrier to specific issues and difficulties percolating all the way to the board and being openly discussed. Although being only one factor among many, fear did play a part in making dialogs more difficult, in particular as pressures grew (Vuori and Huy, 2016). Rather than confront and communicate an uncomfortable reality, middle managers would now more often fall into a denial and cover-up mode. The CORE drivers for this period are summarized in Figure 7.4.

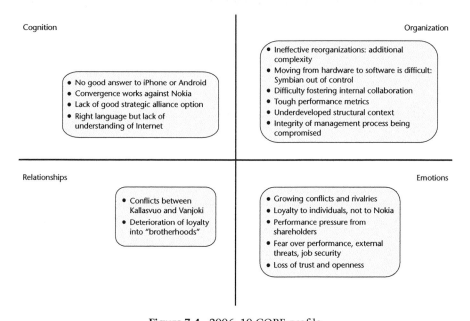

Figure 7.4. 2006–10 CORE profile

References

Elizabeth Altman and Mary Tripsas, "Product to Platform Transitions: Organizational Identity Implications," in *Oxford Handbook of Creativity, Innovation, and Entrepreneurship: Multilevel Linkages*, edited by Christina E. Shalley, Michael A. Hitt, and Jing Zhou (Oxford University Press, Oxford, 2015).

Mary Benner, "Securities Analysts and Incumbent Response to Radical Technological Change: Evidence from Digital Photography and Internet Telephony" (*Organization Science*, Vol. 21 Issue 1, January/February 2010) pp. 42–62.

Yves Doz and Keeley Wilson, *Nokia in 2010: What Are the Alliance Options?* (INSEAD Case Study, 2016).

Thomas Eisenmann, Geoffrey Parker, and Marshall Van Alstyne, "Platform Envelopment" (*Strategic Management Journal*, Vol. 32 Issue 12, 2011) pp. 1270–85.

Katja Kolehmainen, "Dynamic Strategic Performance Measurement Systems: Balancing Empowerment and Alignment" (*Long Range Planning*, Vol. 43 Issue 1, 2010) pp. 527–54.

Jaeyong Song, Kyungmook Lee, and Tarun Khanna, "Dynamic Capabilities at Samsung: Optimizing Internal Co-opetition" (*California Management Review*, Vol. 58 Issue 4, Summer 2016) pp. 118–40.

Timo Vuori and Quy Huy, "Distributed Attention and Shared Emotions in the Innovation Process" (*Administrative Science Quarterly*, Vol. 61 Issue 1, March 2016) pp. 9–51.

Aaron Wildavsky, *Speaking Truth to Power: The Art and Craft of Policy Analysis* (Transaction Publishers, New Brunswick, 1987).

Yue Maggie Zhou, "Designing for Complexity: Using Divisions and Hierarchy to Manage Complex Tasks" (*Organization Science*, Vol. 24 Issue 2, 2013) pp. 339–55.

8

Toward a New Alignment?

The debate around Nokia's future platform strategy had been occupying senior managers throughout 2010, and when Elop took over as CEO this was the most urgent matter facing him. An introvert by nature, Elop was highly analytical and known for his fact-based decision making, and so during his early weeks in Nokia he began assessing the relative merits of the three platform options (Symbian/MeeGo, Android, and Microsoft). In November, despite a project review that had left him with more questions than it had answered, he made a preliminary recommendation to the board to invest in MeeGo. However, in the following weeks, while back in Seattle, he also began talking to Microsoft about a possible strategic alliance between the two firms.

Elop had also begun assessing the state of Nokia more generally. Although results posted by the mobile phone business for 2010 showed revenues up 4.5 percent from the previous year and operating profit up 6.8 percent, this represented slowing growth and denoted underlying problems with Nokia's strategy. One of his first acts within days of joining the firm had been to send an email to all staff asking, among other things, what Nokia's strengths were and what problems the firm faced. He received around 2,000 replies and read and personally responded to each one. He also met with operators, suppliers, shareholders, and developers to deepen his sense of the challenges facing Nokia.

On February 7, 2011, in what has since become known as the "burning platform" memo, Elop sent an email to staff outlining his frank assessment of Nokia's position based on his discussions and analysis over the preceding months. That same day, parts of the memo were leaked, and the following day a full copy appeared on the technology web magazine, *Engadet*.[1] Although the email began innocuously enough, with what staff would later realize was Elop's trademark "Hello there," it went on to regale the story of a man on a burning oil platform in the North Sea faced with two difficult choices: stay on the platform and burn, or risk his life by jumping thirty meters into the cold sea. Elop wrote, "We are standing on a burning platform . . . we have multiple points of scorching heat that are fueling a blazing fire around us."

He went on to describe these in terms of Apple changing the industry and dominating the high end; Google being "a gravitational force drawing much of the industry's innovation to its core"; and Chinese OEMs taking away Nokia's dominance in lower end devices. Nokia had lost ground to its competitors and missed big shifts in the industry. "We poured gasoline on our own burning platform. I believe we have lacked accountability and leadership to align and direct the company through these disruptive times. We had a series of misses. We haven't been delivering innovation fast enough. We're not collaborating internally," continued Elop's assessment.

The memo lamented the fact that MeeGo was taking too long to develop, and that on current projections Nokia would only be able to launch one MeeGo product by the end of the year. He described Symbian as "non-competitive" and concluded that "Our competitors aren't taking our market share with devices; they are taking our market share with an entire ecosystem. This means we're going to have to decide how we either build, catalyze or join an ecosystem."

A New Strategy

In London later that same week (on February 11), Elop announced what he called his new "three-pillar" strategy. First, Nokia would continue producing standard mobile phones using Symbian as a "franchise platform" (with the expectation of selling an additional 150 million units). Second, Symbian smartphones would be discontinued by the summer of that year. The final pillar was the announcement of a strategic alliance with Microsoft to create a new ecosystem using the Windows Phone 7 OS on future Nokia smartphones (Microsoft had released its mobile OS four months previously). The two firms would combine their app stores and would work jointly on developing the platform. Microsoft would incorporate Nokia's mapping services into its browser and AdCenter and be free to license its OS to other phone manufacturers.

In an interview with the BBC that day, sitting next to his old boss, Steve Ballmer, Elop explained, "The industry has shifted from a battle of devices to a war of ecosystems.... It's now a three-horse race. We can take our assets and Microsoft's assets and build that third ecosystem."[2]

News of the new strategy sent a shockwave through Nokia. As Erkki Ormala (Nokia's head of technology policy) recalled, "The announcement that Symbian would be discontinued was a shock. Sales and marketing people in particular were devastated as they didn't have a single phone with the Microsoft OS to sell and wouldn't have one for some time. In such a short time, Elop had killed Symbian and abandoned MeeGo, making us entirely dependent upon Microsoft." Reaction from the markets wasn't any more supportive, with Nokia's share price falling 14.7 percent upon the announcement.

To ensure customers using Symbian phones were supported, Nokia outsourced maintenance of the platform to Accenture, transferring around 2,300 Symbian engineers. The agreement with Accenture continued until the beginning of 2014 when support for Symbian was finally withdrawn.

With uncertainty about when the first Nokia-Microsoft phone would be released, and with a MeeGo smartphone (the N9) close to completion, Elop had been persuaded by Nokia's head of design, Marko Ahtisaari, to complete and release the N9 before walking away from the MeeGo partnership with Intel. Talking about this, Ahtisaari told me, "There was a Nokia nostalgia around the N9 and it had a strong design identity." Disappointed with Elop's new strategy, a handful of senior executives left Nokia, including Alberto Torres, who was an enthusiastic believer in MeeGo and had been leading its development.

The loss of some executives was perhaps inevitable, but rather than fill senior positions with outsiders, in a move that was much appreciated internally, Elop undertook a management reshuffle that saw the majority of senior roles taken by Nokians: Jo Harlow moved from Symbian to head Smart Devices, Kai Öistämö was moved from leading the Devices group to become head of strategy, Mary McDowell remained in charge of Mobile Phones, and both Timo Ihamuotila and Juha Äkräs remained in their roles as CFO and head of HR respectively. In October that year, when Elop created a new Location and Commerce division (containing Navteq plus Nokia's other location services operations), another Nokian, Michael Halbherr, was put in charge.

Even though he had shown a degree of cultural and organizational sensitivity in appointing his senior management team, Elop's personal management style wasn't universally applauded by those working most closely with him. A combination of his natural introversion and reliance on email as his primary mode of communication distanced him and frustrated many of his senior colleagues. Describing Elop, Juka Äkräs told me, "In contrast to Kallasvuo, who always tried to understand other people and approached everything by being open, trusting, and supportive, Elop never got to know people. He remained extremely fact-based and distant." With his family still in Seattle, Elop was constantly traveling between Finland and the West Coast of the US and his senior colleagues noticed this taking its toll, as Elop became progressively less strategic and more reactive—something they put down to a combination of jet lag, tiredness, and a difficult job.

Middle managers and engineers further down the organization had initially been very supportive of Elop. Finally, they felt Nokia had someone at the helm who understood software and spoke their language. He had a more open and inclusive style of management—his regular (some would say constant) emails kept everyone in the loop and the fact that he personally responded to emails was greatly valued. However, their hope and optimism was short-lived.

For decades, Nokia's managers had done everything in their power to avoid heavy job losses in any of the company's businesses, particularly in Finland where Nokia was the country's main employer of highly skilled workers. Although shrinking market share and decreasing revenues had been threatening jobs at Nokia for some time, Elop's new strategy would inevitably lead to significant reductions in headcount, and these began in April 2011. By June the following year 21,500 staff had been made redundant globally—Finland saw a personnel reduction of almost 44 percent, with many jobs being lost due to the closure and downsizing of R&D sites. To try and support those staff who lost their jobs, a program called "Bridge" was put in place. As well as providing support for job searches, Bridge also funded retraining and provided grants and support services for new business start-ups—including businesses based on ideas that had been developed in Nokia but were being dropped due to the new strategy.

Working with Microsoft

For over a decade, senior managers at Nokia had viewed Microsoft as the most likely disrupter to their industry—the prospect of Microsoft coming to dominate mobile communications in much the same way that it had the PC industry was a fear never far from strategic discussions. And so, when considering Nokia's platform options prior to Elop's arrival in Nokia, senior managers had been very wary of an alliance with Microsoft and concerned about how they could work with the Seattle firm without being dominated by them. The new CEO's experience of Microsoft not only calmed nerves within Nokia, but would prove an advantage in designing the interfaces between the two firms in the new alliance. Roles were mapped to ensure executives and senior engineers had counterparts in the other firm as a primary point of contact for agreeing policy, product architecture, features, and development schedules. This mapping resulted in some new roles being created within Nokia.

Despite the specter of job losses looming large, a new air of optimism began to permeate Nokia. After years of indecision, there was now a defined platform strategy (even if it wasn't the preferred option for many Nokians), and as the alliance got underway the discipline, quality, and speed with which their Microsoft counterparts worked impressed Nokia's engineers. In fact, the first two Nokia Windows OS phones, the mid-range Lumia 710 and high-end 800, were announced in early October 2011 (with release dates scheduled for November and December 2011 respectively).

The honeymoon period didn't last long though. As release dates for the first Lumia devices drew closer, fundamental problems with Microsoft's Windows OS began to emerge and it became increasingly apparent within Nokia that the software being developed by their new partner was not as advanced as they had been led to believe. It supported fewer features than had been available with Symbian: the support for different languages was limited and didn't come close to the requirements of many of Nokia's operator customers; it didn't support video calls; multimedia messages for sending pictures only worked on a handful of standards; it wasn't compatible with games consoles or other devices; security was basic and didn't meet the requirements of business users; and the Windows OS was only designed for touchscreens and didn't support qwerty keyboards on phones (which was a common design feature at the time on mid-range and lower end phones that Nokia sold in huge volumes in emerging markets).

Nokia engineers became increasingly frustrated with these shortcomings. This frustration rapidly turned into disillusionment, as their Microsoft colleagues dismissed any concerns they raised and instead plowed ahead making all of the design and development decisions without heeding the warnings and concerns raised by their Nokia counterparts.

The software limitations plaguing the Lumia range were exacerbated by marketing and distribution problems in the key US market. The iPhone and Android had already established such a strong grip on the market that the three large operators, AT&T, Verizon, and T-Mobile, showed little interest in the arrival of the third ecosystem. Similarly, the Windows platform had failed to attract the numbers of app developers needed to make it a viable and attractive alternative to entice customers away from the iPhone or Android ecosystems they had become used to. Even though the pricing of Lumia phones was very competitive, their launch failed to have an impact with either critics or consumers.

The End of MeeGo at Nokia

Two months prior to the troubled launch of the first Lumia phone, in September 2011, Nokia had released its N9 based on the MeeGo platform. Ironically, the N9 was a success with critics, lauded for its elegant design, ease of use, and browsing speed. The general consensus among reviewers was that the N9 seemed to have recaptured the true spirit of Nokia. While most lamented the fact that Nokia would not be releasing more phones in this range, they seem to have overlooked a critical point and one which Elop had been only too aware of in making his decision to discontinue the development of MeeGo: no matter how good the N9 and MeeGo were, competing in this new "war of ecosystems" would mean building an entire platform ecosystem from scratch in a very short time frame to rival the now entrenched iOS and Android platforms. The very fact that no one (not even Microsoft) has subsequently succeeded in achieving this speaks volumes as to the near impossibility of this task. And so, despite its technical and design achievements, sales of the N9 were understandably poor, as the appeal of a smartphone running what was about to become an abandoned OS was limited.

Struggling to Find a Place in the New Competition

In 2011, as Nokia was finding its feet with the Microsoft alliance, operating profit in the mobile phone businesses dropped sharply to 884 million euros, down 75 percent from the previous year. Performance didn't improve the following year, as Apple consolidated its hold on the high end of the smartphone market and Samsung Android phones came to dominate the low to middle ground. Symbian sales in emerging economies also dropped away, as consumers had little appetite to buy a phone with an OS that was being phased out and Chinese producers were out-innovating Nokia at the low end and undercutting prices at the same time.

Reflecting on this troubled period, CFO Timo Ihamuotila explained, "What we missed was that customers would not readily migrate to a different type of user interface. The Windows user interface was really too different from Symbian and if customers had to learn a new interface they might as well switch to another brand on a different ecosystem. We overestimated brand loyalty and weren't innovative enough." As the depth and breadth of Nokia's troubles were becoming clear, in May 2012, after twenty-seven years at Nokia, Ollila stepped down as chairman of the group. He was replaced by Risto Siilasmaa.

Siilasmaa was a tech entrepreneur, co-founder of cyber-security firm F-Secure, and one of Finland's few dotcom billionaires. F-Secure provided security software for Nokia phones, and in 1999 Kallasvuo joined the board of F-Secure followed in 2005 by Baldauf. Through these connections, Ollila and Siilasmaa became acquainted, and in 2008 Ollila invited Siilasmaa to join Nokia's board.

On taking over as chairman, Siilasmaa took a different approach to his predecessor. He knew Nokia was in trouble and believed the board had a decisive role to play in steering the firm back to calmer waters, and so immediately set about changing the way the board worked. At the first meeting he chaired, the directors agreed to a new set of seven operating principles which included being open, honest, and direct, engaging much more deeply with management, and investing time and effort in data analysis to map out future scenarios. All directors would also need to increase the time they spent working on Nokia by a third. As Siilasmaa felt a key role for the board was to define strategy, with the CEO focusing on implementing that strategy, much more of the board's time would be devoted to strategic issues and less to compliance.

Based on his experience of running a smaller, more entrepreneurial and flexible company, Siilasmaa believed it was crucial that the tone of board meetings reflect a shift away from the selling of ideas toward honest, open dialog. He saw it as critical to undo what he observed had become an entrenched culture of keeping bad news from percolating upwards through Nokia's management hierarchy and ultimately to the board, and so he had regular meetings with executive managers, all of which had to begin with a piece of "bad news." Siilasmaa had developed a heuristic in which he perceived "good news as being bad news," because only good news implied something has been missed or hidden. Conversely, "bad news is good news" because it stimulates dialog, problem solving, and constructive action!

As it happened, the board didn't have to look far for bad news as throughout 2012 the position of Nokia's phone businesses worsened. Revenues for the year were down 34.5 percent to 15,686 million euros, and for the first time in the business' history an operating loss was recorded of 1,100 million euros. Having dropped as low as US$1.6 during the summer, Nokia Group's share price closed the year at just under US$4, with the group's market capitalization having fallen 91 percent in the twelve years from 2000. Toward the end of 2012, the first fully Nokia-designed Lumia phone, the 920, was launched to positive reviews and so it was hoped this would revive sales. When the expected sales volumes didn't materialize, it became clear that the market had rejected a Microsoft OS platform and Elop's three-pillar strategy had failed.

Selling the Phones Business to Save the Group

Over the course of 2012, Nokia's board became progressively more concerned about the viability of Nokia's phones business and about the intentions of its strategic partner to move into the devices arena on its own. Mid-year, Microsoft had announced it would launch the Surface range of tablets and Steve Ballmer played up Microsoft's move into devices in his letter to shareholders ahead of the company's AGM that fall. The feeling in Nokia's board, according to Siilasmaa, was that "If Microsoft could go into competition with HP and Dell, who were their number one partners, then why not us too? When we approached them about their intentions, Microsoft didn't deny the possibility of doing a smartphone by themselves."

Microsoft indicated they wanted to talk and Nokia's board were keen to understand what their Seattle partner was thinking. So in February 2013, Siilasmaa and Ballmer met in Barcelona and began discussing a possible sale of Nokia's phone business to Microsoft. Over the coming year, Nokia's board would meet no fewer than thirty-four times to discuss the sale within the broader context of Nokia's survival.

Steve Ballmer and Microsoft executives believed that by acquiring Nokia's phone businesses the Seattle firm would have the opportunity to build a strong ecosystem and compete head-on with its rival Apple in both proprietary hardware and software. It would be able to offer its own services, such as Skype and Office, seamlessly integrated into its devices. Even though Nokia was in trouble, Microsoft recognized that Nokia's phone business still had strong global brand and a large installed base—which would be easier to exploit than building a business from scratch.

The discussions between Nokia and Microsoft teetered on the brink of failure a number of times before Siilasmaa and Ballmer finally shook hands on a deal they were both happy with. Unfortunately, Microsoft's board had been caught by surprise at the proposed acquisition and rejected the deal. A few months later on September 3, 2013, with Microsoft's board now in agreement, the acquisition of Nokia's phone businesses for 5.44 billion euros (just over US$7 billion) was announced. After a meteoric rise, the fall of its phones business had been so severe that, to save the rest of the company, Nokia's board had agreed its sale.

Nokia Reborn

Just as twenty-three years earlier Nokia had transformed itself from a diversified conglomerate on the cusp of bankruptcy to being the brightest star in the global mobile communications industry, the sale of its faltering phone business marked a turning point in the renewal of the firm.

During the short period between the announcement and closing of the deal to sell the mobile phones business to Microsoft, Nokia's board had come up with a new vision and strategy for the company. They had come to the conclusion that the very change in the industry that had brought about the demise of its phone business presented a significant growth opportunity for Nokia Siemens Networks (NSN)—the joint venture company that had absorbed the infrastructure businesses of Nokia and Siemens back in 2006. The growth in mobile phone usage, and in particular wireless Internet traffic, was leading to network operators looking to introduce new very high-speed networks—known as 5G.

With the new infrastructure-focused strategy in sight, while negotiations with Microsoft over the sale of the phone business were underway, Nokia's board had approached Siemens to acquire their share of the joint venture, NSN. Nokia, however, did not have the funds to buy out Siemens, and so Siilasmaa had made it a precondition of his continuing negotiations with

Microsoft that the US firm provide a commercial loan to Nokia of US$1.5 billion to fund the buy-out.

This was a period of true uncertainty for Nokia. Until the buy-out from Siemens was concluded, NSN was still an independent entity, and if the sale of the phone business to Microsoft failed for some reason then Nokia would be left with a business which could sink the entire company. Using this time in limbo to plan for the future, Nokia's board outlined a new organizational structure and selected a new management team to lead the company. At the beginning of July 2013, just two months before the announcement of the sale of their phones business to Microsoft, Nokia acquired Siemens' share of NSN, renaming the infrastructure business Nokia Solutions and Networks.

This marked the beginning of a real turnaround for Nokia. From recording the biggest loss in the firm's recent history in 2012, Nokia posted an operating profit of 672 million euros in 2013. In May 2014, (once the sale of Nokia's phone business to Microsoft was complete), Rajeev Suri moved from heading Nokia Solutions and Networks to become CEO of Nokia. Suri had joined Nokia in 1995 and worked in a range of functions and regions within the infrastructure business.

As Nokia began to strengthen its position in infrastructure, its performance in 2014 was up on the previous year, with operating profit more than doubling to 1,412 million euros. With a clear strategy now in place and a return to financial health, 2015 was an important year for Nokia. On April 15, it announced the acquisition of Alcatel-Lucent through a share purchase worth 15.6 billion euros to create the world's second-largest infrastructure firm, just behind Ericsson.

The Alcatel-Lucent deal gave the combined group one of the strongest R&D capabilities in the industry through the combination of Bell Labs in the US with Nokia Technologies. It also put Nokia in a very strong position in the US market—an area in which it had been weak for some time. In a press release the day the purchase was closed (in January 2016), Suri wrote, "Today's pace of technological change, driven by the transition to 5G, the Internet of Things and the cloud, is demanding extraordinary new capabilities from the network. Combining with Alcatel-Lucent comes at just the right time: we can align our product and technology roadmaps for the next generation of network technology at the outset, allowing us to take full advantage of the coming opportunities... Nokia has the global scale, innovation muscle and end-to-end portfolio to lead this change." The other big landmark, redefining and focusing Nokia in 2015, was the sale of its mapping business HERE (previously Navteq) to a consortium of Audi, BMW, and Daimler for 2.8 billion euros.

In October 2015, in anticipation of the completion of the Alcatel-Lucent acquisition, Suri announced a new structure for the group. The networks business would be organized into four business groups: Mobile Networks,

Fixed Networks, Applications and Analytics, and IP Optical networks. With this synergistic grouping, Nokia planned to be able to deliver hardware, software, and solutions for every type of communication network. Ironically, with the phone business gone, Nokia would continue to live up to its promise of "connecting people."

Commentary

Events during Stephen Elop's tenure as CEO of Nokia remain very controversial in Finland to this day, in particular his decisions to drop Symbian and stop developing MeeGo, and instead commit to collaborating with Microsoft around a Windows platform. A more positive perspective on his actions suggests that by signaling the end of Symbian he merely did what was really required—he put an end to procrastination and delays, and that was perhaps something only someone new to Nokia could do.

One has to ask, however, whether there could have been a better approach than the "burning platform" memo? Over the previous years, Kallasvuo had grown increasingly frustrated with only being able to "prune the Symbian tree"—i.e. to reduce the number of distinct versions of Symbian used in Nokia's product range. This had proved a slow and not entirely successful process, as by 2010 Symbian was still so unwieldy and portability of applications across versions so uncertain that application developers were abandoning it. Symbian was obsolete and now outperformed by both iOS and Android. It was clear that, despite all his efforts, Kallasvuo had failed to gain much traction internally over the problems with Symbian.

Elop's "burning platform" memo, sent to all staff, delivered a stark message internally and, once it was leaked, the outside world was also under no illusions about the problems at Nokia. Even though many developers at Nokia were still attached to Symbian, customers started to desert the platform. This signaled its end, and the armies of Symbian developers in Nokia rapidly began to shrink and were finally disbanded. Given the inertia of a very large installed base, this process should ideally have taken place more progressively over a few years. However, internal inertia proved Symbian's downfall, as vested interests within Nokia had for too long propelled the continuation of Symbian development and stifled the development of its replacement.

If Elop's handling of the end of Symbian raised a "how?" (or more exactly, "how fast?") question, his other, even more controversial decision about its replacement, raised "what?" and "why?" questions. Many defenders of Symbian and MeeGo in Finland have fallen back on conspiracy theories to explain Elop's decisions, along the lines of, "what else would you expect from a Microsoft executive than to favor Microsoft?" Yet there is no real support for this "Trojan Horse" hypothesis except, perhaps, that Elop's past familiarity with Microsoft would have instinctively influenced his judgment. The reality was far more prosaic. Although Elop himself was not interviewed for our research, and has otherwise remained tight-lipped about his tenure at Nokia, it seems the train of events, once again, was a series of partial commitments over time.

At the end of the summer 2010, Elop was reported to have convened a senior management retreat to review the status of MeeGo. He apparently prefaced the meeting by saying he didn't want a rosy picture painted but sought an honest assessment, including the worst-case scenario. MeeGo project members saw this as an opportunity to reset expectations to a more realistic level, after the forced and exaggerated optimism that had prevailed in recent years. Their presentation was sobering. In short, a lot remained to be done to introduce MeeGo, even if they initially relied on an Apple-like approach of releasing a single product family. Over the Christmas holidays back in Seattle, with time to reflect, the idea of a Microsoft-Nokia alliance was said to have gained salience in his mind.

With the benefit of hindsight, dropping MeeGo entirely was perhaps a hasty decision, as an Android-compatible MeeGo, which would have brought portability and a critical mass of apps, could have overcome the inherent problems of building a third ecosystem. But at the time it was probably difficult for Elop to disentangle quickly what were real technical challenges for MeeGo from the fact the project was overstaffed and suffered from bureaucratic shackles. In any event, MeeGo was spun out into a new entity, Jolla, run by some of MeeGo's long-standing developers.

In assessing the Elop era, the conspiracy theorists go one step further and suggest that Microsoft misrepresented its own capabilities to Nokia and hid the fact that Windows Mobile 7 had numerous weaknesses that were hard to remedy. Once again, the truth may have been more mundane. At the time, Microsoft suffered from many of the same bureaucratic ailments as Nokia, and its CEO, Steve Ballmer, who was under growing pressure, was very demanding. Under these conditions, it would not be surprising if Microsoft's engineers had just been overly optimistic about their ability to complete and improve Windows Mobile 7 quickly. They did in fact work eagerly and diligently toward that goal.

Amid all this change, managers at Nokia also underestimated both the power and the limits of their brand. Customers liked and were familiar with Nokia's distinctive user interface and that famous ringtone! Although different types of user interfaces to Nokia's scrolling menus were in some respects superior, Nokia underestimated the discontinuity that adopting a new interface would impose on its customers. Faced with having to adapt to a new Microsoft interface many Nokia customers decided to switch to Android or

Apple. While customers had remained loyal to Nokia even though the quality of its products had been declining for some years, that loyalty did not extend to a Nokia-Microsoft alliance.

The combination of the accelerated demise of Symbian (and with it the abrupt end of Nokia's existing range of phones), Microsoft's failure to deliver on its improvement commitments for Windows Mobile, and the rapid loss of large numbers of once-loyal customers deterred by the high switching costs of moving to a new OS, would sound the death knell for Nokia's mobile phones business.

Faced with this intractable problem, Nokia once again demonstrated considerable strategic agility—not by saving its mobile phone business but by selling it. And, luckily, timing was on Nokia's side. When Steve Ballmer first put the deal he had made with Siilasmaa to acquire Nokia's mobile phone operations to Microsoft's board, to his great surprise it was rejected. Microsoft's board were not actually against the proposal per se, but concerned about Ballmer's independence—they felt insufficiently involved in Microsoft's strategic decisions and had some genuine doubts about the firm's involvement in hardware. When a more convincingly argued proposal was put before Microsoft's board a few months later, it was accepted. In the interim, a cash-strapped Nokia had negotiated to purchase Siemens' 50 percent share in NSN for a very good price. Paradoxically, had Microsoft made its 5.44 billion euro commitment to acquire the phone business after Ballmer's initial proposal, a cash-rich Nokia would have been in a weaker position to negotiate a favorable deal with Siemens.

By focusing on the loss of its phone business, it is easy to overlook the fact that Nokia had successfully extricated itself from a very dangerous situation. When I interviewed Timo Ihamuotila, then CFO of Nokia, the first thing he asked me when I walked into his office was, "Of the many companies that entered the mobile phone business on the basis of the innovations in radio loop technologies, how many are left today?" As I searched for the elusive answer, he added, "None. Alcatel, Philips, Siemens, Motorola, Ericsson . . . they are all gone from mobile phones. We were the last, and we stayed too long."

Nokia had come full circle in exiting mobile phones.

Notes

1. For the full text of the "burning platform" memo, see <https://www.engadget.com/2011/02/08/nokia-ceo-stephen-elop-rallies-troops-in-brutally-honest-burnin/#>.
2. To watch the interview, see <http://www.bbc.com/news/business-12427680>.

9

The Astronomer's Perspective

The exploration journey at Nokia we have reported and analyzed in this book, started with a fundamental theoretical "whodunit?" question about strategic management with competing hypotheses: How much do executive decisions and commitments matter to strategic outcomes? And would population ecology arguments or an evolutionary perspective provide stronger explanations of Nokia's rise and fall in mobile phones than strategic management?

In reflecting on the story we have narrated, a more nuanced assessment than an "either/or" answer emerges. Rather than compete, the different perspectives complement each other. In short, all matter, but not equally strongly at each point in time. Considering the flow of unfolding events presented in previous chapters, it is clear that a few key decisions made in the early 1990s explain Nokia's success, while decisions mostly made in the 2001–5 period and often based on heuristics inherited from the past largely shaped Nokia's subsequent decline. These latter decisions set in motion a course of events leading to a stunted evolution toward strategic stasis, and made escaping from it nearly impossible. Strategic stasis arose from a hyper-stable configuration of activities resulting from unintended interplay between decisions made independently from each other in the early 2000s. Key leadership appointments in the mid-2000s further reinforced the strategic stasis that was by now gripping Nokia.

This strategic stasis proved impossible to break until a new CEO, Stephen Elop, was appointed in the fall of 2010 and took drastic measures, such as issuing the "burning platform" memo that dramatized the crisis Nokia faced, and heralded the end of the Symbian OS in February 2011. By then, no matter whether Elop's choices were good or bad, external selection played the major role. In essence, the increasingly important third-party application developers abandoned Nokia in favor of Apple and Google. And end users followed. Even if the Nokia-Microsoft collaboration had succeeded better and faster than it did, and provided less of a challenge in user interface and ease of migration from Symbian, by then it was too late to build a third application and content ecosystem to challenge Apple and Google. The same would have been true of a continuation of MeeGo, should that route have been chosen.

We can now begin to answer our central question, first in explaining the successes of the 1990s and then exploring and explaining the decline and downfall of the 2000s.

Explaining the Early Success

Explaining success at Nokia, like elsewhere, is less difficult and controversial than exploring failure. Even so, success is more fortuitous than human beings looking for repeatable rather than serendipitous patterns would like to believe. Although corporate leaders typically assign success to their own brilliance, dispassionate analysis would suggest this is rarely the case (Gaba et al., 2010).

However, Nokia's success in mobile phones was neither the fruit of a repeatable recipe, nor an accidental, fortuitous occurrence. It resulted from the interplay of many successful steps, which contributed to Finland's emergence as an innovation ecosystem for mobile telephony, much to the surprise of the rest of the world. These steps resulted from the converging actions of many different actors in Finland: Nokia's visionary CEOs, Westerlund and Kairamo, and then Ollila and his "dream team." But also the heads of Tekes, Sitra, and many Finnish civil servants, regulators, and policymakers who sought economic modernization, military leaders who saw the value of mobile radio communication, and educators who quickly built outstanding technical universities. Innovators and scientists also played a key role, Yrjö Neuvo in particular. Finland, as a small, highly networked society, with a strong collective identity, provided fertile terrain for Nokia to succeed.

Nokia's success was also the result of a remarkable feat of associative thinking in its leadership, committing it to becoming a technology-based global telecom equipment company, rather than a flailing Finnish—or even European—conglomerate. Nokians "connected more dots" more quickly than their early competitors and, at the beginning of the 1990s, had indeed achieved a form of industry "intellectual leadership" in mobile communication that Gary Hamel and others would encourage them to attempt to rekindle a few years later.

Strategic foresight and intellectual leadership would have no value if not acted upon. Nokia was successful in transforming ambition and vision into concrete product development roadmaps and programs, and adhering to them. Serendipity did play a role in bringing to Nokia (with the Technophone acquisition) a manufacturing leader, Frank McGovern, who had deep experience in deploying Japanese manufacturing excellence in Europe and was passionate about building new skills. Nokia survived the supply chain chaos that resulted from extremely fast (and unplanned) growth and used the opportunity to become stronger and more rigorous, and to build a scalable supply chain system on the back of an SAP ERP innovation. As Andy Grove used to say when he was heading Intel, "In a crisis weak companies disappear, others barely survive, but strong companies use the opportunity to become even stronger." This set Nokia on its extraordinary growth trajectory in the late 1900s and to industry leadership.

At the time though, Nokia's mobile phones business model was remarkably simple: designing, engineering, and manufacturing products (three areas where it excelled) and then selling them to telecom service operators and other distributors worldwide, largely on the back of the spreading deregulation of telecom services and the success of the GSM standard. Nokia managed to build one of the top brands in the world—best known and best liked—without having to engage in complex marketing efforts. In mobile phones Nokia was in a sellers' market (where many of their new products were "on allocation"—i.e. rationed quantities delivered to operators eager for more). The intrinsic value to consumers of mobile phones and the ambition of mobile service operators were "pulling" Nokia's growth, and also that of its major competitors, most notably Motorola and Ericsson.

Understanding the Decline

In short, in a first phase leading to the decline, pre-2005, managerial volition played the most critical role. The second phase, until 2011, resulted from the interplay of the consequences of these decisions leading to strategic stasis (the result of a stunted evolution). This led to a third phase when environmental selection forces had become too strong for Nokia's management to stem disaster, except by divesting the phones business to Microsoft. Table 9.1 provides a summary view of key causes of difficulties during each phase, which we will now discuss in more detail.

Phase 1: Management Volition

Poor management choices contributed to strategic stasis. In 2000, to go for product differentiation and proliferation based on hardware features without fully recognizing the demands Symbian's integrated architecture would put on software development was a management decision. Implementing a new organizational structure in 2004 and not anticipating the possible difficulties for middle managers operating in a matrix organization in which product lines carried profit and loss responsibility but depended on horizontal

Table 9.1. Three phases toward strategic failure

2000–6	2006–10	2010–13
Phase 1: Why were decisions in 2001–6 "bad" in their consequences?	**Phase 2:** How did strategic stasis emerge?	**Phase 3:** Why was strategic stasis hyper-stable (and so hard to break)?
■ Relying on inherited heuristics	■ Inefficient resource-draining matrix	■ High tensions, vested interests
■ Fragmented, narrowly bound decisions and "creeping commitments"	■ Product-centric cognition	■ Interpersonal conflicts
■ Adolescent company	■ Strategic vacuum at the top	■ Weak leadership
■ Global but parochial management	■ Intellectual understanding, practical action deficiencies	■ "Après moi le déluge"
	■ Cultural misfit, geographic factors	
Primacy of management volition	**Primacy of (stunted) evolution, strategic stasis**	**Primacy of environmental selection**

Source: Adapted from Doz (unpublished).

"platform" units for most activities and resources, can be seen as an oversight. Not preparing staff for the matrix and not designing a full structural context were shortcomings.

Key leadership appointments in 2004–6 led to management heuristics which shifted commitments in the wrong direction, reinforcing a hardware product-orientation and cost-reduction priority at the very moment when they should have been questioned. Software application-based differentiation and value enhancement would have been better forward-looking choices. But by that time, the key leaders who could have changed the strategic direction of the company were leaving or had been sidetracked. Leaders in power post-2004 were less strategic and more oriented toward "management by numbers," incremental decisions, and delegation to old, trusted phone business executives. And they had unleashed the entrepreneurial energy of the product line executives without balancing that energy with collaborative skills and concerns for collective success.

Formal power remained concentrated in the person of Ollila himself, the artisan of Nokia's success in mobile telecom equipment in the 1990s, who was simultaneously CEO and chairman, but whose interest and understanding in managing Nokia in a complex post-Internet era were no longer as great as they had been in the 1990s. And when he became chairman only, he was keen to step back and let Kallasvuo and his management run the company. A strategic vacuum developed at the top, and key strategic arenas, such as the New Business Development Forum, were discontinued or lost influence. Strategic awareness and sensitivity declined.

Heuristics from Crisis-Driven Learning

Earlier experience influenced decisions being made as Nokia's leadership and senior management developed a set of strong heuristics from traumatic experiences and crises, the solutions to which became "principles" for future action. These principles sometimes resulted from unconscious or unintended learning (Hedberg et al., 1976; Miller and Friesen, 1980). In emerging adolescent companies that have grown very fast, traumatic events (at the individual level) are particularly important: lessons drawn from them become permanently "imprinted," guiding future action into repetitive patterns even if they have been forgotten, or taken for granted.

In Nokia's recent history, a number of such traumatic events stand out. In the 1980s, the failure of the conglomerate strategy and the crisis in the late 1980s led to a strong "every tub on its own bottom" approach, and beyond acquisitions and divestitures Nokia did not manage resource allocation strategically. The logic of financial control rather than strategic control came to prevail (Goold et al., 1993). The infighting between business group heads that followed Kairamo's sudden death was another traumatic event, the ugliness of which led the young executives on the "dream team" to swear never to engage in interpersonal conflicts and commit to doing their best in acting as a team. Failure in consumer electronics, where Nokia had unsuccessfully attempted to assemble a coherent business from the acquisition of many weak companies, led to an enduring aversion toward acquisitions.

Another strong and critical set of heuristics stems from NMP's remarkably simple and powerful business model of the 1990s. To successfully implement it, Nokia had to design outstanding products of high quality and build and deliver them at low cost. Hence the key tenets of Nokia's strategic context were: the primacy of a product orientation (reflected in product roadmaps and well-timed and adhered-to introduction schedules); tight cost control (leading to a bill of materials culture and intense unit cost-reduction efforts); an efficient supply system; and an orientation toward product families with common core kernels and varied features (a way to achieve product differentiation without losing scale efficiencies). This shaped a very robust but also rigid context, both strategic and organizational. It was a good fit for the environment of the 1990s, and provided powerful and scalable simplicity (Siggelkow, 2002).

The 1995 logistics crisis was clearly a traumatic event, leading to tighter controls and an emphasis on "management by numbers" (that would later come to prevail over the management by values favored by Ollila and his team in the early 1990s). The "Cannes crisis," as the 2004 boycott of Nokia by major European operators came to be known, provided yet another example of a traumatic event. Here the lesson was, essentially, not to encroach on operators' territory, around services and consumer relations in particular.

The excessive reliance on trusted executives, and the belief that "good men could do anything," was yet another key heuristic. This had perhaps been true among a tightly knit "band of brothers" reporting to the "dream team" and running a relatively simple business that was a runaway success in the 1990s. But by the 2000s it had serious toxic side effects. Management rotations led to executives having to develop new understandings and capabilities, perhaps a well-intentioned policy in principle (although skeptics would suspect this was also a way for Ollila to prevent others from developing deep domain competence and a stable power base and be tempted to challenge his power), but one that weakened the capability to execute key leadership roles effectively. Key executives would also read the specifics of rotations with an interpersonal and political lens, not a developmental and professional one. This bred growing skepticism and suspicion. It also resulted in personal trust in people trumping professional competence. Trust is necessarily backward-looking, built over time, and fragile, not an incentive for bold action and strong initiative. No wonder trusted lieutenants from the core traditional mobile phone business, whose skills were ill suited to new challenges, came to hold key positions, whereas the heralds of change were kept at bay.

Figure 9.1 outlines the various traumatic events and shows each of them providing an additional "layer" of learning. As in a sedimentation process, the earlier layers harden and become unquestionable heuristics for future action. The fact that, under duress, earlier learning is reactivated and more recent learning forgotten, further contributed to this hardening of heuristics into providing a very strong momentum for the continuity of behavior and action (Miller and Friesen, 1980).

Once imprinted, a heuristic is extremely difficult to change. The strategic rationale for it is easily forgotten and the steps from strategy to orthodoxy are not easily visible or reversible (see Figure 9.2). Gandhi put this more poetically:

> Your beliefs become your thoughts,
> Your thoughts become your words,
> Your words become your actions,
> Your actions become your habits,
> Your habits become your values,
> Your values become your destiny.

Throughout the 1980–2010 period, things were happening very fast. Nokia's executives were seldom given the time to sit back and question emerging orthodoxies. They did not reflect in depth about how their organization actually worked and whether this would be effective in the future, as both Nokia's business model and its organization were rapidly becoming more complex. By inclination and culture, they were not likely to dwell on organizational

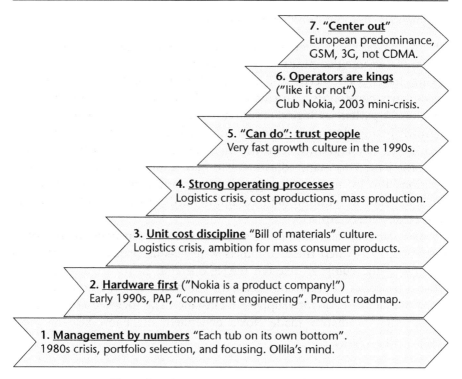

Figure 9.1. From traumatic events to heuristics

choices, and lacked the first-hand experience of senior positions in other complex companies to understand their importance. Baldauf, who had displayed thoughtful organizational design skills in the late 1980s, was running Nokia Networks throughout the period and by 2004 was about to move on to other interests outside Nokia, as was Alahuhta, who had anticipated the need to prepare managers to operate in a matrix organization.

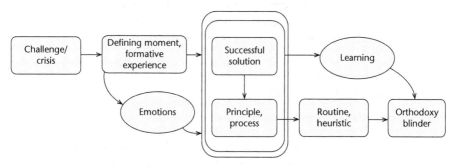

Figure 9.2. Growing "sacred cows"

Fragmented Decisions and "Creeping Commitments"

In our conversations over recent years, Ala-Pietilä suggested Nokia was a victim of "creeping commitments" (a term he used in referring to the most taxing challenges he faced). And indeed Nokia was subject to significant path-dependency constraints, particularly around Symbian, as discussed in earlier chapters. A pattern of logical decisions, each made in good faith but in a narrowly bounded context, yielded inconsistent and even destructive results. Each decision was framed narrowly and influenced by heuristics inherited from the past. This made adjustment to new realities difficult. Fragmented decisions also led to the development of creeping commitments: decisions made in a narrow frame would have unintended consequences that severely restricted further adaptation.

Nokia's strategy for mobile phones also became very dependent on that of its customers, even when these customers were making poor choices. Powerful customers—the European telecom service operators in particular—reinforced Nokia's heuristics by imposing their own commitment to "third-generation" (3G) GSM standards, on their suppliers for instance. This triggered a co-evolution process that ultimately made Nokia dependent on a few key operators (Burgelman, 2002).

Global Company, Parochial Management

Nokia succeeded globally in a light-footed way very fast in the 1990s, and started to hire non-Finns as managers. However, its culture, processes, and decision making remained very home-centric. This was possible because simple "voice" phones were largely universal products, apart from technical standards in North America and North East Asia and differences in languages for user interfaces.

When multimedia phones and the shift of Internet-driven innovation to North America and Asia called for more diversity, Nokia remained largely home-centric in its top management, and was unable to integrate voices and knowledge from a periphery that was now leading the industry.

Phase 2: Stunted Evolution

When Strategy Follows Structure

As we stressed in previous chapters, although Nokia did not develop a full structural context, elements of context came to drive commitments. The financial control perspective adopted in considering the corporate role and defining how to run Nokia in the 1980s remained embedded even though the business portfolio contained only two closely related businesses. Breaking up NMP into groups and product lines restored the distinct corporate management roles of a conglomerate but in a matrix organization where common resources were to be shared. To entrust the allocation of these scarce resources to committees, where consensus and commitment were supposed to emerge, proved unrealistic given the strong vertical reporting orientation and the culture and norms of financial control.

The 2004 implementation of a matrix organization became a formidable constraint on future adaptation. In the drift toward strategic stasis, this is perhaps the most portentous decision and watershed point.

The renewed priority given to core mid-range phones after 2006 (smartphone volumes being seen as too small to justify major commitments, and entry phones being seen as insufficiently profitable) created a pull to the middle, making differentiation more and more difficult. Advanced multimedia capabilities, for instance for online gaming, were insufficient. As for Enterprise Solutions, being short of a major software development effort (e.g. for encryption and safe communication), network integration, and a dedicated sales team for major accounts, it was not given a chance to succeed.

The context structured around the product units mediated perceptions of the external environment, and froze these along a hardware device (product) perspective. These product-centric cognitive representations prevented the development of new platform and ecosystem capabilities (Gavetti, 2005). The lack of broad and varied experience of other industries and businesses among Nokia's senior management also limited their ability to learn about this new environment by analogy, as they had no reference point to grasp how critical software now was (Gavetti et al., 2005).

Dissolution of the Strategic Context

While the structural context was remarkably stable, enduring, and rigid, the strategic context—providing meaning and guidance to resource allocation decisions—weakened and ultimately reached a meltdown stage in 2010. Had Nokia mapped out a new strategic trajectory this would have had to be done by the early 2000s. But beyond the vague ambition of becoming an "Internet company" no such trajectory was defined, no new strategic context was articulated to make the ambition tangible, and over a few years strategic context lost its relevance. So lots of individual initiatives were taken but without an overriding integrative strategic context.

To expect a new strategic context to grow from the integration of emergent "bottom-up" initiatives was unrealistic. The structural context, shaped around financial discipline at the product line level, would naturally deselect any proposal that did not conform to the dominant hardware product logic. Put differently, the "autonomous" initiatives' loop, as described by Burgelman (1983), did not work, except to proliferate variants and derivatives of existing products. The structural context led to a shortening of time horizons and narrowed the field of vision among mid-level and senior executives. By the mid-2000s, individual products had a three-year total cycle: one year in development, three months of launch (during which developers were measured on sales volume), and another eighteen months or so of maturity and decline. This short cycle was driven by a set of measures that reinforced a product-by-product (families in some cases), short- to medium-term orientation. Overall, strategic thinking suffered and became more fragmented.

Horizontal platform managers, busy negotiating resource allocation to support their efforts with competing product line projects, lost the slack and freedom to focus seriously on renewal. Furthermore, their own staff were so focused on a current skills set (Symbian-based development, selling to operators, etc.) that they were not keen to be challenged or to renew their skills. There was little focus on long-term competence-development strategies.

Adaptive mechanisms that would lead middle-management action to precede top management's strategic awareness (Burgelman, 1994) also did not operate because resource reallocation fluidity (Doz and Kosonen, 2008) was lacking. The bulk of software developers were involved with Symbian, and had staked their careers largely on its success. For them to shift their efforts to a different OS environment was too great a departure from their skill base, and even from their practice identity (Carlile, 2002). Geography also played a role. Phones were being developed in Oulu—a Baltic town in northern Finland with few other employment opportunities. In contrast, smartphone development at Nokia originated from Tampere, a major industrial and technology center much closer to Helsinki.

Obviously, short of springing up from autonomous operating managers' initiatives, strategic context renewal could also conceivably be achieved top down. Unfortunately, by the late 2000s, except for Vanjoki, Nokia did not have in its senior management the familiarity and the expertise to readily grasp the strategic implications of the development of the Internet. Some members of the board had this insight but may not have been able to devote enough time to Nokia for their knowledge and understanding to be communicated and absorbed effectively.

Cultural Misfits?

Observers of Finnish culture and industry who have strong external reference points (for instance senior Finnish consultants at major international consulting firms) have argued that the demands of an effective agile organization were not consistent with the functioning of a matrix organization in the context of Finnish culture. Finland has a strong tendency toward consensus, and when this is sought between numerous internal stakeholders without clear and speedy rules for decision making, deliberation within a matrix organization will be slow. Many people privy to Nokia's decision-making processes, such as strategic partners and key suppliers, argue that Nokia's decisions were ineffective not so much because they were mistaken but because they were not timely. Until around 2000, Nokia was often a visionary ahead of its time, but later fell victim to a form of "matrix paralysis" which heralded its descent to the role of follower.

Phase 3: Environmental Selection

While strategic context declined, structural context ultimately collapsed. Competition for scarce competencies—foremost software development— and lack of true market segment differentiation, pitted product line executives against one another. Instead of top management making difficult choices and expressing clear priorities, all development budgets were cut. Faced with tough demands and budget restrictions they were unaccustomed to, together with a top management who did not make clear choices, product line executives started to provide optimistic forecasts for their achievements and to cut corners in product development (Vuori and Huy, 2016). Now fearing top management retribution (although Nokia had never laid people off they could now see the looming risk), some started gaming the reporting and control systems. This undermined the whole reliability of product planning, budgeting, and product performance management, and put an end to trust and transparency in management. The reliability of structural context had collapsed. Ineffective reorganizations that neither lowered frictions or resolved conflicts discouraged managers and staff. Visible conflicts between top executives then further weakened morale.

Unknowingly a new CEO was to deliver the *coup de grâce* to Nokia's mobile phone business, by starkly highlighting the problems Nokia was facing and abruptly announcing the end of Nokia's commitment to Symbian. Nokia's handset sales quickly tumbled.

Despite some valiant "last-ditch" efforts, such as the first MeeGo phone which emphasized the classic Nokia design and style, internal focus had been irretrievably lost. No matter how pressing the challenges identified by executives, they had no chance of success: they had been squeezed out by environmental forces. As we discussed in Chapter 8, the game for platform leadership has a "winner takes all" set of characteristics. Ironically, and analogous to the PC experience, Apple was once again playing a vertical solution game, but this time one that was open and attractive to application developers and made space for Google's Android as a dominant standard, fulfilling the Microsoft Windows role. There was no longer room for either MeeGo or Microsoft mobile. Application developers had voted with their feet and it was now too late for network operators, despite their stated desire for a third platform, to attempt to reverse the emergence of this duopoly.

So, in this third phase of decline, environmental selection had come to prevail, and managerial actions may well have hastened collapse in accordance with population ecologists' predictions (e.g. Hannan and Freeman, 1984).

Concluding Notes

Environmental selection inevitably leads us to a wider question, Could Nokia's mobile phone business have been saved? Although counterfactual reasoning is always fraught with difficulty, let us nonetheless volunteer a hypothesis. A more determined and earlier move to follow the shift of the center of innovation to California—for argument's sake, an acquisition to bring in software architecture and project management skills, much as Technophone had earlier brought manufacturing skills—might have saved Nokia. There is no close comparator, but the experience of SAP in responding to the Internet with a strong move to Silicon Valley may offer a reference point. Had Nokia built MeeGo earlier and faster, without becoming entangled in geographic rivalries in Finland, MeeGo might have become a platform in time.

A deeper question is: But would it have been worth it? The issue here is even more difficult. The two winning platforms monetize their strengths through services, and only partly from hardware sales for Apple and not at all for Google. The value of the iPhone now comes more from its application base than from distinctive features of the hardware itself (where Xiaomi and Huawei have taken the lead). A hardware-only approach would not have been worth it for Nokia—the ever-faster churning of competitors' positions makes it difficult to be profitable and build sustained competitive advantage. Yet neither did Nokia have the skills to become a strong media content provider. So perhaps, indeed, Nokia's core problem was that it simply kept doing what it excelled at for too long before exiting.

More than speculating around the possibility of roads not taken and other potential futures for Nokia, interesting as this might be, what is really important, and was a large part of our motivation for this research, is what managerial warnings and advice we can draw from having analyzed the "Grand Waltz" experience Nokia went through. In Appendix 1 we try to distill and summarize, in capsule form, the major lessons one can draw from Nokia's story.

References

Robert Burgelman, "Corporate Entrepreneurship and Strategic Management: Insights from a Process Study" (*Management Science*, Vol. 29 Issue 12, December 1983) pp. 1349–64.

Robert Burgelman, "Fading Memories: A Process Theory of Strategic Business Exit in Dynamic Environments" (*Administrative Science Quarterly*, Vol. 39 Issue 1, March 1994) pp. 24–56.

Robert Burgelman, "Strategy as Vector and the Inertia of Co-Evolutionary Lock-In" (*Administrative Science Quarterly*, Vol. 47 Issue 1, 2002) pp. 325–57.

Paul Carlile, "A Pragmatic View of Knowledge and Boundaries: Boundary Objects in New Product Development" (*Organization Science*, Vol. 13 Issue 4, July–August 2002) pp. 442–55.

Yves Doz, "Strategic Stasis: The Failure of Strategy Process" (working paper, unpublished).

Yves Doz and Mikko Kosonen, *Fast Strategy: How Strategic Agility Will Help You Stay Ahead of the Game* (Wharton School Publishing, Harlow, 2008).

Anil Gaba, Spyros Makridakis, and Robin Hogarth, *Dance with Chance: Making Luck Work for You* (Oneworld Publications, Oxford, 2010).

Giovanni Gavetti, "Cognition and Hierarchy: Rethinking the Microfoundations of Capabilities' Development" (*Organization Science*, Vol. 16 Issue 6, November–December 2005) pp. 599–617.

Giovanni Gavetti, Daniel Levinthal, and Jan Rivkin, "Strategy Making in Novel and Complex Worlds: The Power of Analogy" (*Strategic Management Journal*, Vol. 26 Issue 1, 2005) pp. 691–712.

Michael Goold, Andrew Campbell, and Kathleen Luchs, "Strategies and Styles Revisited: Strategic Planning and Financial Control" (*Long Range Planning*, Vol. 26 Issue 5, October 1993) pp. 49–60.

Michael Hannan and John Freeman, "Structural Inertia and Organizational Change" (*American Sociological Review*, Vol. 49 Issue 2, April 1984) pp. 149–64.

Bo Hedberg, Paul Nystrom, and William Starbuck, "Camping on Seesaws: Prescriptions for a Self-Designing Organization" (*Administrative Science Quarterly*, Vol. 21 Issue 1, 1976) pp. 41–65.

Danny Miller and Peter Friesen, "Momentum and Revolution in Organizational Adaptation" (*Academy of Management Journal*, Vol. 23 Issue 4, 1980) pp. 591–614.

Nicolaj Siggelkow, "Misperceiving Interactions among Complements and Substitutes: Organizational Consequences" (*Management Science*, Vol. 48 Issue 7, 2002) pp. 900–16.

Timo Vuori and Quy Huy, "Distributed Attention and Shared Emotions in the Innovation Process" (*Administrative Science Quarterly*, Vol. 61 Issue 1, March 2016) pp. 9–51.

Management Lessons

In this appendix we aim to put in perspective key generalizable managerial observations we can draw from the Nokia story, based on our CORE framework. Our hope is that you will find them of value in your own leadership work. Not all of them will be equally relevant to your specific individual circumstances of course, but you may alight on some that give you food for thought.

Cognition

Sources of Rigidity

As companies mature, their strategy making naturally becomes more rigid. Our observations, at Nokia and elsewhere, suggest that a few sources of rigidity need to be watched particularly carefully:

- Success begets failure because of basic attribution mistakes: we usually attribute success to our merits and failure to overwhelming external forces. This leads us to become overconfident, lower our guard in watching for possible impending changes, and implicitly believe the future can be extrapolated from past and current situations.

- Success also breeds conservatism: i.e. a concern with protecting what we have achieved and a tendency to become risk-averse, in particular toward new opportunities in areas we are not thoroughly familiar with.

- Successful past commitments leave a legacy: a large installed base with loyal customers reluctant to incur switching costs and a large staff proficient with and committed to specific technologies, processes, and know-how become a source of active inertia, defending the status quo and denying the need for change. Incumbent companies easily become hostage to their past commitments.

- Our existing business model and day-to-day operational requirements drive us to cultivate certain capabilities and ignore others. When changes take place, we may well face a capability trap, where we find all we can do is more of the same. We may also face a divergence between our capability scope (where our capabilities should take us next), and market scope—the proverbial "What business are we (or ought we to be) in?" Both matter—there is no point being in an attractive business without the right capabilities, nor letting our capabilities drive us toward risky and unprofitable opportunities.

- Outside parties, customers, major shareholders, strategic partners, industry pundits, and regulators can excessively and unduly influence one's sense-making, particularly in adhering to a "being close to customers" logic.

- In facing a discontinuity, such as the advent of Internet-based communications, it is not just strategic choices that need to change, but the way they are made and the way we think of strategy (e.g. from convergence to envelopment, from products to ecosystems, from market competition to collaboration for value creation and competition for value capture). A new reality of a different nature calls for a new strategy-making paradigm.

Barriers to Foresight

So, we constantly need to free our organizations from the past, and actively seek to develop a new, forward-looking understanding. Obvious as this is in theory, it is hard to practice as:

- Failure of cognition may not result from ignorance or lack of information, or even poor foresight, but from inadequate sense-making—i.e. not making effective sense of available information.

- Sense-making is often inadequate because cognitive frames are inherited from past experiences that are no longer appropriate and fail to direct attention to critical aspects of the current predicament. It becomes an "unknown unknowns" challenge.

- This makes poor sense-making hard to detect, in particular because "using the right words" does not necessarily denote true understanding of a situation. It is possible to speak intelligently of something without understanding it and its strategic consequences.

- Shedding and forgetting rather than accumulating and layering orthodoxies (that become decision-making heuristics) is a key process that we often overlook. Periodically reviewing our key tacit and taken-for-granted assumptions is thus a very healthy practice.

The Value of Cognitive Diversity and Openness to the World

- Differences and complementarities in the perspectives and thought processes of members of the top team are a significant asset, provided this diversity is effectively reconciled and perspectives are integrated into a common collective commitment. This calls for a dialog rather than debate about which individual idea or proposal is best. Too little diversity in cognition, communication style, and attitude toward time leads to "group think," while too much leads to irreconcilable differences, conflicts, and either a rush to action or procrastination.

- Openness to information and sense-making from the outside is important. This may happen naturally in the home country of a company. However, as a company internationalizes, learning from a periphery which is more distant geographically and culturally becomes increasingly difficult. This requires purposive and deliberate sensing for new information and knowledge, and attention to how these are conveyed back to the center. It also calls for more participative strategy development processes. Failure to do so results in a company becoming or remaining excessively home-centric.

- Ethnocentricity in the composition of management reinforces a narrow framing tendency, and needs to be offset by active international recruiting and making sure foreign managers do not run into a "glass ceiling" as their career progresses.

Organization

- First and foremost, there is a need for harmony between the following three factors: (1) the different elements in the actual external environment of a business—i.e. its customers, competitors, evolving technologies, regulatory context, and effective business models; (2) how this external environment is made sense of, and how management perceptions are framed and articulated into a shared, accurate, and meaningful strategic understanding of the company's position that can inform, orient, and guide management decisions; and (3), how structure, systems, and processes guide managers in decisions and actions. The structure of the organization, its decision rules and processes, and its measurements, rewards, and punishments all shape, filter, and drive managers' perceptions and their responses to external requirements. In particular, they shape key resource allocation decisions, such as new product development. This forms a structural context to resource commitments.

- As companies grow in size and complexity, and as they mature, the architecture of the structural context becomes increasingly important in shaping and driving increasingly decentralized decisions on the part of middle managers.

- A key role of an effective and coherent structural context is to overcome silos and integrate many decisions, including decisions on tuning management systems, so they fit together and provide a common direction.

- To unleash entrepreneurship without proper corresponding integrative mechanisms leads to conflicts, stasis, and stalemates.

- Mismatches between (sometimes implicit) internal governance logics, such as conglomerate-like financial control, and the nature and extent of interdependencies, mainly around shared resources and common customers, lead to customer dissatisfaction and internal paralysis.

The Difficulties of Reorganization

- Process trumps structure. "Reorganizing" to redirect strategy, for instance toward new opportunities, remains ineffective without attention to enabling and optimizing key strategic processes (such as resource allocation, product policy, sales priorities, etc.) and providing the right incentives for managers to support these processes and work accordingly.

- Reorganizing needs to be forward-looking, intercepting forthcoming strategic requirements rather than remedying past pain points. Problem-solving reorganization is not only short-sighted but even backward-looking. Addressing pain points may be needed to keep commitment and show concern for employees, but should not drive organizational choices.

- To count on middle managers in core businesses undertaking "bottom-up" renewal initiatives is more than often illusory, particularly in an integrated dominant core business. Room for such initiatives is limited and incentives, career progression concerns, as well as narrow attention focus (on mostly operational tasks) limit self-initiated renewal activities. Lack of business "adjacencies" and of bridging technologies toward new, more distant opportunities further constrains such initiatives.

- Corporate venturing may not bring renewal, and not just for reasons of scope. There may be a time horizon mismatch, with long-term ambitions and mid-term measurements. Or there may be a lack of "bridging" technologies and possible intermediate market definitions. Finally, there may not be room for "in-market" experiments between where we are and exploiting new opportunities.

- As a company grows, the loyalty of its members needs to shift from loyalty to individuals (founder, turnaround CEO) to loyalty to the organization, as an institution, and to the integrity of its processes. If a company grows very fast it may not have the time needed for that transformation.

- Complex organizations put high demands on their members, in particular collaboration and integrative win–win bargaining around the management of interdependencies. These demands may be too strong for some. Introducing a complex organization—such as a matrix—without attention to preparing and training those that will have to make it work, may lead to very disappointing results, often exactly the opposite of what the matrix organization was meant to achieve.

- Strong and enduring "frictions" in a complex organization are highly damaging. They slow down decisions, make them painful to reach, and weaken commitments. This may become lethal in fast-moving environments. At the individual level, they not only breed frustration, resistance, and anger, they also turn competitive energies inward against colleagues. Personal "wear and tear" is high, and the best people usually leave. The cultural fabric of the organization is also easily torn.

Relationships

- A very simple business model, and its attending activity system, is a source of rigidity, but so is a very complex one. In a simple model, every element and relationship counts, and departing from the current efficiency optimum is difficult. Any change carries a risk. In a complex business model, all the causal intricacies of how its various components and relationships work together may not be fully understood. If the business model grew in complexity over time, its systemic properties will not all be known and so any change will face a high degree of uncertainty.

- Personal likes and dislikes and individual self-interest will always find their way into clouding assessments and decisions. To deny this and pretend to pursue the common good is at best naïve, and more usually Machiavellian (making self-interest parade as common interest).

- So, as a business grows and matures, so does the need to build institutionally fair processes that contain self-interest and provide checks and balances to regulate the self-interested search for power.

- In a mature business, process trumps people—i.e. tasks, roles, responsibilities, and relationships are well specified and understood by all. But in a new or adolescent business individuals are of paramount importance. Changes in key appointments and roles have a stronger impact and will result in unintended consequences. It is difficult to find a balance between leaving executives in place for too long with the risk they become barons, and moving them but risking damage to relationships and commitment.

- One of the greatest dangers is that, as a company matures and keeps succeeding, the key people, who would have had the flexibility and openness to change its course and reform roles, responsibilities, and relationships in the organization, leave. Their successors do not know how to drive change.

- The board has a role to play in preventing personal ambition and power from becoming dominant factors. This requires an independent board, willing and able to challenge the CEO on both process issues (How are strategic decisions made?) and substantive issues (How wise and timely are they?). In many companies, the evolution of board composition and governance methods may not be up to this requirement. Successful CEOs may also dull directors' attention.

- Shareholders and boards are sometimes ambivalent about narcissistic tendencies in leaders. These provide the drive, energy, stamina, and the will to win that are often essential to success as a CEO. But colleagues and subordinates may bear the brunt of difficult personalities and, over time, lose commitment.

Emotions

- Articulating powerful ethical mission statements (or, if you are skeptical, "slogans") can be a powerful and emotional source of commitment and energy. In other words, "doing good" (for the world) not just "doing well" (for shareholders) matters.

- Management systems and processes have to acknowledge the irrepressible influence of emotions, and thus leave some room for them to be legitimately expressed.

- Measurement, assessment, and reward systems carry perhaps the highest and most obvious emotional content. Approaches to assessment that give a strong role to personal evaluations by superiors require trust, transparency, and mutual understanding to be effective. They also require a strong-enough substantive basis for a well-founded assessment. If work is highly fragmented on multiple projects, as in a "software factory," assessment becomes difficult and its outcome uncertain.

Conversely, an assessment system that puts all the emphasis on numbers may be resented as being blind to individual originality and ignoring the development potential of individuals. Here too, it is a question of balance—being too qualitative or too quantitative are both sources of demotivation.

- In managing change, we often tend to overlook the importance of deep emotional working identity and self-worth issues. The most delicate barrier to change is not intellectual (Does this change make sense?) or self-interest (Will I benefit from it, is it in my interest?), but emotional (Will it challenge, compromise, devalue my professional identity, and compromise my self-esteem? Will I know how to play by the new rules it implements?). So, in implementing change, this emotional challenge needs to be addressed first—at the skills and behavior level—before rejigging management systems and processes, or explaining why change is needed strategically.

- Emotional engagement is not easily scalable, in other words we can be emotionally committed to our small team, to a boss we like, to our subunit, to our business perhaps, but seldom to a large organization. Middle managers thus have to play a key role as "emotional relays" up and down and also sideways. Neglecting the importance of this role leads to a loss of engagement.

Chronology of Key Events by Chapter

Chapter 2

1912	Finnish Cable Works (FCW) founded
1930	FCW enters Finnish telecoms market, developing and manufacturing phones and switches
1935	FCW wins Finnish military communications contract
1960	FCW under CEO Westerlund establishes electronics group
1963	FCW develop their first radiophone
1967	Nokia Corporation formed through merger of FCW, Finnish Rubber Works (est. 1889) and Nokia (forest products company, est. 1865)
1967	Westerlund, head of FCW, becomes first CEO of Nokia Corp
1977	Kari Kairamo becomes CEO
1978	Joint venture with Televa
1979	Joint venture formed with Solera for radiophones, creating Mobira
1982	Mobira 450 launched—first dedicated car phone
1982	Nokia produces the world's first fully digital, local telephone exchange with Finnish state telecoms company Televa
1983	Entered US market to sell mobile phones under Tandy brand name, alliance with Tandy/Radio Shack
1984	Nokia gains full control of Mobira
1986	Three-tier governance structure introduced to distance shareholders from operations
1986	DX2000 fully digital switch launched
1986	Portable version of Mobira 450 launched
1987	Nokia acquires Televa from Finnish state
1988	Nokia has 12 percent global market share for handsets
1988	Kairamo's suicide
1988	Simo Vuorilehto, ex-COO, appointed as CEO
1990	Output—500,000 units
1991	Nokia in trouble—orders dry up
1991	Bank shareholder tries to sell Nokia to Ericsson

Chapter 3

1991	Vuorilehto asked to retire (leaves 1992) along with COO
1991	First company to provide fully functional commercial GSM network, Radiolinja gains license, Nokia builds network
1991	Anssi Vanjoki hired from 3M to build brand and lead marketing
1991	Acquire Technophone
1992	Ollila becomes president and CEO
1992	Nokia in financial crisis
1992	Annual Transformation—Urgency for Change—Vision 2000
1992	Ala-Pietilä replaces Ollila as head of NMP
1992	Commercialize first fully specified GSM mobile phone
1992	Offsite for twenty-five execs "The Nokia Way" (Values)
1993	Annual Transformation—Nokia Values kicked off
1993	Finland joins EU
1993	Output—2.5 million units
1993	Frank Nuovo from the Pasadena School of Design joins (not full-time until 1995)
1994	Annual Transformation—Excellence in Execution theme
1994	Output—five million units
1994	Nokia 2100 launched with new rounded design (Nuovo)
1994	Divestment of non-Telecoms businesses agreed
1994	Listed on NYSE

Chapter 4

1995	Annual Transformation—Intellectual Leadership
1995	Output—eleven million units
1995–6	Logistics crisis
1996	NVB established
1996	Strategy Panel established
1997	Senior management task force to come up with strategic options to ease tensions between NMP and NTC
1997	Launched Club Nokia
1997	NMP establish Mobile Data Unit at Tampere R&D site
1998	Management team reorganization with Alahuhta head of NMP, Baldauf head of NTC, Ala-Pietilä named Nokia deputy-president and head of NVO. Ollila becomes chairman of board in addition to CEO
1998	NTC changes name to NET (Nokia Networks)
1998	NVO established
1998	Overtakes Motorola to become number-one handset producer globally
1998	Market segmentation approach begins

Chapter 5

1996	First Communicator smart phone launched (begun 1992 outside NMP as sunk works project)

1997   WAP Consortium founded

1998   Symbian Consortium founded

1999   Vanjoki presents camera phone concept at GSM World Congress in Cannes

2000   Launched first phone with Symbian OS (9210 Communicator)

2000   Set up DCU under Vanjoki

2001   Slowdown in industry (dotcom crash and overspend on 3G licenses)

2001   Ollila scheduled to step down as CEO but asked to stay on five more years by board

2001   Series 60 Symbian user interface launched

2001   Market segmentation approach deepened with micro-segmentation

2002   Nokia's first camera phone (7650) launched

2002   NMP reorganizes into nine value domains

2002   Strategic analysis of enterprise market potential launched

2003   Visual radio project begins

2003   Announce Enterprise Solutions Group (US-based) will be established

Chapter 6

2004   Reorganization into matrix

2004   Kallasvuo appointed head of mobile phones

2004   Operators boycott Nokia

2004   Club Nokia closed down and development of Nokia-branded services ends

2004   Enterprise Solutions and Multimedia established as separate business groups

2004   Alahuhta resigns

2005   Baldauf resigns

2005   Ala-Pietilä resigns

2005   Neuvo—long-time tech guru retires/resigns

2005   Focus on cost control

2006   Petti Korhonen, CTO and head of Tech platforms, resigns

Chapter 7

2006   Kallasvuo becomes CEO

2006   Merger of NET network activities with Siemens to create NSN

2007   N800 Internet tablet running Maemo OS launched

2007   Apple launch first iPhone

2008   Reorganization to create single Devices and Services group

2008   Bob Ianucci joins as CTO (lasts eight months)—succession of short-lived CTOs follows

2008   Ojanperä made CTO on top of strategy role

2008   Google launch Android

2008   Acquire Trolltech (for Qt)

2008   Fifty-seven versions of Symbian OS in use

2009   N97 touchscreen smartphone released

2010   Alliance with Intel to develop MeeGo OS jointly (based on Maemo)

2010   Reorganization creating Mobile Solutions group for smartphones and software

2010   Internal debate begun about OS platform options
2010   Board decide Kallasvuo has to go
2010   Stephen Elop appointed CEO
2010   Vanjoki resigns

Chapter 8

2011   "Burning platform" memo sent to all staff by Elop (February)
2011   Elop announced "three-pillar" strategy—alliance with Microsoft (February)
2011   Maintenance of Symbian outsourced to Accenture
2011   Mass redundancies commence
2011   N9 phone running MeeGo launched
2011   Operating profit down 75 percent year-on-year
2011   Nokia launched first Windows 7.5 phones, the Lumia 710 and 800
2012   Ollila steps down as chairman, replaced by Siilasmaa
2013   Siilasmaa and Microsoft CEO Steve Ballmer meet in Barcelona to discuss sale of NMP (February)
2013   Nokia acquires Siemens' share of NSN with loan from Microsoft (July)
2013   Nokia and Microsoft boards agree to the acquisition of Nokia mobile phones for 5.44 billion euros (September)
2014   Rajeev Suri becomes CEO of Nokia
2015   Nokia acquires Alcatel-Lucent

APPENDIX 3

Abbreviations

BCG	Boston Consulting Group	
CDMA	Code Division Multiple Access	*Protocol used in 2G and 3G wireless communications*
CEO	Chief executive officer	
CEPT	Confederation of European Posts and Telecommunications	*Regulatory and standards body representing Europe's monopoly state telecoms firms*
CFO	Chief financial officer	
COO	Chief operating officer	
CTO	Chief technology officer	
DCU	Digital Convergence Unit	*Dedicated group focusing on data activities established in 2000*
ERP	Enterprise Resource Planning	*Integrated software to manage multiple back office functions*
ES	Enterprise Solutions group	*New business group announced by Nokia in 2003*
FCC	Federal Communications Commission	*US telecoms regulator*
FCW	Finnish Cable Works	*Company involved in merger to create Nokia in 1967*
FDMA	Frequency Division Multiple Access	*Radio frequency access protocol*
FIM	Finnish markka	*Finnish currency prior to adopting the euro*
GPRS	General Packet Radio Service	*Service for delivering mobile data*
GSM	Global System for Mobile Communications	*Pan-European digital standard set up 1982*
HR	Human resources	
ICT	Information and communication technology	
IMD	International Institute for Management Development	*Business school based in Lausanne, Switzerland*
iOS		*Apple's mobile operating system*
IT	Information technology	
M	Multimedia group	*Unit established under matrix reorganization in 1994*
MMS	Multimedia Messaging Service	
MP	Mobile Phones group	*Unit established under matrix reorganization in 1994*
NCS	Nokia Cellular Systems	*A subunit of NTC*
NET	Nokia Networks	*Nokia's infrastructure business group (name changed from NTC in 1998)*

NMP	Nokia Mobile Phones	*Nokia's phone business group*
NMT	Nordic Mobile Telephone Network	*Cross-border network established in 1981, with roaming between Sweden, Norway, Finland, and Denmark*
NRC	Nokia Research Center	
NSN	Nokia Siemens Networks	*Joint venture absorbing infrastructure business of Nokia and Siemens created in 2006*
NTC	Nokia Telecommunications	*Nokia's infrastructure business group (renamed NET in 1998)*
NTT	Nippon Telegraph and Telephone	
NVB	New Venture Board	*Established in 1996 to focus on new ventures*
NVO	Nokia Ventures Organization	*Venture portfolio established in 1998—NVB activities moved into NVO*
OEM	Original equipment manufacturer	
OS	Operating system	*Underlying software on computer or device*
PCM	Pulse Code Modulation	*Technology for transforming analog signals to digital*
PDA	Personal digital assistant	*Handheld computer popular from mid-1980s until advent of smartphones*
PTT	Postal, Telegraph, and Telephone	*Government monopoly responsible for these services; most now privatized*
SMS	Short Message Service	
TDMA	Time Division Multiple Access	*Radio frequency access protocol*
VTT	Technical Research Centre of Finland Ltd	
WAP	Wireless Access Protocol	*Established in 1997 to create mobile Internet standards*

Who's Who

Ahtisaari, Marko	Joined Nokia in 2002 and held a number of design and strategy roles until leaving to pursue entrepreneurial activities in 2006. Returned to Nokia as head of design in 2009. He left the firm in 2013.
Äkräs, Juha	Spent twenty-one years at Nokia from 1993 to 2014. Undertook a wide range of roles including customer services and strategy within Nokia Telecommunications, head of core networks, and ultimately head of HR.
Alahuhta, Matti	Member of the senior management group known as the "dream team." Originally joined Nokia in 1975 and returned to the company in 1984 after a stint at Rank Xerox. Held various positions including head of Nokia Telecommunications and later head of NMP. Left Nokia in 2004.
Ala-Pietilä, Pekka	Member of the senior management group known as the "dream team." Joined Nokia in 1985 undertaking a number of roles including marketing and strategic planning before becoming head of NMP in 1992 at the age of thirty-five. From 1998 he was president of Nokia. He left the firm in 2005.
Anderson, Erik	Joined Nokia in 1994 and worked in a range of design- and strategy-focused roles culminating in being head of the Tampere R&D site. He left the firm in 2014.
Baldauf, Sari	Member of the senior management group known as the "dream team." Joined Nokia in 1983 in corporate strategic planning. Moved to Nokia Telecoms in 1986 and undertook a range of strategy and planning roles before becoming head of NCS in 1992. She was moved to head Nokia Networks in 1998 where she remained until leaving Nokia in 2005.
Davies, Charles	Joined Nokia from Psion in 1993 as CTO of Symbian. He left the firm at the beginning of 2010.
Elop, Stephen	Appointed CEO of Nokia (from Microsoft) in 2010—the first non-Finn and external candidate to hold the role. At the helm during the sale of Nokia's mobile phone business to Microsoft and remained head of the business (now Microsoft Devices) until 2015.
Green, Richard	CTO of Nokia for two years from 2010.
Halbherr, Michael	Joined Nokia in 2006 with responsibility for the Ovi store. Moved to head Nokia's location-based services until leaving the firm in 2014.
Harlow, Jo	Joined Nokia in 2003, and undertook a range of marketing roles before moving into project management. Her last role before Microsoft acquired Nokia was executive vice president of Smart Devices.
Ianucci, Bob	Joined Nokia in 2004 as head of NRC before a brief stint as CTO for nine months in 2008. He left Nokia the following year.
Ihamuotila, Timo	Joined Nokia in a finance-related function for three years from 1993 and then returned to the firm in 1999. Held a number of roles in Treasury before becoming CFO, a position he held for seven years until his departure in 2016.

Isokallio, Kalle	Joined Nokia in 1981 and held a number of roles until being appointed president in 1990 by his father-in-law and chairman of the board, Mika Tiivola. The appointment lasted only eighteen months until both he and Tiivola were pushed out.
Jaaksi, Ari	Joined Nokia in 1998 to head mobile browsers. In 2003 moved to become vice president of MeeGo Devices. He left Nokia in 2010.
Kairamo, Kari	Charismatic CEO of Nokia from 1977 to 1988, largely credited with transforming Nokia through internal reorganization, acquisitions, and internationalization. Joined Nokia in 1970 working in exports of forestry products and undertook a number of expatriate positions.
Kallasvuo, Olli-Pekka	Member of the senior management group known as the "dream team." He joined Nokia in 1980 as corporate counsel and in 1988 moved to finance, becoming CFO in 1992. In January 2004 he was appointed head of the Mobile Phones group. He became group CEO in June 2006 and served four years in that role until being removed by the board in 2010.
Korhonen, Pertti	Spent nineteen years at Nokia from 1987 to 2006. He joined the firm as a design engineer and quickly gained prominence for his handling of the logistics crisis. He later held senior management positions in product and technology development.
Koski, Timo	Regarded as an early technology visionary, he joined Nokia in 1983 and in 1986 became a member of the Internal Board driving internationalization and the move into electronics. He died in London in April 1988, aged forty, of a brain hemorrhage.
Kosonen, Mikko	Joined Nokia in 1984 as a business analyst, and over the next twenty-three years held various positions in planning, business development, and strategy. For nine years from 1996, he was head of strategy and business infrastructure.
Lindholm, Christian	Spent a decade at Nokia from 1995 working on user interfaces.
McDowell, Mary	Hired in 2004 to head the new Enterprise business group. Moved into a strategy role before becoming head of Mobile Phones in 2010. She left Nokia in 2012.
Moilanen, Mikko	Joined Nokia in 1992 and held a number of roles including product program manager, strategy development, and R&D leadership as well as special programs before leaving in 2009.
Neuvo, Yrjö	After twenty-five years as an academic researcher and professor in Finland and the US, he joined Nokia in 1993. Widely regarded in the industry as a technology guru, he headed Nokia's research until leaving the firm in 2006.
Nuovo, Frank	Spent eleven years at Nokia as head of design from 1995.
Öistämö, Kai	Joined Nokia in 1991 in the consumer electronics unit before moving to the mobile phones business, taking on various management and technical roles. From 2006 he led the Mobile Phones and then Devices group before becoming head of strategy in 2010. He left Nokia in 2014.
Ojanperä, Tero	Spent twenty-one years at Nokia from 1990. During this time he held various senior roles including head of Nokia Research Center, chief strategy officer, and CTO. His last role was heading Nokia's services group.
Ollila, Jorma	Head of the senior management group know as the "dream team." He joined Nokia in 1985 as head of international operations, becoming the group's CFO in 1986, and in 1990 took charge of NMP. He became CEO in 1992 and remained in that role until 2006. He also held the position of chairman of the board from 1998 to May 2012.
Ormala, Erkki	Joined Nokia in 1999 as head of technology policy and remained in that role until leaving the firm in 2013.
Paajanen, Reijo	Joined Nokia (Mobira) in 1981 and held a number of research and R&D leadership roles of particular note, pushing the agenda around wireless data. He left Nokia in 2000.

Putkiranta, Juha	Joined Nokia in 1997. Held roles in business development, marketing, supply chain, and operations. His final role before leaving Nokia in 2014 was to lead the post-acquisition integration for Devices and Services.
Savander, Niklas	Joined Nokia in the networks business in 1997. Moved into the mobile phone business in 2001 and held number of senior roles in R&D and management. He left Nokia in 2012.
Siilasmaa, Risto	A tech entrepreneur, he joined Nokia's board in 2008. He took over as chairman in 2012 and played a pivotal role in the sale of Nokia's mobile phone business to Microsoft. At the time of publication he still holds that role.
Suri, Rajeev	Joined Nokia in the network infrastructure business in 1995, holding senior roles in India, Asia Pacific, and the UK. In 2007 he became head of Global Services at NSN and in 2009 became CEO (and remained in this role when Nokia bought out Siemens).
Terho, Mikko	Joined Nokia in 1983 in R&D in Tampere. He was acknowledged for his significant contribution to the field of digital convergence in particular, and the mobile industry in general, by being made a Nokia Fellow in 2007. He left Nokia in 2012.
Torres, Alberto	Joined Nokia as a strategist in 2004. Later roles included heading the Vertu prestige brand and from 2010 leading MeeGo. He left Nokia in 2011.
Vanjoki, Anssi	Widely regarded as a technology visionary pushing Nokia's innovation agenda around digital convergence, he joined in 1991 and held a wide range of roles including head of markets and head of multimedia. A candidate for CEO, he left the firm in 2010 when the board selected Stephen Elop.
Vuorilehto, Simo	After being president of Nokia, he took over as CEO after Kairamo's death in 1998. He was also chairman of the board from 1988 to 1990. He retired from Nokia in 1992.
Westerlund, Björn	Joined a predecessor of Nokia in 1936 and rose to become the first CEO of the newly merged company. He was responsible for taking Nokia into consumer electronics and laying the foundations for the mobile telecoms firm it later became. He retired from Nokia in 1977.

Compiled from data from numerous sources including interviews, LinkedIn profiles, and Bloomberg Executive Profiles.

APPENDIX 5

Selected Financial and Personnel Data

Section 1.01 Year	1996	1997	1998	1999	2000	2001	2002	2003	2004*	2005	2006	2007**	2008***	2009	2010	2011	2012
Revenues	6,613	8,849	13,326	19,772	30,376	31,191	30,016	29,455	29,371	34,191	41,121	51,058	50,710	40,084	42,446	38,659	30,176
Networks	2,242	3,166	4,390	5,673	7,714	7,534	6,539	5,620	6,431	6,557	7,453	13,393	15,309	12,574	12,661	14,041	13,779
NMP	3,629	4,649	8,070	13,182	21,887	23,158	23,211	23,618	23,036	27,653	33,677	3	35,099	27,853	29,134	23,943	15,686
NMP (%)	55	53	61	67	72	74	77	80	78	81	82	0	69	69	69	62	52
Operating Profit	717	1,422	2,489	3,908	5,776	3,362	4,780	5,011	4,326	4,639	5,488	7,985	4,966	1,197	2,070	−1,073	−2,303
Networks	501	682	960	1,082	1,358	−73	−49	−219	884	855	808	−1,308	−301	−1,639	−686	−300	−799
NMP	241	645	1,540	3,099	4,879	4,521	5,201	5,483	3,751	4,170	5,161	7,931	5,816	3,314	3,540	884	−1,100
NMP (%)	34	45	62	79	84	134	109	109	87	90	94	99	117	277	171		
Personnel	31,766	35,490	41,091	51,177	58,708	57,716	52,714	51,605	53,511	56,896	68,483	112,262	125,829	123,553	132,427	130,050	97,798
Networks	12,558	15,710	19,280	22,804	23,508	22,040	18,463	16,115	15,463	17,676	21,061	58,423	60,295	63,927	66,160	73,686	58,411
Networks (%)	40	44	47	45	40	38	35	31	29	31	31	52	48	52	50	57	60
NMP	10,927	12,631	16,064	20,975	27,353	27,320	26,090	27,196	****				61,130	54,773	58,712	49,406	32,986
NMP (%)	34	36	39	41	47	47	49	53					49	44	44	38	
In Finland	17,999	19,342	20,978	23,155	24,495	23,653	22,615	22,626			23,894	23,015	23,320	21,559	19,841	16,970	11,767
Outside Finland	13,767	16,148	20,113	28,022	34,213	34,063	30,099	28,979			44,589	89,247	102,509	101,994	112,586	113,080	86,031

Unless otherwise indicated, figures are reported in million euros

* NMP reported as MP, M, and ES ** Siemens merger *** MP, M, and ES reported as Devices and Services **** Matrix and common functions mean it's not possible to break down figures until 2008

Data collated from Nokia annual reports

The Research

Although this book is very much a product of collaboration between its authors—we both organized, analyzed, and conceptualized a large amount of both primary and secondary research data, and then of course planned and wrote the manuscript together—over the course of many years it was Yves alone who undertook the research. As mentioned in the Preface, to reflect this and maintain the authenticity of conversations and events described, we decided to recount these using the first person singular throughout the book. Similarly, we felt it made sense for Yves to address the reader directly in this appendix, elucidating the long research process he undertook.

Background

The genesis of this book goes back twenty years, but it did not start as a research project, or with a book in mind at all. Back in 1996, I had the good fortune to be asked to contribute to a "learning expedition" being organized by INSEAD's Euro Asia Center for Nokia in Japan. This was part of a series of seminars and learning expeditions held by Nokia once a year for a subset of its most senior executives. At the seminar, I met for the first time a number of senior executives including Sari Baldauf, who, among various roles, was responsible for Asia in Nokia at the time, and Mikko Kosonen, a seminar participant who later became a co-author and friend of mine. Over the course of that seminar, it quickly became apparent that Nokia, amazingly successful as it then was, needed to become more sensitive and better able to draw insight and knowledge from distant locations. It had grown very quickly from being a Finnish and Nordic company to becoming a global giant.

Coincidentally, I was on a sabbatical at Stanford that same year and co-authoring a book—*Alliance Advantage* (Doz and Hamel, 1998)—with Gary Hamel, summarizing research we had done in preceding years on alliance management and competitiveness. Gary was still involved with Nokia, following the "intellectual leadership" exercise, a project on core competencies, and the launch of new ventures. Gary and I shared an interest in the management of multinational companies and a frustration that most of these were overly reliant on their home country for innovation. In our conversations, we coined the phrase "reversing the knowledge flow," anticipating research on reverse innovation (Govindarajan and Trimble, 2012) by some years. Inspired by the example of Nestlé, a pioneer in performing R&D in a distributed fashion with multiple innovation centers spread around the world rather than just in Switzerland, we decided to research how multinationals could transform themselves into networks of geographically dispersed innovation sources around the world.

As the issues we had unearthed at the seminar in Japan became clearer to Nokia's top management, Nokia became a sponsor for this research. Nokia put in place a steering committee chaired by Matti Alahuhta to interact with our research team (two INSEAD colleagues, Jose Santos and Peter Williamson, and myself supported by some INSEAD researchers and Strategos consultants). We did not research Nokia in that project—we were looking for leading-edge practices that we found with ST Microelectronics, Polygram, Unilever, and a few others—but we did interact closely with the steering committee.

The work was highly relevant to Nokia and contributed to internal debates about important decisions. For instance, at the time, as mentioned in Jorma Ollila's memoirs, he and the top team were considering relocating corporate headquarters outside Finland, London being a prime candidate location. The issue of whether (and how) to internationalize senior management ranks also featured prominently in these deliberations. In the end, Nokia's top team made a clear decision to remain based in Helsinki (selected functions such as finance could move to key financial centers, and New York was ultimately chosen).

In 2004, Mikko Kosonen "knocked on my door" with the following proposition, "I have been given a year off—a Sabbatical of sorts—to research and reflect on how incumbent companies adjust to disruption, for instance traditional IT companies and the Internet." His concern was obviously with the future of Nokia, as he felt that many staff members were not aware of how transformative a change the Internet would bring. So, together we researched a number of companies, including Accenture, Canon, HP, IBM, Intel, Oracle, and SAP, but with a particular emphasis on Nokia as well. Beyond a new series of exchanges with Nokia's leadership and newly appointed CEO, Olli-Pekka Kallasvuo, in 2006 this collaboration led to a book titled *Fast Strategy* (Doz and Kosonen, 2008a) and several articles. Mikko Kosonen and I were asked to study how our findings on other companies would apply to Nokia, and build a two-day top management workshop to present and discuss our results. In the run-up to that workshop, we developed and circulated a survey to almost 3,000 Nokians. The company they portrayed was deeply siloed and fragmented; a far cry from its heyday of the 1990s. Over the same time frame, I was also running a series of seminars for Nokia executives on strategic alliances and the need for ecosystem thinking and strategizing.

So, it was through specific interventions and interactions with senior Nokians over a long period that I became intimately familiar with the firm, specific projects (such as camera phones and visual radio), its management processes, its strengths, and the challenges it faced. But only in 2015 and 2016, through the interviews specifically carried out for this book, did I take the full measure of how damaging and debilitating the conflicts within the organization put in place in 2004 and changed again in 2008, had really become.

Research Methods

This book is based on several complementary approaches to research. My early work with Nokia, from the first seminar in Japan to the research done with Mikko Kosonen in the mid-2000s, was key to understanding the pre-2004 dynamics, the evolution of strategic agility at Nokia in the 1990s (Doz and Kosonen, 2008a, 2008b, 2011), and the state of the organization up to 2006. Over that period I also developed and taught a number of case studies on Nokia (Symbian, Nokia in 2010 for INSEAD, and some others only used internally at Nokia, such as Calypso and visual radio), which provided insight and had the advantage of not being retrospective reconstructions ten or fifteen years after the fact.

This early work allowed me to identify key periods and decision points in Nokia's recent history (from around 1992 when Jorma Ollila took over as CEO and made the decision to focus on mobile telecoms).

Research solely for this book began in earnest at the beginning of 2015 with interviews of former senior executives at Nokia. Although much of the literature assumes that managers throughout the organization affect the way a firm perceives and responds to its environment and suggests that a broad constellation of executives guides the choices of the firm (Barr, 1998), in the case of Nokia, relatively few top managers made key strategic and structural decisions, and they were not always acting in unison in some form of strategic consensus. Therefore, I decided to focus on the perspectives and behavior of these top managers. Others (including Vuori and Huy, 2016), focused on middle management, and so researching top managers would complement these earlier studies. Beyond the most senior executives, I also interviewed senior managers who could shed light on specific issues, for instance that of delays in software development and new operating systems.

With only one exception, all executives contacted for interview responded positively. Some were interviewed several times, to deepen the insight they provided or to address specific questions that arose in the course of the research. In addition the current chairman of the board was interviewed a number of times. In contrast to the positive responses of executive managers and the current chairman to being interviewed, several past board members of Nokia we contacted all declined to be interviewed. This left Jorma Ollila as the only first-hand source of information on the actual functioning of the board and Nokia's governance in crucial years to 2012. However, for the record, Ollila had been keen we interview other board members and had provided contact details so that we may try and set up interviews.

My interviewing approach moved from broadly purposive to theoretical sampling in the course of the research (Locke, 2001). I began with interviewees who could provide rich and insightful narratives, and later selected interviewees, including some additional interviews with early informants, as a function of specific, core empirical and theoretical questions that were progressively emerging in the course of the research.

To limit the ever-present risk of retrospective rationalizations or ad hoc theorizing on the part of managers (telling how things should have been in principle, not how they really were and who actually did what), and also in some cases of emotional distortions (some nerves are still raw about painful episodes in the downfall among former executives concerned with their personal image), the interviews were focused on the interviewees' involvement in specific episodes, and on their descriptive rendering of what happened in these episodes.

I adopted a "courtroom" style of interviewing, pushing for concrete illustrations to increase the data's validity (Eisenhardt and Graebner, 2007). Interview transcripts were fed back to interviewees for review, and intermediate summaries of findings were provided to them for discussion after the interviews were completed. These provided the basis for further clarifying conversations. The factual narratives, as well as many of the interpretations, were actually rather close between interviewees, despite strong emotional undertones. This made data-checking relatively simple. Testimonies were cross-checked with written sources and with other accounts, in particular around conflicting areas which remain contentious today.

Several non-Finn interviewees also provided a different cultural perspective in addition to their insights on specific episodes they were involved in. A list of managers I interviewed in 2015–16 appears at the end of this appendix. Other former executives also provided additional insights but requested not to be mentioned by name. A few outside observers also contributed deep insights, for example Martti Häikiö (for an excellent history of early years see his 2002 book, *Nokia: The Inside Story*), plus a number of Finnish academics who had researched various aspects of Nokia's history and management. I also spoke to a number of former senior executives from other players in the mobile communications industry.

While a global company like Nokia will always attract interest in the English-language international press, we recognized that due to the prominent role of Nokia in its home country there was potentially a greater body of insight and scrutiny of the firm in Finnish-language press and publications. To ensure these sources were not overlooked, in 2014 we engaged a Finnish researcher to read, assess, summarize, and translate public domain sources relating to each of the periods and key decision points I had identified. At the same time, an INSEAD researcher undertook a similar exercise for English-language publications. The results of this secondary source research were grouped by period and specific events.

We had to wade our way through an abundant but often misleading literature (for a review, see Laamanen et al., 2016). In reviewing this rich resource we were sensitive to several challenges. First, managers, and to a lesser extent observers, usually attribute success to their own efforts and perspicacity, and failure to uncontrollable outside events. Second, as in the aphorism "History is written by the victors," interpretations can be multiple and self-serving, and compete for attention and credibility among executives. They can also be politically motivated, years after the facts. Third, observers and analysts tend to single out a subset of causal relationships, or even a single factor, to the detriment of other explanatory factors. Fourth, obviously not all observers and researchers enjoy quality access, and this leads them to bias, oversimplification, and misleading interpretations. Given the amazing success of Nokia in mobile phones and its rapid collapse, we also need to guard against a natural tendency among ex-Nokia managers and observers alike to reify the success and vilify the failure. Success begets a search for heroes and failure a search for villains and scapegoats. Our approach was to avoid both the risk of hagiography and that of condemnation.

To test the validity of emerging findings, in the fall of 2015 I circulated a list of key critical steps in the history of Nokia's involvement in mobile phones and a short summary of key findings, to the former leaders of Nokia. I then had a meeting with each of them separately to listen to and discuss their observations and feedback. Although some of the findings were obviously disquieting to some, all validated the conclusions I had reached, sometimes after a rich dialog deepening our (theirs, and my) understanding of the conclusions.

At the beginning of 2016, my co-author, Keeley Wilson (with whom I have worked on many projects over the last decade and a half), joined the project. Through careful reading of all of the interview transcripts and notes (beginning with those from earlier projects in 2005 to the 2015 interviews) in conjunction with the secondary sources identified in 2014, case studies, more recent publications, and banking analyst reports from 1994 onwards, we drew up a very detailed chronology of events both internal and external which had an impact on Nokia. This not only helped us to start articulating our findings and begin tentative conceptualizations, but the exercise also enabled us to identify contradictions and missing pieces.

From these, we arranged further interviews and undertook additional data collection from secondary sources. All factual data used in the narrative sections of each chapter was cross-checked against multiple sources (both secondary, and in many instances verifications of factual events with interviewees). Given this approach and the fact this data is in the public domain, we did not feel it necessary or appropriate to provide references to all of the sources we used.

The interplay between analyses, interpretation, and conceptualization on the one hand, and data on the other, became iterative, in a patient "to and fro" between data and concepts. Colleagues and informants with whom we discussed the emerging findings, or who read excerpts of the manuscript, also helped by pointing to gaps or underdeveloped areas, for instance the fact that Nokia—although it very quickly became a global company—remained in many ways deeply ethnocentric.

In June 2016 we held a workshop in Helsinki where all the interviewees (except the two chairmen of the board) were invited, together with a few Finnish academics who had developed good insights into Nokia. In that workshop I presented my main findings and observations, validated them, and was able to gain a few new insights from the resulting dialog. This led us to revisit some data, and selectively focus on other issues we had underemphasized. Shortly after, in the summer of 2016 I provided personal feedback to Jorma Ollila (former CEO and chairman) and Risto Siilasmaa (the current chairman), as well as to a few former senior executives who had not been able to participate in the workshop in June.

Last but not least, conversations with colleagues, in Finland, INSEAD, and elsewhere also nourished our reflections. A few Finnish researchers have obviously developed deep insights about Nokia and their papers, and the informal conversations with them, were very useful. So were conversations with INSEAD colleague Jose Santos, and of course Mikko Kosonen, who acted as a key informant and sounding board for many points in the argument, both descriptive and conceptual.

Alphabetical List of Interviewees

	Year(s) interviewed
Ahtisaari, Marko	2015
Äkräs, Juha	2015, 2016
Alahuhta, Matti	2006, 2015, 2016
Ala-Pietilä, Pekka	2005, 2006, 2015
Ali-Yrkkö, Jyrki	2015
Baldauf, Sari	2005, 2015
Baril, Jean-François	2015
Ihamuotila, Timo	2015
Kallasvuo, Olli-Pekka	2005, 2015, 2016
Korhonen, Pertti	2005, 2015
Kosonen, Mikko	2005, 2006, 2015, 2016
Laine, Paula	2015
Malmi, Teemu	2015
Ojanperä, Tero	2015
Ollila, Jorma	2005, 2015, 2016
Ormala, Erkki	2015
Putkiranta, Juha	2015
Siilasmaa, Risto	2015, 2016
Terho, Mikko	2015
Torres, Alberto	2015
Vanjoki, Anssi	2005, 2015, 2016

References

Pamela Barr, "Adapting to Unfamiliar Environmental Events: A Look at the Evolution of Interpretation and Its Role in Strategic Change" (*Organization Science*, Vol. 9 Issue 6, November/December 1998) pp. 644–69.

Yves Doz and Gary Hamel, *Alliance Advantage: The Art of Creating Value through Partnering* (Harvard Business School Press, Cambridge, MA, 1998).

Yves Doz and Mikko Kosonen, *Fast Strategy: How Strategic Agility Will Help You Stay Ahead of the Game* (Wharton School Publishing, Harlow, 2008a).

Yves Doz and Mikko Kosonen, "The Dynamics of Strategic Agility: Nokia's Rollercoaster Experience" (*California Management Review*, Vol. 50 Issue 3, Spring 2008b) pp. 95–118.

Yves Doz and Mikko Kosonen, "Letter to the Editor—Nokia and Strategic Agility: A Postscript" (*California Management Review*, Vol. 53 Issue 4, Summer 2011) pp. 154–6.

Kathleen Eisenhardt and Melissa Graebner, "Theory Building from Cases: Opportunities and Challenges" (*Academy of Management Journal*, Vol. 50 Issue 1, February 2007) pp. 25–32.

Vijay Govindarajan and Chris Trimble, *Reverse Innovation: Create Far From Home, Win Everywhere* (Harvard Business School Press Books, Boston, April 2012).

Martti Häikiö, *Nokia: The Inside Story* (Pearson Education, London, 2002).

Tomi Laamanen, Juha-Antti Lamberg, and Eero Vaara, "Explanations of Success and Failure in Management Learning: What Can We Learn from Nokia's Rise and Fall?" (*Academy of Management Learning & Education*, Vol. 15 Issue 1, 2016) pp. 2–25.

Karen D. Locke, *Grounded Theory in Management Research* (Sage Publications, London, 2001).

Timo Vuori and Quy Huy, "Distributed Attention and Shared Emotions in the Innovation Process" (*Administrative Science Quarterly*, Vol. 61 Issue 1, March 2016) pp. 9–51.

Index